ADAPTING PSYCHOLOGICAL TESTS AND MEASUREMENT INSTRUMENTS FOR CROSS-CULTURAL RESEARCH

Adapting Psychological Tests and Measurement Instruments for Cross-Cultural Research provides an easy-to-read overview of the methodological issues and best practices for cross-cultural adaptation of psychological instruments.

Although the development of cross-cultural test adaption methodology has advanced in recent years, the discussion is often pitched at an expert level and requires an advanced knowledge of statistics, psychometrics and scientific methodology. This book, however, introduces the history and concepts of cross-cultural psychometrics in a pedagogic and simple manner. It evaluates key ethical, cultural, methodological and legal issues in cross-cultural psychometrics and provides a guide to test adaptation, data analysis and interpretation.

Written in an accessible manner, this book builds an understanding of the methodological, ethical and legal complexities of cross-cultural test adaptation and presents methods for test adaptation, including the basic statistical procedures for evaluating the equivalence of test versions. It would be the ideal companion for undergraduate students and those new to psychometrics.

Prof. Dr. Vladimir Hedrih is a full professor of psychology at the University of Niš in Serbia. He is the author of the undergraduate university course called "Cross-cultural adaptation of psychological measurement instruments" and has been teaching it for over a decade.

ADAPTING PSYCHOLOGICAL TESTS AND MEASUREMENT INSTRUMENTS FOR CROSS-CULTURAL RESEARCH

An Introduction

Vladimir Hedrih

Routledge
Taylor & Francis Group
LONDON AND NEW YORK

First published 2020
by Routledge
2 Park Square, Milton Park, Abingdon, Oxon OX14 4RN

and by Routledge
52 Vanderbilt Avenue, New York, NY 10017

Routledge is an imprint of the Taylor & Francis Group, an informa business

British Library Cataloguing-in-Publication Data
A catalogue record for this book is available from the British Library

Library of Congress Cataloging-in-Publication Data
A catalog record for this book has been requested

ISBN: 978-0-367-21003-8 (hbk)
ISBN: 978-0-367-21004-5 (pbk)
ISBN: 978-0-429-26478-8 (ebk)

Typeset in Bembo
by Apex CoVantage, LLC

MIX
Paper from responsible sources
FSC™ C013985
www.fsc.org

Printed in the United Kingdom
by Henry Ling Limited

CONTENTS

PREFACE

Dear readers,

No matter whether he or she is working in practice or in research, every psychologist will sooner rather than later encounter tests that have been adapted to or from a foreign language. Many psychologists worldwide are also familiar with a situation where they need a test in a specific language, either their own or some foreign, and know of a test that would be perfect for that need, but it either does not exist in that language or there is no data about interpreting the results in that language. Sometimes, a psychologist will have a test in an appropriate language available, but will not be sure whether that test is valid and how it can be used. This will often be the case in regions like Europe, with its multitudes of languages in a limited geographical area, but also in many other regions of the world, and especially in multicultural areas with dynamic flows of people and businesses.

In spite of this, knowledge of good standards and practices for the adaptation of psychological tests is permeating slowly into the world's psychological community. At the time I conceived this book, most texts on the topic were either written for readers from the scientific community who already have advanced knowledge of psychometrics and test adaptation or contained only general principles and standards on the matter. The topic was almost not covered at all in university curricula of psychology studies. Hoping to change this, almost a decade ago, I created a course titled "Cross-cultural Adaptation of Psychological Measurement Instruments" and included it in the curricula of bachelor studies of psychology in my university. The course required students to master the basic principles of adapting tests for use in another language or culture. The course required students to create their own adaptation of an existing test in their language into a foreign language and then to travel to that foreign country, collect data and make a report on the functioning of the adapted version. Thanks to our geographical position, two foreign countries with different languages were available within a two-hour drive, and multiple more if we extended travel time a bit. After years on working on that course, I prepared a textbook for it.

The book before you is based on that book, in the meaning that the goal of this book is also to introduce the reader with basic concepts, issues, procedures and good practices for adapting psychological tests for another language or culture. And to do that in a way that is easy to follow and understand for students of psychology, but also for psychologists and casual readers. Compared to the original textbook it has been somewhat updated and modified to present key issues in a way that is more relevant for the English-speaking readership. It requires the reader to have a basic understanding of psychological statistics and psychometrics, and be familiar with concepts like reliability and validity, latent variables and manifest variables, factor analysis, test theory, measurement error and the like.

Enjoy.

The author

1
CULTURE

Culture as a concept

For issues related to cross-cultural adaptation of psychological measurement instruments, culture is a central concept. Culture can be considered a frame that gives meaning to behaviors, gestures, words and relationships between people. It represents a general context in which all of these happen. For example, if we see two people on a street encompassing each other with their hands, culture will determine whether we will perceive these two persons as two people in romantic love embracing each other, or as close friends who have not seen each other for a long time greeting each other. Culture will also determine whether we will see this gesture as an expression of friendship, or of domination, or whether we will perceive this as an ongoing fight and the two persons fighting each other. Geert Hofstede (Hofstede, 2011, p. 3) defines culture as "the collective programming of the mind that distinguishes the members of one group or category of people from others", although there are many other definitions. Straub et al. (2003) divide **definitions of culture** into several categories: 1) definitions based on common values, 2) definitions based on problem solving and 3) general, all-encompassing definitions. These first two categories comprise the central part of what people typically understand as culture.

Hofstede et al. represent **manifestations of culture** as a group of concentric circles:

- In the innermost, central circle are common values defined as "wide, non-specific feelings for good and bad, beautiful and ugly, normal and abnormal, rational and irrational". They state that these values create feelings that are often unconscious and that are rarely subject to discussion, but which still manifest in behavior.

- The second circle are rituals – collective actions that are practically superfluous, but are essential from the social standpoint, and are therefore performed for their own sake.
- The third circle of manifestations of culture represents heroes – "persons, alive or dead, real or imaginary who possess characteristics highly prized in the cultures and who thus serve as models for behavior".
- The fourth and the widest circle represents symbols – "words, gestures, pictures and objects that carry a certain meaning within a culture".
- These authors consider symbols, heroes and rituals to be examples of "practices" or common behaviors because these three types of manifestations of culture are visible to an external observer, "although their cultural meaning lies in the way they are perceived by insiders" (Hofstede, Neuijen, Ohayv, & Sanders, 1990, p. 291).

From the description of what culture is, it is clear that culture is a collective phenomenon first. Common values require a community for which these values would be common. But how large does a community need to be so that it can be justifiably considered to possess a culture of its own? We know that individual persons are not all the same, but that they differ in many things, including values, and surely in all these other constructs that comprise manifestations of culture. And also, when we observe any larger natural group of people, how do we know if all members of that group belong to the same culture?

In common speech, culture is primarily tied to ethnic groups, nations or sometimes to groups of people speaking the same language. However, aside from such uses of the term culture, there is also the concept of "organizational culture" and the concept of subculture. The concept of subculture refers to a smaller group of people that are part of some bigger, usually national, culture, but who have some specific cultural characteristics of their own. The concept of "professional culture" is also being used ever more and this is a concept based on the data of ever-increasing body of research showing that, in many aspects, people working in same professions from different countries may be more similar than even people from the same country working in different professions.

Considering such a wide scope of the concept of culture, it should be noted, as was noted by Straub et al (Straub et al., 2003), that there are individual differences between people within each group, and that they do not all accept the same values literally or to the same extent. These authors also state that the same person may accept an array of different cultural patterns, i.e., that influences of different cultures may manifest themselves in the same person. In accordance with this, they suggest that each individual be considered a combination of cultures or subcultures it belongs to. Aside from the national culture, these cultures should include cultural patterns of different collective identities the person accepts, such as gender, profession, sports club and of other smaller social groups cultural norms of which the person accepts. These authors believe that, within this approach, which they consider to be based on the social identity theory, culture should be assessed on the individual level, by examining the individual. In this way, culture would be studied as an individual phenomenon, and conclusions about the culture of the entire group could then be based on the aggregation of individual data.

A question that than arises is which definition or what scope of culture should be taken into account and applied in the practice of psychological testing? Taking into account only cultures of large social groups, such as nations, would potentially lead to psychological testing practices providing inadequate results for many individuals whose culturally determined psychological characteristics differ from those typical for the majority of their compatriots. On the other hand, adopting an approach that would take into account cultural differences on the individual level would make the process of psychological testing so complicated that psychological testing would probably be impossible without the use of complex software, if even then. It is quite probable that such a practice would also compromise one of the key requirements of psychological testing – the requirement that psychological tests be administered, scored and interpreted in the same way for all test-takers.

A solution that is the most common in practice is that the criterion for the maximum size of the social group is the language. In the maximum variant, a test is, without any additional adaptations, used on test-takers who speak the same first language. If test-takers do not share the same first language,[1] most psychologists would now agree that assessing them with the same test would be problematic at least, and that the test should be adapted to the first language of test-takers. And while it is up to debate whether it is justified to create special adaptations of a test for smaller social groups, the need to create different language versions of a test for people who speak different languages is an issue about which there is more or less a general consensus.

Culture, language and psychological testing

Why is culture important for the practice of psychological testing? For a psychological test to function as intended, it is necessary that it be administered, scored and interpreted in the same way for all participants. For test scores to be valid, it is necessary that responses of the test-taker to stimuli in the test (test items) be influenced or incited by the same psychological trait or construct – the trait or construct the test was designed to measure in the test-taker. If it so happened that the same item produced responses influenced by one psychological trait in one group of test-takers and responses caused by some other, completely different, psychological trait in another group of test-takers, that would completely compromise the integrity of the testing procedure. In the same way, if differences in familiarity with test contents, which of themselves are not the construct that the test proposes to measure, caused certain items to be harder or easier for test-takers with the same level of the measured trait from one population then for test-takers from another population, this would represent a source of variability of test scores that would seriously compromise the validity of conclusions drawn from the test. For example, if some general information test contained an item asking the test-taker to name the US state in which Salt Lake City is located, such an item would be much easier for test-takers living in Utah, USA, then for test-takers living for example in England, UK with the same level of the measured trait or construct.

Culture, as a framework that gives meaning to actions, words and objects, critically influences ways in which a person will interpret the meaning of various elements of the psychological test as well as the meaning of the test as a whole. Cultural differences cause or may cause two different persons to attach different meaning to the same elements of a psychological test, and in that way cause the psychological test to function differently for these two persons.

From a practical standpoint, cultural differences create problems for the practice of psychological testing by causing the same test to sometimes function differently when used on test-takers belonging to different cultures. For these reasons, modern standards for psychological testing (International Test Comission, 2017) proscribe that the equivalent functioning of a test in two cultures or in two different populations may not be presumed in advance, but must be empirically verified. Aside from that, differences between cultures, as well as properties of each culture are not static, but tend to change over time. For this reason, the equivalence of functioning of the same test in different cultures must be periodically reexamined.

When considering the relationship between culture and language, it should be noted that language need not represent a border of a culture. Although language and culture are often equated in everyday life, in the sense that members of the same culture speak the same language, this need not be always the case. It may be possible that speakers of the same or of very similar languages belong to cultures that are so different that the validity of a test that works fine in one group would be completely compromised in the other group without adaptation. In the same way, it might be possible to find groups that speak different languages, but whose cultures are similar enough for psychological tests that are valid in one group to function adequately in the other with only a simple translation to the other language.

Related to this issue, one very important factor that needs to be taken into account is **globalization.** Globalization is typically defined as an increased interaction between people through growth of international flow of money, people and ideas (https://en.wikipedia.org/wiki/Globalization). The start of globalization is usually placed in modern times and is especially related to the expansion of internet, but there are authors who believe that we should look for the first moments of globalization in the European "Age of Discovery", particularly in the time period when European sailors discovered the Americas and set forth exploring and conquering the world. Although the concept of globalization seems to primarily refer to the process of economic integration and strengthening of international exchange, it also has important social and cultural aspects. Through increased communication, travel and exchange between cultures, globalization, on one side, increases differences between inhabitants of one territory, i.e., inside national groups, and on the other hand, reduces differences between cultures throughout the planet.

Increases in differences between inhabitants of a certain territory happens because, through communications and exchange of cultural contents, individuals obtain an opportunity to adopt cultural norms and values that are dominant in some other, often geographically distant, social groups. Aside from that, moving of people through emigration and immigration leads to a situation in which a single territory that was once ethnically, culturally and linguistically relatively homogenous, now hosts members of different cultures who bring with them their values and other aspects of their culture. Reduction of differences between cultures happens through multiple mechanisms:

- Members of various cultures throughout the world are now **exposed to same cultural products or contents** (movies, music, media contents) thanks to the availability of international exchange of cultural products, thus producing an opportunity to change the properties of the domestic culture by adopting cultural elements contained in these cultural products.
- People **learn foreign languages** (currently, mostly English), in order to be able to understand people who do not speak their language. Through this activity, they adopt and become aware of concepts contained in the foreign language, which might not even exist in their own language. They also become aware of connotative meanings of words and expressions in the foreign language.
- People **more often meet people belonging to cultures different from their own** and have more opportunities to communicate either directly or through communication devices. Communication and exchange allows people to be acquainted with properties of other cultures, and, through time, this creates opportunities for synchronization of values and other elements that comprise culture.
- The synchronization of characteristics happens through **intentional creation of similar or compatible national institutions with the goal of making international flow of people, ideas and capital easier** – this process can be observed in various areas from the organization of government administrations, through laws and their contents, to the synchronization of educational systems and systems of professional qualifications. For example, in many European countries, one of the requirements for a university study program to be accredited is that its contents must be similar enough to contents of programs that educate people for the same professions in foreign countries (one of the components of the Bologna process – https://ec.europa.eu/education/policies/higher-education/bologna-process-and-european-higher-education-area_en). The national laws of most countries are often required to be in line with various international treaties, conventions or norms of various international organizations, and this causes them to be similar to laws regulating the same area in other countries.

In this way, there are less and less large differences between societies of various countries, and through this, between cultures. This trend is visible in some areas even when psychological constructs, i.e., functioning of psychological test, is in question (Hedrih, Stošić, Simić, & Ilieva, 2016). For example, in the area of vocational interests assessed through the scope of Holland's theory, during the second half of the 20th century, researchers often obtained results showing inadequacy of this theory in various countries. In contrast, in the first two decades of the 21st century, such results seem to be much rarer. Even studies in some countries where negative results were previously obtained, for example in China, now produce results that confirm the validity of both this theory, and of tests based upon it (Long, Adams, & Tracey, 2005).

We should also be aware that **effects of globalization do not seem to reach all parts of a society equally**. While there are parts of society, i.e., groups of people who are intensively involved in the process of international or intercultural communication and exchange, there are also parts of the society these processes reach much more slowly or not at all. In less developed, poorer strata of a society, among nonintegrated, isolated or semi-isolated social groups, as well as among the older or less-educated people, we can expect these effects to be much less pronounced than in, for example, groups of young people, educated in the scope of the official school system and who grow up in places and in conditions that provide them ample opportunities to come into contact with foreigners and foreign cultural contents.

We can conclude from everything previously listed that in a large number of practical situations, the decision if two persons should be treated as belonging to a single culture or as members of different cultures depends on multiple factors. However, one factor that surely represents a clear border when psychological tests and psychological testing are in question is the language the person speaks. It is probably self-evident that there is no point in administering a psychological test to a test-taker if the said test is in a language the test-taker does not understand. For this reason, from a psychometrics point of view, language represents a hard border, marking a line at which test adaptation is obligatory. But creating a version of a test in another language is far from being an issue that can always be solved by a simple translation.

Unlike most other materials, where the goal of the translation process is to produce a translation that is "as accurate as possible", with psychological tests, accuracy of the translation is not as important as obtaining a version of a test that is "psychologically" identical to the original. Each psychological test is composed of a series of stimuli, i.e., items, each of which is carefully selected so that, when administered to a test-taker, it produces a response caused by the very psychological trait or construct the test proposes to measure. If translated stimuli (items) in the new language version of the test no longer produce responses caused by the trait or construct the test proposes to measure, such language version of the test is of no practical use, even though it might be very accurately translated. This is the reason why the process of creating a new language version of a test is termed adaptation and not translation. From a psychometrics standpoint, the same test that is adapted into another language is always treated as a different, separate test from the original. The equivalence of these two tests – the original test and the adaptation of that test to a new language – is something that needs to be empirically verified and documented, and absolutely not something that can be taken for granted in advance (AERA, APA, & NCME, 2006; International Test Comission, 2017).

Culture, psychological constructs, emics and etics

Most psychological theories are formulated so that they imply that psychological constructs, the existence of which they propose, exist in all people everywhere, although no real verification of such strong general claims can be found in the scientific literature.

Although there are many studies exploring the existence of a specific construct or a set of constructs in different countries, such studies rarely produce uniformly confirmative evidence for all populations. It typically remains unknown why results on different samples differ. An answer to the question of whether the cause of differences is an inadequate test adaptation, a lack of standardized or equal testing conditions, differences in data collection procedures, nonequivalence or nonexistence of the examined construct in at least some of the studied groups, or something else entirely is usually answered through speculation or by making assumptions that are usually not really explored.

Even when positive results are obtained – results that confirm the equivalence of constructs in studied cultures – such results can often be ascribed to the fact that very "globalized" samples were examined (university students, for example), and sometimes even by the fact that members of "different" cultures were in fact residents, or even more frequently students in the same country, usually the US, who are, by some criteria, of foreign origin, even though they speak the local language, usually English, and are integrated into the society of that country. It also often happens that tests used in such studies were also in English.

All of this shows that we cannot just assume in advance that all psychological constructs exist in all human populations, i.e., in all cultures. It should also not be assumed in advance that all psychological constructs function the same in all cultures, even when there is evidence that these constructs exist as such in all studied cultures. While it is certainly possible that there are constructs that are equal in all cultures, it is also highly probable that there are constructs that are unique for a particular culture, or a group of people. For this reason, the existence of equal psychological constructs in different cultures is something that needs to be empirically verified.

Concepts of an **emic** and an **etic** are two concepts that are very important for the study of the existence and functioning of psychological constructs. These two concepts came to the area of cross-cultural psychology from the area of anthropology, where concepts of emic and etic approach are used. In anthropology, the etic approach demands that the system used for describing studied phenomena be such that it is equally valid in all cultures, thus enabling the description of similarities and differences between studied cultures. The etic approach is based on the pancultural or metacultural approach to studying culture. As an opposite to this, there is the emic approach, in which the researcher tries to describe phenomena the way they are perceived by his/her study participants, i.e., in ways that are specific for the culture under study (Helfrich, 1999).

When discussing **emics** and **etics** in the context of psychology, the word "emic" is used to refer to constructs that are universal, i.e., that exist in all of the studied cultures. The word emic is used for a construct that is specific for a culture, i.e., for a construct that exists in only one culture or only in a group of cultures, but not in all of the studied cultures. The former implies that whether a construct will be treated as an emic or an etic depends on the concrete group of cultures that are studied. In limited groups of cultures, it is easier to obtain etics. For example, studies that compare the measurement equivalence of Croatian and Serbian version of psychological tests typically yield results confirming the equivalence of constructs measured by the tests (e.g., Hedrih & Šverko, 2007; Šverko & Hedrih, 2010). Croatia and Serbia are two neighboring countries in the Balkans region of Europe. Languages spoken there are mutually completely intelligible, but formally considered to be different languages.

Emic and etic approaches can also be applied to the practice of exploring measurement properties of tests. In the scope of the etic approach, one can study if a test has the same measurement properties (for example, factor structure) in all studied groups. One can assume the so-called pancultural approach and study to what extent do measurement properties of a test on samples from a certain (cultural) group correspond to measurement properties obtained on all groups taken together, controlled or not for intergroup differences. Or one can assume a multigroup approach and study if the measurement properties of a test in all individual groups correspond to the same properties in some reference group or to the assumptions of the theoretical model the test is based on.

The emic approach is based on the assumption that studied constructs are group-specific, and that a study should start by asking which psychological constructs the test measures in a given group. However, as psychological tests, by their nature, are not samples of general human behavior, but rather sets of stimuli strictly selected for their capacity to produce responses caused by a specific construct that is known in advance, studying what a test might measure, after we have already established that it does not measure what it was designed to measure, has little theoretical justification. It would be like a person buying a phone in a store, and after establishing that it does not work as a phone, starting to think about what else aside from the phone the said nonfunctional phone might be good for (instead of returning it to the store and asking for a replacement).

The way the emic approach is applied to the practice of studying measurement properties of psychological tests in different cultures is either through identifying constructs that are specific for a given culture or by identifying changes that need to be incorporated into the theoretical model for each of the groups in order to make the theoretical model valid in all groups.

For example, inspired by psycho-lexical studies in various countries around the globe that served as basis for the Big Five personality model, Smederevac (Smederevac, 2000) conducted a psycho-lexical study of the Serbian language in the scope of her PhD research. Psycho-lexical studies of this type are conducted by extracting words that can serve as personality descriptions from dictionaries of a certain language.[2] Test items are then created based on those words and these items are formatted into a questionnaire that is administered to study participants. An exploratory factor analysis of responses is then conducted and this is the basis for conclusions about latent traits causing covariances between responses. Results of this particular study showed that the obtained factors have a lot in common with the Big Five, but that they also have some specificities. To summarize, this author used a sample of personality-describing words from the vocabulary of a local language to conduct a research study. The goal of this research study was the identification of latent traits specific for that culture. This is an example of a procedure for identifying factors that are specific for a certain culture and an application of the emic approach.

Another possible form of the emic approach proposes that parameters of the theoretical model that is the basis of the test should be allowed to vary between cultures/groups, and then the changes to the theoretical model that are necessary are studied so that it becomes valid in the studied culture. For example, in the study of the functioning of the Serbian version of the Multidimensional Jealousy Scale (MJS) (Pfeiffer & Wong, 1989), after concluding that the empirical structure of the scale does not conform to the original theoretical model, authors of the study (Tošić Radev & Hedrih, 2017) proposed certain changes to the model properties in order to obtain a model that adequately describes the empirical structure on the studied group. In this case, these changes consisted in different specifications for two items, which were allowed to load on one more factor from the test, and in the inclusion of several correlated residuals into the model, i.e., correlations between items that did not originate from the constructs the test proposes to measure (see Figure 1.1).

One more possibility is to combine the emic and the etic approach. In this approach, it is possible to create a test that measures constructs that are considered to be universal, i.e., that represent etics, and then also plan for the same test to measure some constructs that are specific for local cultures, i.e., that are emics. In the case of cross-cultural application of this test, this would mean that some constructs measured by the test will be the same in all cultures, while some of the constructs the test measures will differ between cultures/test versions.

For example, Cheung et al (Cheung et al., 2011) set into the construction of the Chinese Personality Assessment Inventory – (CPAI and CPAI 2) with the goal to also include some personality characteristics specific for the Chinese population into the inventory. For this purpose, they analyzed a sample of Chinese literary works (folk stories, novels, sayings, but also some Chinese psychological publications) searching them for personality descriptions. They then used these personality descriptions as the basis for formulating test items that were intended to "capture" personality traits that are specifically Chinese. On the other hand, the remaining test items were based on the contents of similar foreign personality inventories, in order to include traits that they expected to function as etics. They ended up with

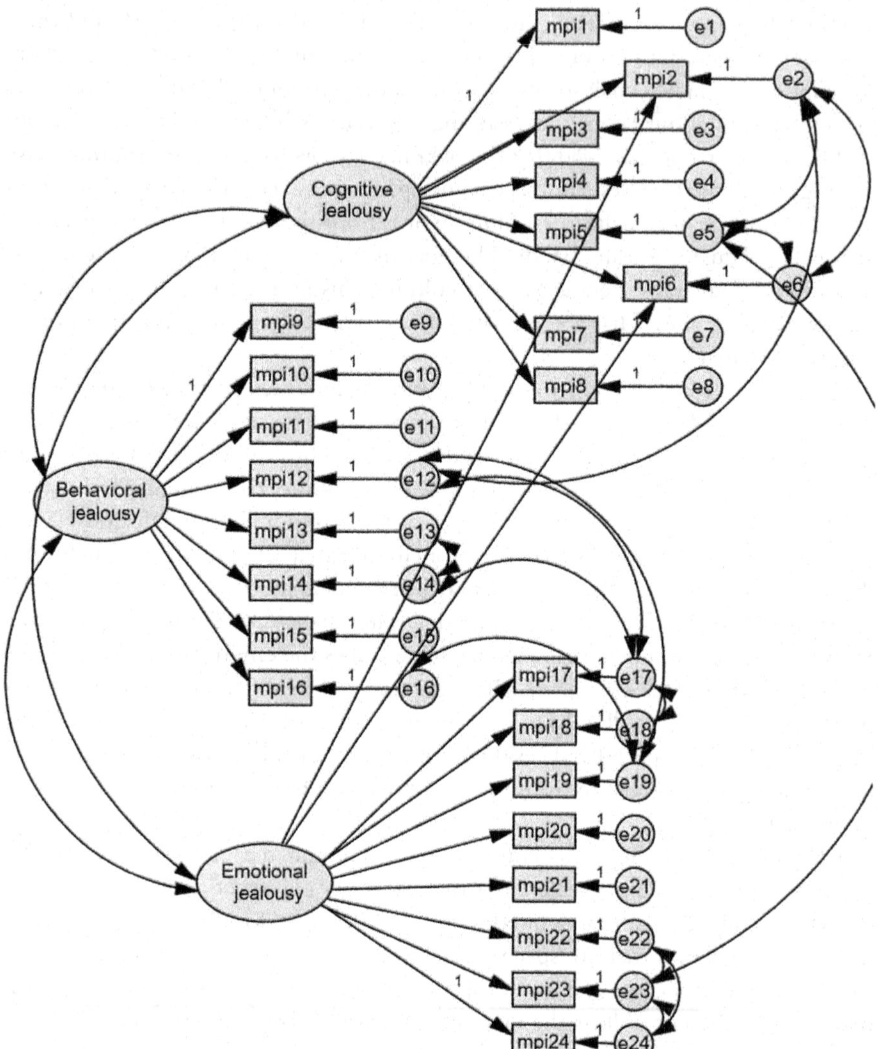

FIGURE 1.1 Changes to the theoretical structure of MJS proposed by Tošić Radev and Hedrih for the Serbian population. The original theoretical model proposes that each of the latent variables loads eight items – the first eight should be loaded with cognitive, second eight on behavioral and the last group of eight items should be loaded on emotional jealousy. Relations between emotional jealousy and items two and six, as well as the correlated residuals, are changes proposed by authors of the Serbian version.

Source: Tošić Radev & Hedrih, 2017

28 scale of "normal" personality traits and 12 clinical traits, that together comprise a certain number of higher order factors – four personality factors of normal personality and two factors representing clinically relevant traits. A common factor analysis of these measures with the measures of the NEO-FFI inventory measuring the Big Five personality traits according to the "Western" model revealed a separate factor that the authors named Interpersonal Connectedness. This factor did not have loadings on any of the Big Five model traits. On the other hand, they noticed that their inventory – the first version of CPAI – does not contain measures that correspond to Openness to Experience (O) from the Big Five model. For this reason, they added items specifically created to measure this trait to CPAI 2, in spite of the fact that this trait did not appear at all in the contents of the initial version of the test. However, even after adding the special scale intended to measure the O dimension, items that comprised this scale did not form a separate factor, but loaded on other factors that were identified earlier. The authors concluded that, although the Chinese can recognize properties that form the O dimension, these properties do not form a separate factor, as is the case in the West. They stated that their results show that the status of the O dimension as an etic is problematic to say the least, when the Chinese culture is taken into consideration, i.e., that this dimension should not be treated as an etic. This was an example of a case where authors combined an attempt to obtain personality traits that are culture-specific (based on personality descriptions from Chinese literature and psychological publications) with an attempt to reproduce factors that are already confirmed in foreign cultures, and which are proposed as universal in the international psychological literature (items inspired by foreign tests and the O scale). This is thus an example of a combination of an etic and an emic approach.

How do we actually know that a construct is an etic? Given that every psychological construct is first identified in one culture, how can we know if that construct is something specific for that culture, i.e., an emic, or if it is something that is universal for all cultures, i.e., an etic? A logical answer to this question is that we need to make an empirical trial and determine if the construct we identified in one culture functions equally in other cultures. But how can this be done? Before empirical verifications are made, it is not known if the construct identified in one culture will work in another. What can be done is to create an instrument for measuring that construct in the other culture, based on the instrument that is already known to function well in the culture or cultures in which the existence of the construct is confirmed and then conduct a study to see if this instrument will work the same in the new culture. Alternatively, and based on the knowledge about this new/other culture, it might be possible to create a test that would be used for studying the existence of the construct and then see if the test created in this way functions on the studied population in a way that confirms the existence of the studied construct in it.

Any of these two methods creates a situation in which a construct is treated as an etic even though its cross-cultural equivalence is unknown, i.e., something is treated as an etic before there is available evidence to verify if it indeed is an etic.

For this reason, constructs that are treated in this way in a new culture are called "enforced etics". An **enforced etic** is a psychological construct which has not yet been found to be culturally universal, but the cultural universality of which is under investigation. Instruments for measuring an enforced etic are constructed or adapted for the new culture based on the assumption that the measured construct exists in that culture, although this is yet unknown, but is to be verified. If an investigation carried out in this way confirms the existence of the enforced etic in the new culture and the test created to measure it functions adequately, this construct is no longer considered an enforced etic, but can, with full justification, be concluded that the construct is an etic in the studied culture.

For example, in the already described study of the multidimensional jealousy (Tošić Radev & Hedrih, 2017), authors first created an adaptation of the existing English version of the test into Serbian, starting from the assumption that the three-dimensional construct of jealousy that has already been confirmed in studies in other countries, also functions in the Serbian population. In that phase, the three-dimensional jealousy construct had the status of enforced etic. Had the later conducted study shown that the construct so defined functions in an identical way in the Serbian culture, that would merit a conclusion that this construct of jealousy is invariant in both the original US culture (in which it was first obtained) and the Serbian culture, i.e., that it is an etic for those cultures.[3] So, in order to establish if a construct may be considered an etic, it must necessarily pass through an enforced etic phase.

Dimensions of cultural differences

After we made the conclusion that there indeed might be cultural differences between various populations, the next question that arises is if these differences can somehow be systematized. Is the best we can do to simply accept that cultures differ and to then proceed to make a list of all the different cultures or is it possible to find a system in those differences? Apart from the finding that two cultures differ, can we also uncover characteristics in which they differ? By posing this question, we start discussing the issue of dimensions of cultural differences. We ask ourselves if it is possible to identify some more general dimensions, i.e., variables that define continuums along which cultural differences are distributed.

When discussing a possible systematization of cultural differences, i.e., identification of possible dimensions along which cultures differ, a lot of authors start from the US anthropologist Edward Hall (Gong, 2009; Hall, 1976; Kim, Pan, & Park, 1998) who proposed that cultures can be divided into high-context and low-context cultures, according to the way their members acquire information and knowledge and into polychronic vs. monochronic cultures, according to the way members of a culture relate to time.

In **high-context cultures**, people are taught and expected to obtain information from the context. These cultures are characterized by high interconnectedness and very close relations between people. There is a clear social hierarchy and the individual is expected to keep their personal feelings strongly controlled. Communication typically consists of simple messages that carry deep meaning (Kim et al., 1998), and individuals are expected to understand this meaning based on the detailed knowledge of the context, i.e., of people, their relations and the situation. The context is considered to be the medium that contains the information a person needs in order to decide how to act. Members of cultures like this tend to communicate indirectly, rather than directly.

An opposite of this are **low-context cultures** that are characterized by strong individualization of their members, a somewhat alienated relationship with the society and weak involvement into relations with other members of the culture. The social system and the social hierarchy impose less demands on individuals and, due to this, communication tends to be more explicit and more often impersonal (Kim et al., 1998). It is expected in these cultures that all important pieces of information be explicitly communicated and written, to be expressed verbally, so they can be understood even by people who do not understand the context.

Citing the 1999 work of Morden, Gong (Gong, 2009) states that high-context cultures include the Japanese, Chinese, cultures of Roman people, Arab, African, Indian, Korean and cultures of countries of south-east Asia. Low-context cultures include cultures of Slavic peoples, cultures of the Benelux, British, Australian, New Zealand, South Africa, cultures of the US and Canada, German, Swiss and Austrian cultures.

When considering polychronic and monochronic cultures, this categorization is based on the way members of a culture organize time. In **monochronic cultures** people believe that activities should be performed sequentially, one at a time. People in these cultures tend to be punctual and organize their time around detailed schedules which they strictly respect. In **polychronic cultures** people believe that multiple activities can be performed simultaneously, and act accordingly. They are much more laid back about time issues and, typically, do not worry much about the time a process takes. They are more oriented toward end results then toward strict adherence to a timetable.

According to Morden, who is cited by Gong (Gong, 2009), monochronic cultures include German, Austrian, Swiss, culture of white people of the Anglo-Saxon decent in the US, Finish, Scandinavian, British, Australian (culture of white people in Australia), New Zealand, Canadian, South African, Japanese, Dutch, Belgian, Korean, Taiwanese and the culture of Singapore. According to the same author, polychronic cultures include Slavic culture, Chinese, Italian, Chilean, Portuguese, Spanish, Indian, Polynesian, South American, Arab and cultures of African countries.

Although Hall's categorization of cultures into these groups can be considered a start of a systematic study of dimensions of cultural differences, one much more comprehensive theory of dimensions of cultural differences was proposed by Geert Hofstede (Hofstede, 2011; Hofstede et al., 1990). Hofstede states that he proposed the first version of his theory more or less by accident, when he acquired access to a database containing over 100,000 filled questionnaires that measured values and value-related feelings collected in various branches of IBM around the globe

FIGURE 1.2 Low-context (left) vs. high-context (right) approach to communication. On the left is the low-context case, in which all important pieces of information are verbally expressed on the sticker with the declaration attached to the bottle. One can read from the sticker that the liquid in the bottle is water, the name of the brand is listed, along with the volume, contents, producer and other pieces of information. On the right is the high-context case. Based on the shape of the bottle, the look of its contents and on circumstances under which a person acquired it, i.e., based on context, he/she is expected to know that the bottle contains water. Or maybe schnapps.

in the course of four years in the 1970s. Although the data turned out to be quite confusing on the individual level, as Hofstede reports, a big discovery happened when attention was diverted to correlations between average scores of items on the country level. This study was a turning point in the study of dimensions of cultural differences and is referred to as "the IBM study" in literature.

Inspired by these results, Hofstede repeated his studies on 400 managerial interns from 30 countries who were unrelated to IBM. Results showed that average country scores obtained on this sample are in statistically significant correlations with scores obtained in the IBM study. He concluded from this that scores obtained in the IBM study can be validly used to determine differences between national value systems.

In the years that followed, the IBM study became a reference study for many researchers both in regard to conclusions Hofstede derived from it and in regard to methodology used in it. In the first version, Hofstede's theory proposed four dimensions of cultural differences, but in 2007 and 2010, Hofstede included two more dimensions into the theory. For this reason, the current version of Hofstede's theory proposes the existence of six dimensions of differences between cultures. These dimensions are:

- Power Distance
- Uncertainty Avoidance
- Individualism vs. Collectivism
- Masculinity vs. Femininity
- Long-Term vs. Short-Term Orientation
- Indulgence vs. Restraint

Power distance is defined by Hofstede as the degree to which less powerful members of a society (or of an organization or an institution) accept and expect power to be unequally distributed. It refers to the degree of inequality in power that is acceptable to members of the society who are at the bottom of the social hierarchy. It does not refer to the degree of power differences that those at the top of the social hierarchy would like.

In societies with low power distance, use of power is acceptable only if it is legitimate and this is assessed against whether it is used for good or evil. Societies in which power distance is high tend to accept power as a basic social fact without questioning its legitimacy. In such societies, parents typically teach their children obedience and old people are respected and feared at the same time. Education is centered around teachers, subordinates in organizations expect to be told what to do, while the government tends to be autocratic and is changed violently. Corruption is frequent, scandals are covered up, wealth distribution is uneven and religious institutions emphasize a hierarchy among priest orders. As an opposite to this, in societies with low power distance, parents tend to treat their children as equals, old people are neither feared nor particularly respected, and in places where a hierarchy exists, it is established primarily for practical reasons. In societies like this, subordinates in an organization expect to be consulted, the government of the country tends to be pluralistic, elected by a majority vote and changeable by peaceful means. Corruption tends to be rare and scandals usually mark the end of the political careers of the participants. Wealth distribution in the society tends to be more even, while religion tends to emphasize equality among believers (Hofstede, 2011).

Uncertainty avoidance refers to the degree in which a society tolerates ambiguity, i.e., the degree to which a culture teaches its members to feel unpleasant in situations that are new, not previously known, surprising or generally just different from usual.

Societies with a high level of uncertainty avoidance tend to reduce possibilities for behaviors that are unusual or nontraditional to occur by introducing strict rules, laws and regulations, through non-acceptance of differing opinions and through belief in the absolute truth (religious, philosophical, etc.). In these societies, stress levels are generally high, as well as emotionality, anxiety and neuroticism. People in these societies tend to score lower on subjective health and well-being. So-called "deviant" persons and ideas are not tolerated, because different is considered to be dangerous. People tend to have a pronounced need for clarity and structure. Teachers are expected to know all the answers, and employees keep their jobs even when they do not like them. The need for rules is emotional, even when those rules are not observed. Religion, philosophy and science in these societies are characterized by a belief in final truths, while, in the area of politics, citizens are considered incompetent before the authorities. On the other hand, in societies in which uncertainty avoidance is low, uncertainty is accepted and considered to be an immanent property of the nature of life. In these societies, people tend to be more relaxed, under less stress, less anxious and have better self-control. These societies tolerate "deviant" people and ideas and diversity attracts curiosity. It is acceptable for teachers to not know something, and job change does not represent a particular problem. Members of these societies do not like rules. Religion, philosophy and science of these societies is characterized by relativism and empiricism, while citizens are considered competent before those in power (Hofstede, 2011).

Individualism vs. collectivism refers, according to Hofstede, to the degree in which individuals are integrated into groups (Hofstede, 2011). In individualist cultures, connections between individuals are weak and each individual is expected to take care of him/herself and his/her nuclear family. In collectivist cultures, people are integrated into strong and cohesive groups, usually based on kin, from birth, and these groups protect them through life in exchange for their unquestioning loyalty.

In collectivistic cultures people think of themselves as a part of a collective ("we" instead of "I"), emphasis is on the belonging to a group and maintaining social peace and harmony is considered to be very important. Other people are evaluated based on whether they belong to the same group or not. In these cultures, group membership determines attitudes and goals of an individual in advance, breaking social norms leads to the feeling of shame and first-person speech is avoided. The purpose of education is to teach people how to do things, and maintaining good social relations is more important than accomplishing tasks.

In individualistic cultures, people see themselves as individuals first, right to privacy is very important, and it is considered good and healthy for an individual to be able to speak his/her mind. Other people are seen as individuals and it is expected that every person has an opinion of his/her own. Breaking of norms leads to feelings of guilt and first-person speech is usual. It is believed that the purpose of education is to teach a person how to learn, and accomplishing tasks is considered to be more important than maintaining interpersonal relations.

Masculinity vs. femininity refers to the degree in which there is differentiation in values between males and females. According to Hofestede, value systems of females differ much less between societies than value systems of males. Value systems of males, on the other hand, range from very assertive and competitive, those that are as different from value systems of females as possible, to value systems where modesty and care hold the central point and which therefore differ very little from value systems of women. The consequence of this is that in feminine societies there is very little or no gender differentiation of social roles. In contrast, in masculine societies, there is a pronounced differentiation between male and female social roles.

In masculine societies, males are expected to be assertive and ambitious, more significance is given to work than to family and the society admires strong men. In these societies, fathers deal with facts and mothers with feelings. Girls cry, boys do not cry. Boys fight if they are attacked, girls should not fight. Fathers decide on the size of the family. The number of women holding political positions is very small. Religion is focused on God or gods. Sexuality is a topic of morality, and sex is treated as a subject of achievement. In masculine societies, contents of this dimension often represent a taboo.

In feminine societies, both men and women are expected to be modest and caring, and to achieve a balance between family and work roles. People in these societies sympathize with the weak, and both mothers and fathers deal with both feelings and facts. It is acceptable for both boys and girls to cry, but neither should fight. In these societies, mothers typically decide on the size of the family and there are many women in political positions. Religion tends to be centered on people, sexuality is accepted as a fact and sex is a way of building relationships between people.

According to Hofstede, pronounced masculinity is a characteristic of Japanese and German cultures and countries such as Italy and Mexico, while femininity is a pronounced characteristic of Nordic countries and the Netherlands (Hofstede, 2011).

Long-term vs. short-term orientation is a dimension Hofstede states was obtained from students from 22 countries by using a questionnaire created by Chinese scientists (The Chinese Culture Connection, 1987). Hofstede states that the author of this study was Michael Harris Bond, and he initially named this dimension Confucian work dynamism. Hofstede included it into his model later, with Bond's permission.

Societies on the pole of this dimension that corresponds to long-term orientation value perseverance and thrift, organization of social relations in accordance with social status and the feeling of shame. They believe that a good person adapts to the situation, that what is good and what is evil also depends on the situation, and that the most important events of their lives are yet to take place in the future. Tradition is something that adapts to conditions. Family life is led by common tasks. These countries try to learn from other countries and save a lot in order to have money for investing. Students tend to explain their success as a result of effort, and failure as a result of insufficient efforts. People expect fast economic development of the country. Hofstede states that long-term orientation is a characteristic of East Asian countries, and also the countries of Eastern and Central Europe.

Societies on the pole of this dimension that corresponds to short-term orientation value social relations that are based on reciprocal commitments, respect for tradition, protection of one's "face", i.e., personal credibility and personal stability and steadiness. People in these societies believe that the most important events of their lives have already happened or are happening now. Personal steadiness is important – a good person is always the same and there are universal rules for deciding what is good and what is evil. Tradition is sacred and family life is guided by clear imperatives. A person is expected to be proud of his/her country. Serving others is an important goal. These societies are oriented toward spending. Students attribute their success or lack of success to luck. In poor countries from this group, economic development is slow or there is none. Short-term orientation is a characteristic of the USA, Australia, countries of South America, African and Islamic countries (Hofstede, 2011).

Indulgence vs. restraint is a dimension that differentiates between societies that allow "relatively free gratification of basic and natural human desires related to enjoying life and having fun" (Hofstede, 2011) from societies that control gratification of needs and regulate it through strict social norms.

According to Hofstede, societies on the pole of this dimension corresponding to restraint consist of people who are less happy, people who see themselves as helpless and tend to have an external locus of control. Freedom of speech is not a topic about which people worry much and free time is less important. People from these cultures are less likely to remember positive emotions. Fertility will be lower in countries with this culture if the population is educated, and there will also be less people engaging in sports. In countries with sufficient food, the number of overweight people will be lower, while, in richer countries, sexual behavior norms will be stricter. These countries tend to have a higher number of policemen per capita. Hofstede states that cultures close to this pole are cultures of Eastern Europe, Asia and the Islamic world.

Societies on the pole of this dimension corresponding to indulgence have more people who consider themselves to be happy, and people also tend to perceive that they have more control over their lives. Freedom of speech is considered important as well as free time. It is more likely for people in these countries to remember positive feelings. In countries with an educated population, fertility will be higher, and there are also more people engaging in sports. In countries with sufficient food, there will be more overweight people in the population. In rich countries, norms regulating sexual behavior will be mild. Maintaining order is not a high-priority topic. Hofstede states that cultures closer to this pole can be found in countries of North and South America, the Western Europe and some parts of sub-Saharan Africa (Hofstede, 2011).

******

When considering the practice of cross-cultural adaptation of psychological tests, these dimensions of cultural differences are important because greater differences in test functioning, as well as greater problems with adaptations, should be expected when test versions are created for cultures that differ more on these dimensions. On the other hand, when test adaptation is conducted for cultures that are similar about these properties, the adaptation process can be expected to be simpler and cross-cultural equivalence of test versions more easily achieved.

When working on adapting a test created in one culture for use in another culture, knowledge about the exact differences between these two cultures on these dimensions can be of great help. This is especially important if the content of measured constructs is close to or includes content of dimensions on which cultures differ. Aside from this, knowing the nature and content of differences between two cultures can be invaluable when reflecting on possible reasons for obtaining results showing unequal functioning of test versions created for the two cultures. This will be discussed in more detail in the following chapters.

Notes

1 "First language" is the language a person learns to speak first (in childhood, usually). Formerly known as "native language", "mother tongue", etc.

2 As the total number of words extracted in this way from a dictionary is huge, usually not all words are extracted, but some procedure of sampling the content of the dictionary is used (for example, systematic sampling – every n-th page is sampled for appropriate words and then all the words are extracted from those pages that can be used as personality descriptors).

3 In that study, authors found that although the construct measures did not function on the Serbian sample in the exact same way as in the original, the changes that were needed were not extensive. Based on this, the authors concluded that for all practical purposes the construct in their sample is sufficiently similar to the original, although not identical. As this shows, things are not black and white.

References

AERA, APA, & NCME. (2006). *Standardi za pedagoško i psihološko testiranje*. Zagreb: Naklada Slap.

Cheung, F. M., Van De Vijver, F. J. R., Leong, F. T. L., Cheung, C., Van De Vijver, F. M., & Leong, F. J. R. (2011). Toward a new approach to the study of personality in culture. *American Psychologist, 66*(7), 593–603. https://doi.org/10.1037/a0022389

The Chinese Culture Connection. (1987). Chinese values and the search for culture-free dimensions of culture. *Journal of Cross-Cultural Psychology, 18*(2), 143–164. https://doi.org/10.1177/0022002187018002002

Gong, W. (2009). National culture and global diffusion of business-toconsumer e-commerce. *Cross Cultural Management: An International Journal, 16*(1), 83–101. https://doi.org/10.1108/13527600910930059

Hall, E. T. (1976). *Beyond culture*. Doubleday, New York.

Hedrih, V., Stošić, M., Simić, I., & Ilieva, S. (2016). Evaluation of the hexagonal and spherical model of vocational interests in the young people in Serbia and Bulgaria. *Psihologija, 49*(2), 199–210. https://doi.org/10.2298/PSI1602199H

Hedrih, V., & Šverko, I. (2007). Evaluation of the Holand model of the professional intersts in Croatia and Serbia. *Psihologija, 40*(2). https://doi.org/10.2298/PSI0702227H

Helfrich, H. (1999). Beyond the dilemma of cross-cultural psychology: Resolving the tension between etic and emic approaches the goals of cross-cultural psychology. *Culture & Psychology Copyright ó Sage Publications*, (22).

Hofstede, G. (2011). Dimensionalizing cultures: The Hofstede model in context. *Online Readings in Psychology and Culture, 2*(1). https://doi.org/10.9707/2307-0919.1014

Hofstede, G., Neuijen, B., Ohayv, D. D., & Sanders, G. (1990). Measuring organizational cultures: A qualitative and quantitative study across twenty. *Administrative Science Quarterly, 35*(2), 286–316.

International Test Comission. (2017). *ITC guidelines for translating and adapting tests* (2nd ed.). https://doi.org/10.1027/1901-2276.61.2.29

Kim, D., Pan, Y., & Park, H. S. (1998). High-versus low-context culture: A comparison of Chinese, Korean, and American cultures. *Psychology and Marketing, 15*(6), 507–521. https://doi.org/10.1002/(SICI)1520-6793(199809)15:6 < 507::AID-MAR2 > 3.0.CO;2-A

Long, L., Adams, R. S., & Tracey, T. J. G. (2005). Generalizability of interest structure to China: Application of the personal globe inventory. *Journal of Vocational Behavior, 66*(1), 66–80. https://doi.org/10.1016/j.jvb.2003.12.004

Pfeiffer, S. M., & Wong, P. T. P. (1989). Multidimensional jealousy. *Journal of Social and Personal Relationships, 6*, 181–196.

Smederevac, S. (2000). *Istraživanje faktorske strukture ličnosti na osnovu leksičkih opisa ličnosti u srpskom jeziku*. Univerzitet u Novom Sadu, Novi Sad, Serbia.

Straub, D., Loch, K., Evaristo, R., Karahanna, E., Srite, M., & Evaristo, J. R. (2003, January–March). Toward a theory-based measurement of culture. *Journal of Global Information Management*, 13–23.

Šverko, I., & Hedrih, V. (2010). Evaluacija sfernog i heksagonalnog modela strukture interesa u hrvatskim i srpskim uzorcima. *Suvremena Psihologija, 13*(1), 47–62.

Tošić Radev, M., & Hedrih, V. (2017). Psychometric properties of the multidimensional jealousy scale (MJS) on a Serbian sample. *Psihologija, 50*(4), 521–534. https://doi.org/10.2298/PSI170121012T

2

COPYRIGHT AND AUTHOR'S RIGHTS

Basic concepts – author, copyright and author's rights

In working with psychological tests, and especially when cross-cultural adaptation of psychological tests is in question, the topic of copyright, author's rights and intellectual property is unavoidable. Copyright, author's rights and intellectual property rights refer to a set of legal norms the goal of which is to enable creators of literary, scientific, artistic and other original works to retain control of their work, both while the work is being created and in the time period after the work has been published, i.e., made accessible to public. These rights give the creators of such works exclusive rights to use the work and to allow or deny others the use of the work. These regulations also include a system for enforcement. Psychological tests are such works, and they are protected by these copyright laws. It is therefore important for anyone working with tests to have a basic understanding of the legal regulations contained in copyright laws to enable him/her to navigate test use in a lawful way.

In most of the world, issues of copyright/author's rights are regulated by national law or a group of laws regulating the area. Main provisions of the laws regulating copyright tend to be relatively similar across countries worldwide, because most of them are based on the provisions of conventions regulating copyright on the international level. At this level, copyright/author's rights are protected by a series of conventions, most important of which is the Berne Convention for the Protection of Literary and Artistic Works, usually referred to as just the Berne Convention. This convention was adopted for the first time in Berne, Switzerland in 1886, and has been updated and amended several times. These updates were primarily driven by the development of technologies and ways in which authors' works can be expressed and used. The last update of this convention was in Paris, France in 1971 (Berne Convention for the Protection of Literary and Artistic Works, 1971).

The Berne Convention introduced several concepts that have been mirrored into existing national laws, like for example the rule that copyright protects the author's work from the moment of its creation, without the need to have the work specially registered, or special rights that make up the domain of copyright, time duration of copyright and many other provisions. This convention requires the signatory countries to recognize copyright/author's rights of citizens of all the other signatories of the convention, not only of their own citizens.

Another historically important convention on copyright is the Buenos Aires Convention of 1910. It was signed in Buenos Aires, Argentina and included a number of countries of North and South America. This convention demanded mutual recognition and protection of rights of authors over works that carried a notice stating a reservation of rights. This was commonly done by putting the statement "All rights reserved" on the work, but laws of signatory countries differed in regard to what else was needed for the protection to be in full effect. Signatories of the Buenos Aires Convention collectively joined the Berne Convention in 2000, and the Buenos Aires Convention itself became a part of the Berne Convention with a status of a "special agreement".

The United Kingdom joined the Berne Convention in 1887 and was also signatory to all the later revisions. The United States ratified the convention of Buenos Aires in 1911, and in 1988 joined the Berne Convention (the Paris act/revision of 1971), with the convention coming into force in 1989. Australia joined the Berne Convention through the United Kingdom and, in 1928, after becoming independent, issued the Declaration of Continued Application.

Author's rights and copyright

In the UK, the central act regulating copyright is the Copyright, Designs and Patents Act of 1988, including a number of amendments of later date. In the US, the central act is the Copyright Act of 1976 with numerous later amendments, but there is also a plethora of other legal acts regulating copyright issues in specific areas. These acts are currently published together by the United States Copyright Office as the Copyright Law of the United States and Related Laws Contained in Title 17 of the United States Code (2016). Some US states also have legal provisions further regulating specific copyright issues.

The key concepts of these copyright laws, and laws of all signatories to the Berne Convention, are concepts of the author, copyrighted work and of the copyright owner. A **copyrighted work** is an original creative work fixed in a certain form and it is protected by copyright laws. National laws often define types of creative works that fall into this category. For example, UK law defines copyright works as original literary, dramatic, musical or artistic works, sound recordings, films or broadcasts, and typographical arrangements of published editions (Copyright, Designs, and Patents Act, 1988), while the corresponding US law provides a similar but more comprehensive list of types of copyright works. What is important is that the work needs to be original, meaning that it is something that did not exist previously. This also means that it needs to have at least a minimum complexity for it to be clearly differentiated from works that already exist. Copyright work also needs to be expressed or fixed in a certain physical form – a recording, writing, print, drawing, etc. US copyright law defines that a

> work is "fixed" in a tangible medium of expression when its embodiment in a copy or phonorecord, by or under the authority of the author, is sufficiently permanent or stable to permit it to be perceived, reproduced, or otherwise communicated for a period of more than transitory duration.
>
> *(Copyright Law of the United States and Related Laws Contained in Title 17 of the United States Code, 2016, sec. 101)*

Copyright laws protect the fixed expression or form of creative works. They do not protect the underlying ideas the work is based on, general principles, or general knowledge contained in the work and similar. For example, US copyright law explicitly states that

> In no case does copyright protection for an original work of authorship extend to any idea, procedure, process, system, method of operation, concept, principle, or discovery, regardless of the form in which it is described, explained, illustrated, or embodied in such work.
>
> *(Copyright Law of the United States and Related Laws Contained in Title 17 of the United States Code, 2016, sec. 102)*

The copyright protection of a work is also not dependent on its value. If a creative work is original, it is protected, regardless of any assessment of its artistic, scientific or any other values. Copyright protection starts from the moment the original creative work is produced, i.e., as soon as it is fixed in a certain physical form.

A person that creates a copyrighted work is called an **author**, and a copyright work can have multiple authors. UK law also defines who will be considered the author in works that can have multiple persons involved in their creation. Copyright laws based on the Berne Convention recognize two types of rights of authors – **moral and material/economic rights**.

Moral rights of authors are defined by the Berne Convention, Article 6bis in the following way:

> Independently of the author's economic rights, and even after the transfer of the said rights, the author shall have the right to claim authorship of the work and to object to any distortion, mutilation or other modification of, or other derogatory action in relation to the said work, which would be prejudicial to his honor or reputation.
>
> *(Berne Convention for the Protection of Literary and Artistic Works, 1971)*

The idea behind the existence of moral rights is to secure that the author of a copyright work be identified and that he/she retains control over what happens to his/her work. The Berne Convention, as can be seen from the above citation, recognizes two moral rights of authors that are commonly called the right of paternity or attribution and the right of integrity, but national regulations often list additional moral rights of authors. UK law lists the following moral rights of authors:

- The right to be identified as author (or director) – i.e., the right of paternity is the right of the author to be identified as the author of the work in various circumstances, such as when the work is published, performed, shown in public, when copies are made, etc. UK law requires the author to assert this right and lists various situations where the right is applicable and needs to be observed, and also situations that are exempt from the exercise of this right.
- Right to object to derogatory treatment of work – i.e., the right to integrity; gives the author the right to "not have his work subjected to derogatory treatment" (Copyright, Designs, and Patents Act, 1988). The law states that this right refers to additions, deletions, alterations or adaptations of the work of a character that would be derogatory or would be prejudicial to the honor or reputation of the author, but does not refer to translations. It also lists situations to which this right may apply and those that are exempt from it.
- Right to not have a work falsely attributed to a person – a person has the right to not have a creative work falsely attributed to him/her. This right also includes the right of the author of an original work to not have alterations of this work attributed to him/her.
- Right to privacy of certain photographs and films – means that a person who commissions the taking of a photograph or making a film has to right to not have these materials published or exhibited in public.

In most Berne Convention-based legislation, including UK laws, moral rights are nontransferable, remain in force for the lifetime of the author and provisions are included for the maintenance of some of these rights after the death of the author.

Being a late signatory to the Berne Convention, the copyright laws of the US did not initially include moral rights of authors, but were later amended to include them. Moral rights of paternity and integrity were explicitly introduced in 1990 with the Visual Artists Rights Act, but only for specific types of works of visual art, while other types were excluded. In this law, moral rights are defined as nontransferable, but unlike in other laws based on the Berne Convention, they last only for the lifetime of the author.

Material/economic rights of authors, often referred to as copyright, consist of a set of rights that all represent various forms of the right to allow entities other than the owner of copyright to use the work. They provide the copyright holder with exclusive rights to allow or deny others the right to use his/her copyrighted work. UK law lists the following material rights:

- To copy the work
- To issue copies of the work to the public

- To rent or lend the work
- To perform, show or play the work in public
- To communicate it in public
- To make adaptation of the work and perform any of the operations listed above with that adaptation (Copyright, Designs, and Patents Act, 1988)

US law essentially lists these same rights of the copyright owner under section 106. Laws allow the transfer of material/economic rights and this is typically referred to as the "transfer of copyright".

According to both UK and US laws, the **first copyright holder** is **the author** of the copyrighted work, unless the work is created by an employee in the course of his/her employment. In this case, the employer is the first owner of the copyright if not otherwise agreed. US copyright law goes further in defining this as **a work for hire** and states,

> In the case of a work made for hire, the employer or other person for whom the work was prepared is considered the author for purposes of this title, and, unless the parties have expressly agreed otherwise in a written instrument signed by them, owns all of the rights comprised in the copyright.
>
> *(Copyright Law of the United States and Related Laws Contained in Title 17 of the United States Code, 2016, sec. 206)*

Even though it might seem that the UK and the US laws essentially have the same provisions about copyright ownership, the fact that US laws did not recognize moral rights at first, and later adopted moral rights of authors only for certain types of visual arts, made the US concept of work for hire highly controversial, as it can be interpreted as giving moral rights to the employer, i.e., a person who did not create the copyrighted work. It should be noted that apart from US federal law, there are a number of other company and professional association-level regulations and informal rules in place that regulate the issue of moral rights of authors in the US. For example, the American Psychological Association lists on its webpage a number of practice guidelines for determining authorship, i.e., the allocation of moral rights to creators of a scientific work – www.apa.org/research/responsible/publication/.

Considering the **duration of copyright protection**, the Berne Convention states that it should be the lifetime of the author and 50 years after that, but allows signatories to proscribe longer periods of protection or different periods for specific types of copyrighted works. To that effect, national laws of signatory countries provide different durations of copyright protection. UK and US laws also provide different durations for different types of works.

Although copyright laws give exclusive rights to the copyright holder over the copyrighted work, both the US and UK, along with other signatories of the Berne Convention, allow limited use of the copyright work without the consent of the copyright holder for specific purposes and in ways that do not interfere with the legitimate rights of the copyright holder. In the US, this doctrine is referred to as the **fair use** doctrine and the law states that use of copyrighted work for purposes such as criticism, comment, news reporting, teaching and research is not an infringement of copyright, provided that this use meets certain conditions regarding the nature of the work and its use, size of the part of the copyrighted work that was used, and effect of such use on the potential market or value of the copyrighted work. US law also specifies certain limitations of exclusive rights of the copyright holder in the cases of reproduction of the copyrighted work by libraries and archives and a number of other specific cases (Copyright Law of the United States and Related Laws Contained in Title 17 of the United States Code, 2016). The UK refers to these limitations of copyright protection as **fair dealing**, and the law lists specific acts and situations that are permitted in relation to the specified work, such as certain cases of creation of personal copies of the work for private use, research or private study, making of temporary copies, creating copies for text and data use for non-commercial research, use for criticism, review and news reporting, making alterations and personal copies needed by disabled persons to use the work, some uses by authorized bodies, etc. (Copyright, Designs, and Patents Act, 1988). All this said, the issues of fair use and fair dealing are complex ones and the border between fair use and copyright infringement can sometimes be blurred. Due to this, there are often industry-, area- or profession-specific standards and norms in place detailing what does and what does not constitute fair use in common situations found in that industry, area or profession.

Violations of copyright

Violations of copyright, also called copyright infringements are situations in which a person violates or fails to observe some of the provisions of legal acts regulating copyright or of a contract regulating copyright. Although there are many specific forms in which copyright can be violated, the central point of all violations of copyright always consists of unauthorized use of the copyrighted work or an unauthorized method of using or presenting the copyrighted work. It should be noted, that some of the violations of copyright have such form that they are not and cannot be sanctioned through relevant laws and legal norms.

Violations of copyright have some specific characteristics in comparison to other sorts of violations of rights, because the damage done usually consists either in the violation of the exclusive control the copyright holder has over the use of the protected work or in deceiving other people about the properties of the work. These violations do not usually include the taking of the protected work away from the copyright holder, in a sense that the copyright holder does not possess it anymore. This nature of violations of copyright makes it critically different from the situation of theft, where the owner of the stolen thing, after the theft has occurred, loses control and possession of the stolen object. Violations of copyright can happen even without the author or the copyright holder knowing about them, and in such a way that they do not interfere with any aspect of life of the author/copyright holder or with the exploitation of the protected work. There are also situations in which violations of copyright may result in net benefit for the author – for example, in situations when unauthorized distribution of the work in the markets currently inaccessible to the copyright holder increase the popularity of the work in those markets, so that when the market becomes accessible to the author, he/she is already well-known to consumers there. Apart from this, violations of copyright can also happen unintentionally, for example, in a case when a person independently creates an identical or a very similar expression of an idea, without being acquainted with the fact that such expression of that idea already exists.

Three most well-known and legally punishable categories of copyright violations are **plagiarism, forgery and piracy**.

Plagiarism happens when a person appropriates or copies a protected work of another person in entirety or in part and presents that work as his/her own or includes the protected work into his/her own work without referencing to the real author, i.e., without specifying that it is a protected work of another person.

Probably the most well-known form of plagiarism is the one in which one person intentionally, with premeditation, appropriates the copyrighted work of another person in slightly altered or unaltered form and starts representing it as his/her own. When something like this happens, the copyright and moral rights of the author are obviously violated. Someone who is not the author of the work presents it as his/her own and benefits from it. However, this clear and obvious form of plagiarism is actually not very common.

A much more common, and currently somewhat controversial, phenomenon is when parts of a piece by one author are identical or very similar to the work of another author, while it is not completely clear how this similarity came to be. Sometimes, it really is the case that a person appropriated parts of a copyrighted work of another with the intent to present them as his/her own, but it might also happen that the author who appropriated parts of copyrighted work of another person was simply not sufficiently familiar with referencing standards, i.e., about correct ways in which content taken from others should be marked. Some authors include in this category of violations a situation in which an author regularly marks/references the content taken from another author, but the volume of the content is too large to represent the case of fair use. As there is no uniformly accepted consensus about what exactly does and does not represent fair use, such cases easily become a subject of controversy, where one side claims that plagiarism has happened and the other side refuses such allegations.

Plagiarism causes damage to the original author/copyright holder because the public, not knowing who the real author/copyright holder of a certain work is, might attribute credit for the work to the plagiarist and, consequently, withhold from the original author/copyright holder benefits that he/she would have from using his work. Also, plagiarism causes damage to the society at large by causing the recognition and benefits from a copyrighted work to go to people who did not create the work and who most likely are not even able to create such works. In this way, material and other rewards go to stimulating people who will surely not use that to create new value for the society in the form of new copyrighted works, while those really responsible for the creation of such original works remain unrewarded.

Forgery happens when someone creates or represents a work in such a way that he/she deceives others that some other work is in question or that the work possesses some properties that it does not possess.

Probably the most well-known example of forgery is when producers of certain objects place logos or markings of well-known brands or well-known authors (that have nothing to do with that particular product) with the intent of deceiving others that their product actually belongs to the well-known brand or that it was created by a well-known author. The forger attains additional profits or benefits in this way because buyers, believing that the product really belongs to the brand which they know, trust and respect, buy products from the forger. Products that they would not buy if they really knew who created them. However, in science, and with psychological tests, a typical form of forgery is the forgery of results of scientific research. Forgers falsely represent some aspects of the research that they claim to have carried out or they may falsely represent or falsely interpret the results of the study. The research they claim to have carried out has sometimes not been carried out at all. The forger claims that he/she carried out the research study, when in reality, no study was conducted at all, and all the research data have been made up.

Forgeries in which works of another are falsely represented as being created by the author cause damage to the author because buyers will buy copies of the forgery instead of copies of the original work created by the author, thus taking away from the author's profits from the sale of his work. If, in addition to this, forgeries are of bad quality, i.e., they do not possess declared and expected properties, they can additionally damage the reputation of the author/copyright holder of the original work, especially if buyers do not realize that they purchased a forgery. Bad, low-quality copies of the copyrighted work that the forger puts on the market, and which buyers believe are made by the original author, may create a bad image of the author and this may then damage even the sales or marketability of other original works of this author. When forgery is done by the author of the original work himself, by deceiving users that the work has some properties that it does not have, damage is sustained by users of the work because they remain deprived of the expected effects of this work. Examples of forgery include medicines that do not cure the disease they are declared to cure, approved based on forged testing results; psychological tests that do not measure psychological traits they propose to measure, supported by forged results of research studies that never took place, or had very different characteristics than declared; and computer software that does not perform the function it is declared to perform in its advertising materials.

In the area of psychological testing, one can encounter situations in which little-known authors create tests that they name incorporating the names of existing, widely used and well-known tests, thus deceiving the public and users that their tests are variants of world-famous tests, and hiding the fact that their tests – aside from perhaps the topic – have nothing to do with these famous tests or with their authors. However, it should be noted that sometimes the reason for this occurrence is not a desire to deceive the public or attain material gain at the expense of the author of the original test, but very often the excitement of the author about the second test and the theory it is based on. Situations like this happened relatively often in previous decades, especially in situations where the original test was not available in the country or territory where authors of the new test worked, and these authors were not familiar enough with the topic of copyright.

Piracy happens when someone uses a copyrighted work without the permission of the author/copyright holder and without any other legal right. In many aspects the most benign of all forms of copyright violation, piracy is an act in which a person simply uses the copyrighted work of another without permission. In this type of infringement there is no appropriation of the copyrighted work, there is no attribution of nonexistent properties to the copyrighted work or any other alterations or damaging effects on the copyrighted work – the work is used as-is, users are not deceived about the identity of the author, and signs of authorship/copyright remain on the work. However, as the author or the copyright holder are the only persons to have the right to allow or disallow others the use of their work, anyone who uses the work without their permission or other valid legal basis makes an infringement of copyright of this sort.

Piracy causes damage to the author/copyright holder by depriving them of the earnings they would receive for the use of their work if usage rights were obtained legally.

★★★★★★

Aside from these three types of copyright violations, there are some other behaviors that are in discord with the letter or spirit of legal norms regulating author's rights/copyright or that cause damage to the society at large, and which are encountered in practice. These behaviors are mostly not punishable by law or are such that the current methods of law application cannot result in punishment for these acts. Some of them are prohibited by ethical rules and codes of conduct of various organizations and may be punishable behaviors within organizations that employs the perpetrators.

Underserved authorship represents a situation in which some of the people listed as authors of a creative work did not contribute to the creation of the work substantially or at all. In a typical case, they receive moral rights over the work they did not create. The public is deceived that a person who did not really contribute to the creation of the work is the author of the said work. Situations like this typically arise as a result of an agreement between the real author and the persons acquiring undeserved authorship or as a result of coercion that happens through abuse of power by the person taking undeserved authorship over the real author. A typical example of undeserved authorship happens when two scientists agree that each of them will give the other (undeserved) authorship of the paper he/she has written. In such a case, although each of these two scientists worked only on his/her own paper, through their agreement, they become coauthors of both papers. In a system that evaluates the performance of scientists by counting papers and citations, like is the case in many universities throughout the world, this arrangement creates a clear benefit for such scientists by doubling their output of scientific papers.

Another typical situation in which undeserved authorship occurs is the one where the real author is in a dependent position toward the person taking undeserved authorship and then this person coerces the real author to give him/her undeserved authorship through misuse of power. For example, a head of a scientific organization enforces "an unwritten rule" that he/she must be listed as a coauthor of all papers and works of scientists, especially junior ones, employed at his/her organization. In a similar fashion, there could be a professor at a university or a head of a laboratory who enforces "an unwritten rule" that they must be listed as coauthor of all papers and works of their students or those that are created by using their lab. Sometimes these people enforce this rule by punishing or threatening to punish employees who do not abide by them (for example by firing them, by not extending their contract, through harassment, giving bad evaluations to students and their works, etc.), and sometimes by directly using their power to give themselves the authorship – for example, by creating contracts stating that they are the authors of all results created as a part of their project, or by using their power to list themselves as authors of the scientific work directly, without consulting the real author. A variant of this scenario is also the case where the real author, out of fear of being the victim of abuse of power, or in hope of ingratiating him/herself to the person in power, lists the person in power or even someone else close to the person in power (children, relatives, spouse of the person in power) as a coauthor on their own initiative.

Probably the most benign form of undeserved authorship occurs when a lesser known author agrees with an accomplished author to list him/her as a coauthor of the work in hopes that, thanks to the well-known author being a coauthor, the work will achieve better sales, or become more famous and thus help the less-known author to increase his fame.

Undeserved authorship is an important topic in modern discussions of copyright. As many prominent institutions in the society, especially in the area of science, use creative works of a person as an indicator of competence of that person for various important job and social positions, the existence of undeserved authorship leads to the situation in which essentially incompetent persons come to look competent "on paper", thus allowing them to obtain positions that require competencies that they realistically do not have. Such persons, through incompetent work, cause damage to the organizations and institutions in which they work, and often use their position of power to force those in a dependent position to list them as coauthors of their works, enabling them to increase "their qualifications", thus continuing this vicious cycle. As the position of such a person gets higher, so grows the number of real, competent authors in a position of dependence to the undeserved author. Given that persons like these get their authorships by making others list them as coauthors, and not by creating the original works, if they can attain a position high enough to make a large number of real authors be in a dependent position toward them, they might succeed in obtaining moral rights or even copyright over an opus of works that exceeds even the opuses of the most productive real authors. Such practice usually has a very demotivating effect on real authors, creating a bad social climate in the organization in which these types of undeserved authors work.

In recent decades, the awareness of the problem of undeserved authorship is rising and organizations that deal with original works create various regulations in order to identify and reduce the frequency of undeserved authorship occurrence. For example, some universities, when deciding on promotions or admission of new people into their faculty proscribe that candidates need to have a certain number of publications in which they are the first author. Scientific journals request authors to submit statements about the contribution each of the listed authors made to the manuscript under consideration. Some professors request the students to, along with their group work, submit a statement about which of the students working in the group contributed to which part of the work. Organizations, professional associations and other similar bodies include in their codes of ethics and other normative acts explicit bans for anyone to be declared a coauthor based solely on his/her position in the organizational hierarchy. Also, normative acts and recommendations are created that precisely define what is and what is not a basis for someone to be treated as a coauthor. For example, one very prominent effort in this regard are the recommendations for defining the roles of authors and coauthors of the International Committee of Medical Journal Editors – www.icmje.org/recommendations/browse/roles-and-responsibilities/defining-the-role-of-authors-and-contributors.html, created after noticing a trend of an increasing number of authors per paper in a number of different journals (Eriksson, Godskesen, Andersson, & Helgesson, 2018). Although the existing practices for countering undeserved authorship are far from perfect, these practices do make it more difficult for persons who did not contribute to the creation of an original work to be listed as coauthors.

It should be noted, that none of these examples or situations refer to cases where work-for-hire provisions of the US copyright law apply or are applicable. Also, as right to attribution is explicitly specified by the Berne Convention as the right of the author "to claim authorship of the work", regardless of the economic aspects, undeserved authorship represents a case where people who are not authors claim authorship. As laws that recognize moral rights of authors typically see them as nontransferable, sharing of authorship with a person who is not an author also represents a disregard for the provisions of these laws.

Ghostwriting or writing for others is a form of undeserved authorship in which the real author creates a work for others who then later present it as their own. The real creator of the work remains unknown, and the people who present themselves in public as authors did not really contribute to the creation of the work. European laws directly disallow the transfer of moral rights of authors, including the right of attribution, making ghostwriting a practice outside the legal boundaries in these countries. US law, on the other hand, recognizes the institution of work-for-hire making the issue of the legal status of ghostwriting a little more moot, especially in areas not afforded protection of moral rights by the Visual

Artists Rights Act (Copyright Law of the United States and Related Laws Contained in Title 17 of the United States Code, 2016, sec. 106a).

The name ghostwriting itself seems to point to the textual nature of the work created in this manner, but the phenomenon of ghostwriting can be found in all forms of creative works. Typical examples include situations where unknown and usually little-known authors create original works (musical, textual, graphical, perfumes, software, etc.) for people that are much more known to the public. These people then expect that copies of the creative work for which the public believes to be created by a well-known author will sell much better, as often indeed happens. In such situations, the ghostwriter is paid for his/her work, and sometimes even splits the profits with the person who is listed as the creator of the original work. There are also cases where publishers hire ghostwriters to produce a creative work, and then hire other, well-known persons to be presented to the public as creators of the work. In this way, publishers secure a higher volume of publication for highly selling authors, thus increasing profits.

Ghostwriting may sometimes be **a way to avoid censorship**. In societies in which certain authors are banned from publishing their works because, for example, they are not "in good grace" of the government or the people in power, they may try to avoid this by finding other people who will declare themselves to be authors of their works. A famous alleged case of this type of ghostwriting is the case of the movie *The Bridge on the River Kwai*. The movie was written by Carl Foreman and Michael Wilson ("Michael Wilson [writer], Wikipedia", 2018). As the two of them were on a sort of Hollywood "blacklist" at the time for alleged communist attitudes (during the so-called McCarthy period), they arranged that authorship of the script for this movie be attributed to Pierre Boulle, the writer of the novel of the same name, who, at the time, was not "blacklisted".

A form of ghostwriting that is much more harmful to society happens when anonymous writers create works attributed to other persons, who then use such attributions to deceive others that they possess qualifications that they do not possess. Typical examples of this are so called "paper mills", i.e., individuals or organized groups who offer university students to write their essays, graduate and master papers, and even doctoral dissertations that these students will then submit to the university as their own, and in that way pass exams and acquire professional and scientific degrees that they do not deserve. Another example of this type of ghostwriting is when incompetent persons, who somehow managed to obtain a job in science, get other people to write scientific papers for them, either by paying these anonymous authors or by abusing the power they have over the real authors as their superiors in the organization, their professors or as people on which the ghostwriter is somehow dependent.

In the literature, one can also find claims about cases of ghostwriting coupled with forgery where unethical organizations, often producers of pharmaceutical or medical products, hire anonymous authors to write papers based on made-up research or research results which have been altered so as to benefit the company products, and then proceed to hire well-known scientists or people of authority in the area to agree to have the paper presented or published with these well-known people as authors.

Hiding the copyrighted work from the public happens when an individual or an organization acquire copyright on a creative work with the intent to curb its availability to the public. They may do this with an intent to prevent that work from harming some of their other businesses or reducing profits of other works they possess, and for which this work would represent competition. Sometimes organizations and individuals might intentionally create copyrighted work, which they do not plan to publish at all, for the sole purpose of using copyright on that work to earn money by suing for copyright infringement other persons who, not knowing of the existence of their work, create similar works.

This is related to the phenomenon of **patent squatting**, which is a situation where an individual or an organization registers patents or copyrighted works in order to protect them, and then does not use these patents or works, but waits for someone else to create something similar so they can sue him/her and then earn money through compensation for infringement or obtaining out-of-court settlements. There is also data on a practice where organizations intentionally publish their works on the internet, in such a way that users can download them easily, believing that they are free. After this happens, the organization files charges and demands reparations from the user claiming infringement of copyright. There are also organizations that try to register patents or other forms of intellectual property that they intentionally define as broadly as possible in order to increase chances for someone else in the future to create something similar, so they can then charge him/her for patent or copyright infringement. Such individuals and organizations are commonly referred to as **patent trolls**.

Hiding the copyrighted work from public causes damage both to the author – who is deprived of the recognition he/she would receive if his work was published and used – and to the society at large when the hidden works are something that is useful for the society, such as cheaper medicines for existing diseases, more efficient or better devices for certain purposes, and similar. Aside from this, when copyrighted works are kept for the sole purpose of extorting money from authors of similar works, such behavior may seriously harm the advancement of science and technology by increasing costs and creating risks and insecurity for authors of original works. In contexts like these, authors are no longer sure if their honest creation of new works might get them into trouble, when they will are responsible for copyright or patent infringement, thus creating additional costs connected to the need to constantly search the registers of copyrighted works (patent registers, repositories, etc.), costs of insurance against involuntary copyright or patent infringement (offered by insurance houses that recognized this as a real source of risk), etc. Using these tactics to extort money from naive, uninformed users reduces the general trust in small, unknown publishers, as well as the readiness to use the original works they issue, thereby making the environment harsher for new players on the market of original works, which reducing dynamics and the rate of development of the market in which behaviors like these take place.

Self-plagiarism is when an author publishes a work that he/she tries to present as a new original work, but that is in fact the same or very similar to another of his/her already published works.

Self-plagiarism is probably the most controversial topic in the domain of copyright. On the one hand, unless copyright has been transferred to another party, the author possesses all the rights on his/her work, and that includes the right to copy, change, present and publish. On the other hand, there are numerous situations when users of a copyrighted work expect the author to provide them with a new, original work, different from what was already published, and will consider themselves deceived if a new work that is identical to some old, already published work is presented or sold to them as a new work. If copyright for the work has already been transferred to another party before the author creates a new work that is identical or very similar, a situation may arise where buyers of the copyright of the previous work and the new work are financially harmed because they do not actually possess two different original works, although they paid for two different works. This may also cause financial harm to end users who buy a copy of the new work expecting it to really be something new, but receiving what is essentially just one more copy of the work they may already possess, just misrepresented as a new work.

Another socially detrimental form of self-plagiarism occurs when persons working in areas where competencies or quality of work are evaluated based on the number of works a person creates, publishes or registers the same work multiple times under different names or translated into other languages, falsely presenting them as different creative works. Such examples can be found in the area of science, research and development where scientists, wishing to present themselves as having created more works than they actually have, publish the same work multiple times only in different scientific publications or under different names.

The other extreme end of the issue of self-plagiarism are numerous situations in which there is a legitimate need to repeat parts of a creative work or for repeated publication of a creative work with minor changes. For example, it is possible that a scientist, who became famous for a certain discovery, is invited to present that same discovery in the form of a lecture at multiple scientific conferences. The conference organizers then ask him/her to write the text of that lecture for their conference proceedings. If the scientist accepts these invitations, then, technically, this scientist might be doing the act of self-plagiarism, because the results of that study have already been published in a journal, for example, thanks to which his discovery became famous. The lecture will, of course, be somewhat different from the original journal article, but the presented results will essentially be the same. And this happens after the first conference. At the next conference at which the scientist is asked to present these same famous results, he/she will face a dilemma about whether to search for a new way to deliver the same lecture or to simply use the old one. He/she will also face a dilemma about whether to simply publish the same text of the lecture that he/she published with the previous conference in the proceedings of this conference, just with a remark that the text is the same or similar to the one already published, to allow a reprint of the already published work or to try each time to invent a new way in which to present the old results. He/she may also decide to simply deny the conference organizers the text of his/her lectures with the excuse that it was already published, thus harming the dissemination of results important for science and hence the development of science as a whole. With an increase in the number of presentations of results, the situation becomes more and more absurd. Inventing ever more original ways for presenting the same results becomes completely meaningless, and, after some time, also impossible, while, in fact, originality is not something that is even demanded of the scientist in this case, as he/she is specifically invited to present the same, already published results.

Another controversy with self-plagiarism happens when self-plagiarism is considered to be not only the repeated publication of an identical creative work, but also to include situations when a new creative work repeats elements of previously published works of the same author. The situation becomes more complex when the evaluation of the work for self-plagiarism is done using software tools that provide data on the percent of identical elements (i.e., iThenticate), and the decision on whether to consider the work plagiarism is determined solely on the percentage of content of the work under consideration that is identical to contents of other already published works. When there is no consensus on what percentage of overlap between two creative works is acceptable, and when it is realistically impossible to reduce the assessment of originality to a mere calculation of the quantity of identical content, people who use this method to assess the originality of a creative work typically use arbitrary overlap percentages and limits that they cannot justify in a valid way.

This practice can especially be seen in scientific publications, where editors typically use software tools to assess the content overlap of papers that have been submitted to them with already published papers. Interestingly, except in a few very specific cases of extreme content overlap, editors who do make the decision based on quantitative assessment of content overlap will often publicly deny that they use this method to decide on whether to send paper into review or not, and it might also happen that they try to justify a rejection of paper with other or unclear reasons, when it was really done based on the content overlap. However, in informal communication, one can often hear that such practice exists, and also hear about exact overlap percentages certain editors use for making decisions on whether to consider a paper for publication or reject it due to overlap with already published works. The trouble with practices like this lies in the fact that scientific works are neither novels nor poems, so that one should demand that they be original in their entirety. The standard structure of a scientific paper – SIMRAD – proscribes the parts a scientific paper should consist of as well as what should be written in each part. One can derive from these standards that the original part of the paper – the part that represents its contribution to science – is primarily presented in parts called results and discussion. The theoretical part presents the theoretical basis of the paper and previous studies, and the methodological part presents the research methods used. These two parts contain content that can be very similar to what is available in previously published papers. Authors of scientific papers are always required to present the theoretical basis of the study and previous studies, and these two things usually differ very little from paper to paper if the papers are on the same topic. In the methodological part, the author is expected to describe variables, instruments used and statistical procedures, and there is little sense in describing these differently in each paper that mentions them. In fact, the purpose of scientific papers is best served if identical elements are always described in a standard, identical way, and if series of different but comparable studies uses standardized methods, thus securing comparability of their results. However, the need to prevent self-plagiarism and secure originality for the sole purpose of passing a quantitative software assessment of content originality is in a direct collision with these purposes, causing scientists who focus their studies on a single phenomenon or use a standardized methodology to study various phenomena to be under the risk of being accused of self-plagiarism, and their works rejected as insufficiently original. Scientists of this type will be subjected to demands to make their papers more "original", either by changing something in their approach or method, thus bringing into question the systematic variation of condition or standardization of methodology, which are two basic traits of a good scientific approach. Paradoxically, behavior that has the advancement of science as its goal may in reality hinder the development of science.

Claiming copyright on insignificant parts of a creative work or parts of disputable originality is a situation where the copyright holder of a creative work extends his/her rights to miniscule parts of that work, parts the originality of which is at least disputable and often clearly nonexistent, accusing creators of works that have the same or similar miniscule parts for plagiarism. Although extant legal norms do specify that the holder of copyright for the entire work also possesses rights for all its constituent parts, these norms also require that these parts must be original and expressed in a certain form to enjoy protection. The problem comes from the fact that there is often no indisputable or objective way to determine whether a part of a creative work fulfills these conditions or not. If a dispute on matters like this reaches the court, the defending side can show examples of other works that possess the same or similar elements, but that were created earlier then the work he/she was accused of plagiarizing. However, court processes are tiresome and expensive, and most of these cases do not reach court at all, and are used to harm the reputation of the person who is accused of plagiarism on the basis of identical elements.

Probably the most relevant example of this situation for psychologists are disputes about copyright on individual text items of psychological tests. While it is completely clear that a psychological test as a whole is a creative work enjoying copyright protection, does such protection extend to individual items of a test? Although some tests contain very complex items with original and unique graphical solutions (for example, Rorschach inkblots), most tests, especially verbal tests, do not have such items. Items like "I am satisfied with my life", "I am often full of energy", or "I am a sociable person" and many other similar items can hardly be regarded as original creative works. A huge practical problem would arise if it were possible to copyright individual sentences or words and ban people from using them without the consent of the copyright holder. On the other hand, copyright holders of tests that contain such items and who believe they own them could reply that they are the ones who studied psychometric properties of items containing such sentences and that for that reason they should enjoy copyright on those sentences. A counterargument to this idea is that psychometrical properties are a general idea, and general ideas are not protected by copyright, and that other people – those who use the same sentences in their tests – do their own studies of psychometric properties. In spite of this, one can often hear, especially at scientific conferences and in communication between psychologists who work on psychological test development, statements in which test creators claim copyright to individual sentences – items contained in the test and accusations against creators of other tests that they have "stolen", i.e., plagiarized, these sentence items from them.

Why does copyright infringement occur? The motives of people who violate copyright are very diverse. Just one, probably smaller, situation of copyright infringement occurs because the person doing the copyright infringement wishes to obtain material gain at the expense of the copyright holder. Other situations of copyright infringement may be a consequence of completely different motives, such as:

Unavailability of the copyrighted work – if copies of the work are not available for purchase in a certain territory, people inhabiting this territory might resort to unauthorized copying of the work in order to use it. A typical example are books that are sold-out, movies that are no longer commercially available or any other type of creative work that is, by decision of the copyright holder, available only on a limited territory. This category also includes situations where, due to economic sanctions, certain copyrighted works are unavailable in the country subjected to sanctions. Copyright infringement in these situations may represent efforts of the inhabitants to maintain educational, scientific, technological and professional capacities of the country subjected to sanctions and prevent or reduce technological lagging or decay. Such was, for example, the case of the Federal Republic of Yugoslavia, during the wars of the 1990s.

Avoiding censorship – legal ownership of copies of certain types of creative works may be prohibited in certain countries, so buying copies of these works through regular channels might expose the buyer to legal punishment by authorities. In these cases, people might resort to unauthorized copying of the work in order to protect themselves from punishment. For example, when authorities of a certain country ban a movie, unauthorized copying becomes the only way for people of that country to view it. One such example is the situation in North Korea where, in spite of bans and severe punishments, people smuggle, copy and secretly watch foreign movies, music and other creative works (Lankov, 2009).

Maintaining anonymity – people may sometimes wish to hide the fact that they are users of certain copyrighted works from the public and official records, and the official process of buying a copy of the work often includes recording of personal data (for example through a payment system that transfers the money between bank accounts of the buyer and the seller).

High, unaffordable price – people who have a need to use the copyrighted work, but have no money to buy it, might resort to unauthorized copying and use of the copyrighted work. There exists a debate about whether this form of copyright infringement causes damage or benefit for the copyright holder of the work. On one hand, the copyrighted work is used, while the copyright holder is not paid for it. On the other hand, people who use the copyrighted work in this way would not become buyers of the work if they were denied the opportunity to use it, because they cannot afford it. That means that the copyright holder would not profit if the option of copying were not available. Also, if the option of unauthorized copying became unavailable, it is highly probable that these unauthorized users would switch to using some other similar work that is cheaper or would stop using that kind of copyrighted work at all. Through the unauthorized use of the copyrighted work they become acquainted with the author, thus strengthening the reputation of that author. Additionally, these people will now not switch to using cheaper competitor works, especially if these are of lower quality. And, if the material status of these people at some point improves, it is quite probable that they will become regular users of the copyrighted work they previously used without authorization, because they are now well acquainted with it. In this way, due to unauthorized copying, the copyright holder inadvertently obtained a future market and protected his/her market position from competitors. For example, the understanding about this aspect of unauthorized use is one of the principal reasons why many software companies offer students and educational institutions free or symbolically priced use of their software. While high school and university students often do not have enough money to buy expensive software during that phase of their lives, it is highly probable that they will start buying it once they graduate and become experts, earning enough money to be able to afford such software. The situation is similar with psychological tests, where it is quite customary that test authors/copyright holders allow free use of their tests to psychology students for the purposes of student projects as well as to researchers – their professors – for use in research studies.

There are properties of the copyrighted work that hinder lawful use – copyright holders, sometimes, in an effort to protect their work from unauthorized use, include in the work copy-protection systems that are poorly implemented and that hinder the regular use of the work by lawful buyers. For example, the author of a computer program might include in it a demand that the user be constantly on the internet or, as was a common case in earlier times, demand that the original disk with the program be constantly in the disc reader. Or, there may be some special conditions for use, such as where the software should be installed in order for it to work. In a similar fashion, distributors of psychological tests may insist that test users must use response forms that are exclusively purchased from the test publisher, which must then be periodically ordered and include multiple days of waiting. Or, they may put unreasonable demands on the user – for example the duty to keep a precise archive with all the tests ever used, to give the right to the test publisher to search the user's offices at will, to give out contract fines, etc. In situations like these, people may decide to remove the protection systems themselves or to resort to unauthorized copying and use of the copyrighted work with an intent to avoid the hassle involved with the legal use completely.

Non-acceptance of copyright as such – some people believe that all creative works should be free and that information has to be free. They believe that when a creative work is copied, the author does not lose anything, since he/she retains his/her own copy and that it is unacceptable for authors/copyright holders to have the power to deny others access to their work. These people may then conduct unauthorized copying and distribution of works of other authors. It is important to note that there is a significant number of people around the world that accept the idea that information should be free (Beyer, 2014); that the existing system of copyright/protection of author's rights is inadequate, that it creates bad social consequences by giving too much power to distributers, i.e., copyright holders; and that it is a basis for censorship and repression, while denying access to copyrighted works to the poor or vulnerable social groups. Some supporters of this idea also call for abolishment of the copyright protection system in its entirety (Beyer, 2014). Although this idea might look noble and beneficial for the society at a first glance, it can be argued that if copyright was abolished, production of creative works would inevitably be reduced to "a hobby for the rich", i.e., those who can devote their time to work they will not earn money from, while supporting themselves by some other means. In this way, the number of people engaged in creating original works would be significantly reduced. The idea about free and unlimited access to information has so far been embodied in the form of political parties like the Swedish Pirate party (Piratpartiet), internet portals and organizations devoted to sharing protected contents like WikiLeaks and Pirate Bay, but also in organizations devoted to the creation of free content, like Wikipedia.

Copyright and psychological tests

By their nature, psychological tests are original, creative works of their authors. This means that copyright regulations refer to them as much as to all other creative works. According to this, the author/copyright holder of a psychological test has the exclusive right to allow or deny others its use. He/she also has the exclusive right to define conditions under which use is allowed. These conditions need not be the same for all situations. The author/copyright holder may decide on different conditions for different situations or types of use of the test.

Conditions under which the author/copyright holder of a test allows a certain user the use of the test are typically defined in a document called the **license**. **License** is a document in which the author/copyright holder states which types of use or for what purposes he/she allows, who may use the work – in this case, the psychological test – and under what conditions. Licenses are usually distributed together with a copy of the creative work. Licenses are issued by the author of the test or by the copyright holder, if the copyright for the test has been transferred to some other party. The license may have different forms. It can be in the form of a legal document accompanying the product; it may be very long, with detailed conditions for use, mutual obligations etc.; but it may be also very short and informal, such as in the case of an email in which the author states that he/she allows the person asking for permission to use the work in the way requested. The license may sometimes be displayed in public, for example on a website, and users may be expected to read that license before starting to use the copyrighted work and to also observe its provisions.

When considering psychological tests, authors of the more popular tests will typically work together with a publisher or an organization that professionally works in test distribution. The author usually makes a contract with such an organization, after which the distribution of the test, licensing, deciding on conditions for use and other related issues are handled by this organizations. Sometimes, this transfer of rights also includes the right to modify the test, including the right to create other language versions of said test. However, this is not the case with all psychological tests. This path is most often followed with the more popular tests with authors who are interested in their commercial exploitation. For the majority of psychological tests this is not the case, and their authors keep rather all the rights for those tests, so it is up to authors to decide on allowing others to use their tests.

Although licenses for using psychological test may come in any shape and contain any, including very diverse provisions, in practice, one typically encounters three general types of psychological test distribution, i.e., types of licenses the accompany them. In other words, psychological tests may be:

- Free for use in all conditions and for all purposes.
- Free for use for some purposes, but payment is required for some other purposes.
- Tests that require payment for all uses.

Psychological tests that are free to use in all conditions and for all purposes are tests the authors of which allow anyone to use them free of any charge. Authors of these tests may sometimes create a formal license text in which they specify that the test is free to use and publish that license on their website or include it in the materials accompanying the test. Sometimes there is no formal license accompanying the test, but authors give their permission for use to everyone who contacts them and asks for it. Authors may sometimes allow free use of their test, but require all users to register on their website or send them an email informing them of their intention to use the test. Some authors who distribute their test in this way keep a website with different language versions of the test and an archive of published results, i.e., abstracts and scientific papers in which their test was used. It should be noted that authors who allow free use of their test might do so with the hope that their test will in this way be used by as many people as possible and in as many studies as possible. Aside from the fact that this strategy might allow them to obtain more data on test validity and functioning in various populations than they could gather if they worked by themselves, having a large number of users makes the psychological test well-known or famous in the psychological community. This increases the scientific reputation of the author of the test by also increasing the number of citations the author's publications about the test receive. This may indirectly bring greater benefit to the author than the one he/she would receive if the test usage rights were sold.

It should be noted that there are also test authors/copyright holders who do not require that they be paid money for the use of their test, but require the users to compensate them in another way. They may sometimes demand that the users send them the data they collect with their test, which they would then include in their standardization sample, and they may sometimes require the user to collect additional data from a certain type of respondents for them. In situations like this, the user should be very careful and think thoroughly before accepting. If the user needs the test for conducting research, and the test author/copyright holder asks the user to share the collected data with him/her so the author/copyright holder can also process the data and publish results obtained through the use of the test, the author/copyright holder and the user might find themselves in a conflict about publication rights on the results obtained by using the test, and also about the ownership of the database created from this data. For this reason, it is very important that the test user clarifies and takes into account all issues that might arise before accepting this kind of agreement. Also, it might happen that the cost in time, effort and money of finding test respondents with characteristics required by the author/copyright holder might end up being higher than the value derived from the use of the test. Finally, if the user intends to use the paper in his/her psychological practice, and in this way collects personal information of the test takers, he/she must be aware that an explicit consent must be obtained from all the test takers if a database containing their personal data is to be shared with a third party. Alternatively, the user must take great care to anonymize the database, removing all personal data and/or information that could allow the identity of test takers to be revealed before sharing it with the author/copyright holder of the test.

Psychological tests that are free to use for particular purposes are tests for which their authors/copyright holders allow free use for certain purposes or to certain categories of users, while they request payment for use for some other purposes or other categories of users. Most commonly, authors will allow free use of their test to students for purposes related to their studying (e.g., for student projects, psychometrics courses, etc.), and for scientific research purposes, while requiring payment for using the test in psychological practice or commercial use in general (e.g., for job selection, psychodiagnostics, etc.). The logic behind this type of license says that if the user does not earn any money from using the test, there is no basis for the author to ask for payment; but if the test user earns money from using the test, that it is fair that the profits be shared with the author/copyright holder of the test. Additionally, by allowing free use of the test to students and researchers, the author indirectly benefits by investing in his/her future profit. Students will now use the test for creating student projects and papers, but these same students will finish their studies and start working as psychologists. Given that they already became well acquainted with the test during their studies, and have also became proficient in its use, if the test works well, it is more probable that they will continue to work with this test on their job after graduation than that they will start using some other test they are not familiar with. And then they will also start paying the author/copyright holder for the right to use the test, thus creating profit for the author/copyright holder. By allowing free use of the test to the students, the author/copyright holder created a strong brand, which will later – when students finish their studies and start working – create income for the author/copyright holder. The logic behind allowing free use of the test for research purposes is similar. Researchers that use the test in their research will publish these results in scientific publications, thus making the test more known to the public. The existence of published research studies that examined the functioning of the test or of studies in which the test was used, but which were not conducted by the author or persons connected to the author, increases the public credibility of the test because assessments like these are seen as more objective than the ones published by the author. Widespread use of the test in research might also result in the test being positioned as the right solution for certain types of problems, which in turn also increases reputation of both the test and its author. Good reputation of a test obtained in this way, as well as a higher level of familiarity of psychologists with the test, its optimal usage and properties in general, may then lead to an increase in the number of psychologists who wish to use the test in psychological practice i.e. for purposes for which usage rights must be paid, thus creating increased income for the author/copyright holder. Researchers might also create adaptations to other languages and other populations themselves, and thus do a large amount of work that is needed to allow the author/copyright holder to profit from the use of test in these other populations. To summarize, researchers using the test might greatly contribute to the popularization of the test, thus increasing both the scientific reputation of the author and his/her income from test use and in this way making the free use of the test by researchers profitable, sometimes even very profitable, for the author/copyright holder.

The risk for the author exists in the case when additional research shows that the test is bad and that it does not function as declared, thus ruining the reputation of the test. However, the reputation of a bad test would soon be ruined anyway, and negative results of research with which the author is acquainted provide the author due time and an abundance of data that can be used to identify the causes of bad functioning of the test. These data may show which part of the test does not work as intended – is it due to some items, some scales, or the test as a whole; where exactly are the discrepancies; do the problems persist in all populations or only in some of them; etc. Without these studies, the author/copyright holder, might find him/herself in a situation where users simply stop ordering the test, without any clue as to why that is happening, and especially as to how to correct the problem (because no data is available). These data provide the author a chance to alter, repair or replace the test with a better one in time, thus turning a very probable loss into a chance for future profit.

Tests that require payment for all uses are primarily tests for which the authors have transferred copyright to a publisher or to a company specializing in distribution of psychological tests. These are usually very well-known tests the use of which is already established in psychological practice. Authors/copyright holders may sometimes have different prices for different categories of users, for example, lower or more affordable prices for students, more expensive for commercial use. The payment may be per individual copy of the test, for the right to use the online version (often per test taker), it may be a time-limited license (the right to use the test unlimited number of times in a limited time period) and payment may sometimes be for unlimited use. Some authors/copyright holders might sell to test users the right to create their own copies of the test. In that case, the user specifies in his order the number of copies he/she plans to make, and the copyright holder specifies the price to be paid for the right to create that number of copies. The price may be per copy or for the whole package.

This form of licensing is also often encountered with old, obsolete tests where the publisher applies the so-called "harvesting" strategy. Aware that test users are mostly older psychologists who use the test out of habit, while the younger psychologists use other, newer tests, leading to a decline in demand for this test that follows generational changes, the copyright holder tries to extract as much profit as possible from the aging test by charging for everything they can. This strategy is especially common with tests that used to be very popular, but that no longer have good psychometric characteristics (due to changing population properties for example), or when the test is based on an outdated or refuted theory, or when the test never really had good psychometric properties, but used to pass as acceptable due to weaker psychometric standards and more modest methodology for evaluating tests. The strategy of charging for every use then deters researchers from using the test in research studies (by the fact that it is outdated and has to be paid for) that would inevitably expose its poor psychometric properties, which would probably also focus more public attention to it, thus shortening the remaining commercial life of the test and also the remaining income the publisher can earn from it.

When dealing with tests for which the copyright holder charges for every use, one should be careful and should thoroughly read the license or contract the copyright holder offers. Although catalogues and public information emphasize the price that should be paid in money for the right to use the test, copyright holders are known to include in the contracts and licenses various other demands and rights that the user is expected to give them. They usually state the desire to verify that the test is used according to license as justification for such demands, but these demands may often be such that they enforce various additional duties on the user, make test use harder or give the copyright holder disproportionate rights in relation to the user. These additional rights may include the right of the copyright holder to carry out inspections of the user's company space, the right to charge contractual fines, the obligation of the user to maintain a detailed archive of all used tests, etc. One especially controversial practice for the user happens when the user is just a part of a larger company, multiple parts of which may be using psychological tests (such as when a university professor orders a test for his use in research, but there are other professors and parts of the university that may be using the same test as well), and the said user purchases the right to create a certain number of test copies for him/herself. The copyright holder may then specify in the contract that the said user is responsible for all uses of the test throughout his organization (because the test was sold to the organization the person who will be using it works in) and then control the total number of uses on the organization level, including all the other parts of the organization. This may then create a situation where a part of the organization buys tests but is then denied or hindered in their use, or is given a contractual fine for unauthorized use or exceeded number of uses by some other part of their organization on which they have very little influence. This may then lead to a situation in which, after having paid a substantial amount of money, the user ends up fined for something another part of his/her organization did, or if he/she did not maintain the required archive of used tests diligently enough.

How to obtain a license to use a psychological test. Both students who need a test to fulfill some of their study tasks and researchers who wish to use a test in a research study legally use the test only if they obtain permission for this from the copyright holder of the test. Whether it is a general permission to use the test or permission to use the test for a certain purpose, it is necessary that the purpose for which test is to be used be encompassed by the license. The same goes for the volume of use. The license should either be for unlimited use or, if the use is limited, the number of uses and purpose must be sufficient to cover what the student or researcher plans to do with it. This refers primarily to the number of test takers that the test may be used on.

For tests that are publicly declared to be free for use, obtaining a license is easy – one should only read the license and make sure that it indeed includes the type and volume of use that he/she needs and maybe fulfill some other conditions, like registering or notifying the author about the intention to use the test, for the license to become active. It is usually a good idea to save a copy of the license either in the form of a document or as a screenshot of the webpage with the license text and to also record the data when it was accessed. After this, test use may commence.

If a copy of a test is publicly available or a student or a researcher obtained it in some way, but the test is not accompanied by a license, it is necessary to request one from the author/copyright holder. The same should be done in cases when a student or researcher wishes to obtain from the author/copyright holder both the test and the permission for its use – license. A standard way to do this is to write an email to the author/copyright holder in which the student/researcher will:

Introduce him/herself by full name, and, if the researcher is employed, also with the name of the organization he/she works for. A student should name the university and the study program he/she is enrolled in and also the professor or the course for which the activity he/she needs the test for belongs.

Write exactly what he/she wants with the test. Do you need only to administer the test, or would you need to make alterations to it? Will you be using it in one research study only, or do you need permission to generally use it in your research studies? It is useful to formulate this part of the message to include all other usage situations that the student or researcher might wish to engage in later. If the intention is to use the test in research purposes, it is good to ask the author for the permission to use the test in research without limiting the number of test takers or the number of applications. If the author/copyright holder agrees with such a formulation, that means that he/she permits unlimited use of test in research, and that permissions need not later be asked for again. If your intent is to adapt the test into another language, or to make some alterations to it, this should also be stated in the request. It is very important that this part of the message is very precise and clear about the intended use of the test.

Clearly ask for permission to use the test in the way described above. The message should contain a clear question – a sentence ending with a question mark "?" – asking the author/copyright holder for a permission to use the test. If the author/copyright holder responds with a short text stating that he/she agrees with the request, it must be clear form the text of the message and the response of the author/copyright holder that the author/copyright holder permitted the requested use of the test, and not, for example, he/she just acknowledged the content of the message. Formulation like, "Would you permit me to use the test xy in the way described above?" is OK, as it represents a clear question. Formulation like, "I would like to use your test in the way described above" is not OK, because it is not a clear question.

Ask for any other things needed for the task that includes the test, which the author/copyright holder might be able to provide, like data on the psychometric properties of the test, test manual, rules for interpreting results or scoring, etc. Alternatively, the student or researcher might ask the author/copyright holder to direct them to where he/she could obtain these things, if the author/copyright holder is not able to provide them.

This message should be sent to the author/copyright holder of the test, and if the test has multiple authors who have not transferred copyright to a publisher, it should be sent to one of the authors. This request should not be sent to people who used the test in their research or published texts about it but are not authors, nor to any other category of people who are not copyright holders. When considering tests that are originally in some other language, but you need an adaptation into a particular language different from the original one, the permission should be requested from the author/copyright holder of the original version, but sometimes also from the author/copyright holder of the adapted version. In these cases, the email about permission should first be sent to the author/copyright holder of the original version and then determined if the copyright for the needed version is held by him/her or by someone else. In case the author/copyright holder of the original version is unavailable or does not speak any of the languages in which you could write him/her, it is justified to first write to the author of the adaptation and ask him/her for advice about contacting the author/copyright holder of the original version and obtaining permission to use the test. Sometimes the author of the adaptation has an arrangement with the author/copyright holder of the original version that allow him/her to issue permissions for use of the adaptation, and sometimes the author of the adapted version might be ready to ask the author of the original version for permission on your behalf, if necessary.

After receiving an email described above, most test authors will answer positively, giving their permission to use the test in the way described. Some will do that by explicitly repeating the text of the request and stating that they agree with it, while some authors/copyright holders will simply answer that they agree. Authors will generally be glad to hear that someone wants to use their test, and many of them will be particularly positive about requests coming from students, especially if they are expressed nicely, clearly and in an email message that shows good literacy. However, sometimes it might happen that the message gets bounced from the publicly available email address of the author or that the author/copyright holder does not respond to the message. Sometimes the reason for this is that the author/copyright holder changed his/her email address and you should then verify if the email is correct and look for the current one. If the author/copyright holder does not respond to the message, it is OK to wait for a few days and then send the message again. If this does not help, you could write to some of the other authors of the test, if there is more of them, or consider some other ways to get in contact with the author/copyright holder. One of the options is to send the message from some other email address, located on some other server, as it is possible that your previous emails ended up in spam and were not seen by the author/copyright holder. In most cases, this should resolve the problem. However, sometimes it may happen that the author still does not respond and that you have no way of getting in contact with him/her. Sometimes this might be because the author is no longer working in research, is no longer alive, does not use email any more or simply does not want to respond. In this case, if there are no alternative ways to reach the copyright holder, and there are also no signs that the test is in the public domain or free for use, the valid option is to choose some other test, permission for the use of which is obtainable.

Sometimes it will happen that authors/copyright holders respond, but instead of giving permission, demand payment or some service, or offer a complex contract regulating rights and obligations of the users. My personal opinion is that when you need a test for scientific research or if you are a student who needs the test to fulfill his/her study obligations, you **should not agree to pay for the right to use the test**. For the majority of psychological constructs, and particularly for those most important and most well-known, there are many alternative tests, many of which are free for use. Having that in mind, there is no reason to accept to pay for usage of a test that is noncommercial and that will increase the public familiarity with the test. One should simply choose another test to measure the same psychological constructs. On the other hand, if the author/copyright holder does not demand payment, but asks for some service from the user, the decision about accepting or rejecting such demands should be made after they are carefully considered. If the author/copyright holder asks that you send him papers that you create based on the results obtained with his/her test, there is usually no reason not to accept that. If the author/copyright holder asks that you send him/her the database created by the use of the test, you should carefully consider the content of that database and whether the author/copyright holder of the test will use the data in accordance with the purpose you intend to use them for (e.g., who has publication rights from the database). The conditions should be carefully considered and it is usually not wise to accept any conditions that create financial responsibility for the user about the way test is used or responsibility for the way other people use the test, regardless of whether these other people are connected to the user or not. It is usually not very wise to accept demands of the author/copyright holder to administer test to certain precisely defined categories of test takers for this data to be used by the author/copyright holder if the user is not absolutely certain that this is sufficiently easy to accomplish.

After receiving the permission, text of the license/permission or the email message in which the author/copyright holder gives permission to use the test should be kept as a proof that you are using the test legally.

References

Berne Convention for the Protection of Literary and Artistic Works. (1971). Retrieved from http://global.oup.com/booksites/content/9780198259466/15550001

Beyer, J. L. (2014). The emergence of a freedom of information movement: Anonymous, wikileaks, the pirate party, and Iceland. *Journal of Computer-Mediated Communication*, *19*(2), 141–154. https://doi.org/10.1111/jcc4.12050

Copyright, Designs, and Patents Act. (1988).

Copyright Law of the United States and Related Laws Contained in Title 17 of the United States Code. (2016). United States Congress.

Eriksson, S., Godskesen, T., Andersson, L., & Helgesson, G. (2018). How to counter undeserving authorship. *Insights*, *31*(1). https://doi.org/10.1629/uksg.395

Lankov, A. (2009). Pyongyang strikes back: North Korean policies of 2002–2008 and attempts to reverse "de-stalinization from below". *Asia Policy*, *8*, 47–71.

Wilson, M. (writer). (2018). *Wikipedia*. Retrieved January 2, 2018, from https://en.wikipedia.org/wiki/Michael_Wilson_(writer)

3
TEST ADAPTATION

History

Although there are some earlier authors who wrote about relations between culture and psychological phenomena, the history of interest of psychologists on the effects of culture on differences in functioning of psychological tests started in the second decade of the 20th century in the US. While travelling through Europe, the US psychologist Henry Goddard learned of the Binet-Simon scale and organized its translation into English. As he held the position of a research director at an institution that worked with children with cognitive disorders, he quickly popularized intelligence testing among his colleagues and, as a consequence, psychologists in various US institutions started to use the Binet-Simon scale (Boake, 2002).

One of the places where a pronounced need for methods for assessing intelligence existed was Ellis Island. Located in New York harbor, this island held an immigrant inspection station in which a team of medical doctors was tasked with assessing if the immigrants that arrive asking for residence in the US fulfilled the legal conditions for entry. The conditions defined by the US immigration law of 1882 specified that "lunatics and idiots" could not be admitted into the country. The law of 1907 prohibited the admission of "imbeciles and feebleminded" persons and, in 1917, this formulation was developed into persons with "constitutional psychopathological inferiority" (Kamin, 1974). This was at first interpreted as a demand to test the literacy of immigrants, but with the popularization of the science of "mental testing" there were soon expectations that tests of intellectual abilities be used for this purpose.

An important thing to have in mind is the political and social context in which all of this was happening. The second decade of the 20th century was a time when the world was more or less divided between European colonial powers that reigned sovereignly over numerous colonies in Africa, Asia, America and Australia. The

British Empire was at its peak and it ruled over a large portion of the world. The US was independent, as well as a major part of South America, but Canada and Australia were still colonies of the British Empire. A few years earlier, in Namibia, German colonial authorities conducted a genocide over the Herrero and Nama peoples, creating in its course the concept of death camps, a horror they applied on the people of Europe only a few decades later. In Congo, Belgian colonial authorities and private concessioners had been severing and collecting hands of local people who did not produce and deliver the quantity of rubber or agricultural products they were ordered. Attempts to inform the European public were faced with government censorship. In the meantime, in Europe, the Balkan Wars, World War I and the October Revolution all took place, accompanied by what we would now call massive ethnic cleansings and war crimes against civilians.

Racial theories that spoke about "races" of people and a hierarchy of "races" dominated psychology, anthropology and other social sciences. Psychologists and other social scientists created maps, listed characteristics of people of various races, and used race to explain the existing social hierarchy, stating how "superior", "better quality" races ruled the society due to their special, high abilities, while "lower", more primitive "races" occupied the bottom of the society or consisted of unproductive members of the society, described by various names that we now consider to be defamatory and insulting. Some spoke with disdain about the danger of humanitarian organizations that helped these people, who "would not be able to survive by themselves" to "stay alive and even leave offspring". Psychologists and anthropologists warned about the danger of mixing of "lower races" with the "superior race" (a race to which, as a rule, the writers of such texts belonged) (Grant, 1916), i.e., they warned of the "infiltration of lower races" into the superior race. In their texts, psychologists wrote that some "races" were more intelligent and some less, and that the difference was innate and prophesized intellectual degradation of their "superior race" due to "infiltration" or mixing with "lower races". They called for decisive measures, "based on science", to prevent that (e.g., Brigham, 1923). In Europe, the superior race was considered to be the so-called Nordic race, while the lowest race was the Slavic, so-called Alpine Slavs (Brigham, 1923; Grant, 1916). In the US, the standard race was considered to be the "Whites", while the lowest of the races were the "Negro". In scientific texts, a lot of bad traits were attributed to the "Negro" and they wrote about the danger of degradation of intelligence of the American people due to infiltration of the "Negro blood" into the population (Brigham, 1923).

Psychologists had huge confidence in the newly founded science of "mental testing" and in its instruments – tests of intelligence and mental abilities – and applied them with full confidence in their ability to measure "innate" intelligence. Eugenics, the "science" about "enhancing the genetic qualities of the human population" that provided justifications for genocide over social groups, races and individuals of "lesser value" and that, in the second half of the 20th century, led to campaigns of forced sterilization in the US and Canada, and also to a campaign of taking children away from Aboriginal Australians, was a highly valued branch of biology. The prestigious US Eugenics Society strongly supported the development of "mental testing" and considered "mental tests" to be instruments that would help them achieve their goals (Kamin, 1974). Psychologists working with mental tests were strongly convinced of the power of their tests and that they measured innate cognitive abilities, such as intelligence, which they considered a strictly heritable trait. These are the attitudes that had, as history shows, dominant influence on political decisions in societies of Western Europe and the US, although, it should be noted, there were also differing opinions among scientists of the time.

At that time, the US was also faced with a wave of so-called "new migration". Instead of immigrants from England, Scandinavia and Germany, which theoreticians of the time believed belong to the "master", "Nordic" race, and which were dominant up to that point, the majority of immigrants were becoming people from Southeast Europe, Italy, Poland, Russia, as well as Jews (Kamin, 1974). According to scientific views of the time, these were members of the "Alpine race", primarily "Alpine Slavs", a race to which very bad traits were attributed. This group was considered incapable of governing a state and, because of this, occupied the lower layers of societies in which they lived. The "Mediterranean race", was believed to have obtained bad traits by mixing with other races with bad traits. Scientists of the time perceived these "races", and especially the "Alpine race", as an entity that was spreading, occupying areas that used to be dominated by the "superior" "Nordic race" and called for this spreading to be stopped (e.g., Grant, 1916). It should be noted that it is not the case that scientists of the time believed that members of these "races" were hostile toward members of their "superior race". No, it was about a belief that the genetic properties of members of "lower races" were bad, that they lacked abilities, primarily "intellectual" abilities that were needed to live in a modern industrialized society. In the US, influential scientists believed that the mixing of these "races" with the white population of the US, would accelerate the "intellectual decline of the white races" which they believed was well underway because of the mixing of the "white race" with the "Negro". In these conditions, information about the changing ethnic origin of new waves of immigrants led to public upheaval and calls to introduce selection of immigrants, i.e., to institute a type of "quality control" (Kamin, 1974) of the people admitted into the US.

These are the conditions under which Henry Goddard was invited to Ellis Island to help in the selection of immigrants in regard to their mental abilities. He applied a version of the Binet-Simon scale, adapted into English, on samples of immigrants from which, as he specified, the "obviously feebleminded" and "obviously normal" (Snyderman & Herrnstein, 1983) were excluded. He reported results by ethnic groups and concluded that between 80% and 90% of the test-takers, depending on nationality (Russians, Jews, Hungarians, Italians), were feebleminded. This finding received a strong echo in the public and later psychological texts, where authors cited percentages of "feebleminded" within each ethnic group, but mostly failed to report on the fact that these were preselected groups of borderline test respondents (Kamin, 1974, 1982). This created an impression in the public, both general and professional, that the results showed that in these ethnic groups there are between

80% and 90% of "feebleminded" individuals, thus reinforcing expectations based on racist theories of the time. Although he expressed doubt that purely genetic factors were responsible for the achievement of immigrants, and considered it to rather be more due to environmental factors, Goddard himself stated that these percentages would be only somewhat lower had the testing been done on the entire immigrant population (Snyderman & Herrnstein, 1983). However, Goddard stated in a later article that the application of tests led to a dramatic increase of the percentage of immigrants who had departed – those who were denied permission for entry and residence in the US – which was a result that public of that time wished for. This led to a dramatic increase in the popularity of the young science of "mental testing", which was, in line with the spirit of the time, seen as a way for the US to defend itself from being swarmed by "feebleminded" migrants.

New versions of the Binet-Simon scale were soon developed. The two most famous were versions created by Robert Yerkes and James Bridges, which became known as the Yerkes-Bridges Point Scale examination, and the test by Lewis Terman. The second one, named the Stanford-Binet Intelligence Scale included some new items and scales, and extended the age range of people to which it could be applied to also include adults (instead of children only). As a measure of intelligence, it introduced the intelligence quotient – IQ – instead of the "mental age" of the original Binet-Simon scale. The Stanford-Binet Intelligence Scale soon became the most widely used intelligence measure in the US.

However, even during the testing of immigrants at Ellis Island, medical doctors and psychologists tasked with this testing noticed that the intelligence test developed for testing French schoolchildren was not adequate for testing immigrants who were not French and often had no formal education, meaning that they were also not literate. For this reason they started to create their own tests that they named "performance tests", and which they considered to be adequate for people who "have never been learned" (Knox, 1914).

Somewhere around those years, recruitment and preparations of the US Army for entry into World War I also began, and the US joined this conflict in April 1917. World War I was a conflict that differed very much from all previous ones. The development of military technology changed the character of warfare. Unlike armies of previous times, in which the huge majority of soldiers used relatively simple gear that required little specialization, World War I was the first war that demanded that soldiers be capable of using many various complex pieces of equipment on a large scale. Some of this equipment even required advanced mathematical, logical and other specialized skills (for example, using a tank, a plane, driving a military vehicle or using indirect-fire artillery pieces). It was necessary to select adequate people for all these diverse positions and to recognize adequate people among hundreds of thousands of recruits, many of which were illiterate or without any education, or among immigrants with little or no knowledge of the English language. For the purposes of this selection, psychologists developed a verbal test of intellectual abilities entitled "Army Examination Alpha". However, recognizing that Alpha cannot be used on people who have no mastery of the English language or are not literate, or, to a large extent, on people without any education, they also developed another nonverbal test entitled "Army Examination Beta" or "Army Beta". Alpha and Beta were both group-administered tests, and aside from them the US Army also used two individually administered tests for selection – the Stanford Revision of the Binet-Simon scale, which required knowledge of the English language, and the so-called "performance scale", that did not require knowledge of English (Brigham, 1923).

> When a detachment reported for psychological examination, the first step was that of separating the English-speaking and literate from the non-English speaking or illiterate. Those who were both English speaking and literate were given examination alpha. All others were sent to beta. At the close of examination alpha, all men who had made low scores were sent to beta. After examination beta had been given, the examiners tried to recall for individual examinations all men who had made a low score in beta. In the rush of examining it was impossible to recall all men for individual examinations who should have been given special examinations, and some men were graded on alpha who should have been graded on beta, and vice versa, but most men were properly graded by the rough methods in use.
>
> *(Brigham, 1923, pp. 22–23)*

This was written by Carl Brigham, Assistant Professor of Psychology at Princeton University in his 1923 book in which he presented selection methods and analyses of results obtained on over 100,000 recruits of diverse ethnic and racial backgrounds, differing in the number of years they have been living in the US and in their level of literacy (Brigham, 1923). The total number of soldiers assessed using these tests exceeded two million, but as the technology of the time dictated that all calculations needed to be done by hand and on paper, this number is staggering. Aside from Brigham's book, results of testing were presented in an edited collection prepared by the president of the American Psychological Association at the time, Robert Yerkes, who led the activities of psychological testing of recruits as a major in the US Army.

As the practice of psychological testing of recruits started rather late relative to the time point when the US entered the Great War, and as there was yet no developed system for allocating soldiers based on their psychological characteristics, results of psychological testing did not have too much influence on the real allocation of specialties within the US Army. However, the practice at the Ellis Island as well as the application of various tests on members of diverse social groups during the testing of recruits are the first examples of recognition and massive application of that recognition in practice, that not all people can be adequately tested with same tests and that psychological tests need to be adapted to characteristics of the population they are to be applied on. These examples of mass testing of immigrants in the US also represent the first practical examples of psychological science and practice "descending" among the common people. Psychology, officially the science about human psychological life, and in practice a science about the psychological life of wealthy and educated people from the West, made its first steps in working with poor people with no education.

However, what made these studies famous are their conclusions about the achievement of people of difference "races" and ethnic groups on these tests. Namely, their results showed that the average achievement of "black" recruits is more than one standard deviation below the average achievement of "white" recruits, people whose achievement is in turn almost two standard deviations below the average of "white" officers. Also, these results showed that the average achievement of "white" recruits born abroad is around half a standard deviation lower that the average of "white" recruits born in the US. And, when the category of recruits born abroad is divided into categories by the number of years they have been living in the US, results showed that the average achievement rose with the number of years of residence in the US, making recruits who have been living in the US for more than 20 years have an equal or even somewhat better average achievement than recruits born in the US. Brigham concluded that "army authors" explained this by proposing that immigrants who are not intelligent enough do not manage to make a living in the US, and thus return to their countries of origin, while those who are more intelligent remain, because their intelligence allowed them to make a living and survive in the US. Brigham discarded this explanation as speculation that does not account for the obtained results. He stated that if this were really so, then individuals of lower intelligence would have to be highly represented among the people leaving the US, and that was not the case. He stated that among those who leave the US there were also people who came to the US to earn money, and after achieving that goal, went home with the money they earned. And, he said that such people are surely not unintelligent. He concluded that for this reason the previously mentioned explanation could not explain the differences between immigrants.

After that, he considered a hypothesis that was very important for the topic of this book, and that is the hypothesis that the test used to assess intelligence was somehow constructed to punish people born in countries in which English was not spoken, and that those who had lived in the US longer were more Americanized, thus achieving better results. He tested this hypothesis by comparing the differences between groups with different durations of residence in the US, on Alpha and Beta separately. He reasoned that if the increase in test results was really a consequence of acculturation, i.e., accommodation to the American culture, then an increase in score would happen only on Alpha, the verbal test, but not on those tested with Beta.

It should be noted here that Brigham, as well as Yerkes, strongly believed that the nonverbal tests they used were clear measures of innate intelligence. In test descriptions they gave, they stated that success on the tests could not be influenced by learning or education, but that only the innate abilities of reasoning and drawing conclusions were manifested on the test. Although Brigham, in one place, stated that it s possible that some of the respondents were not up to the "hurry-up attitude frequently called typically American" (Brigham, 1923, p. 96) that was

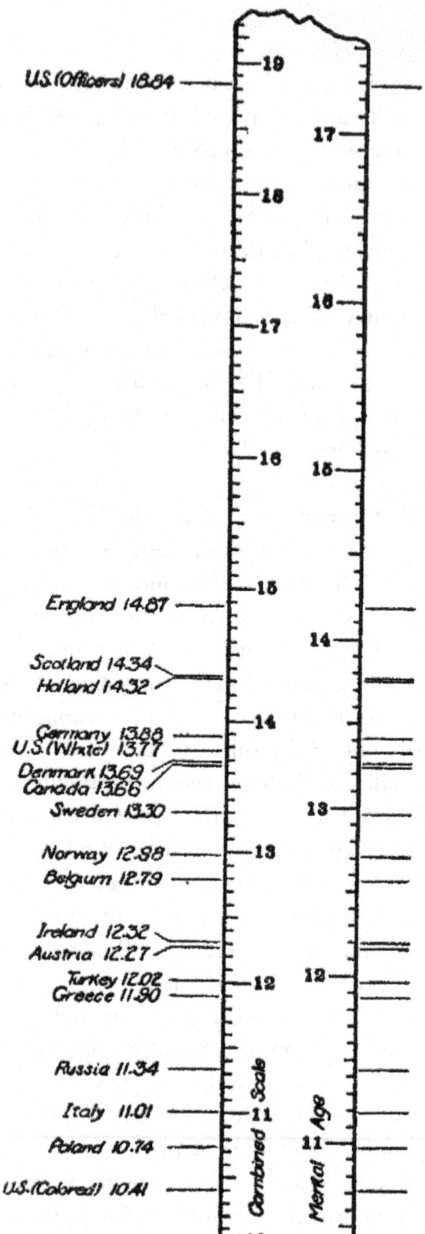

FIGURE 3.1 "The relative standing of the nativity groups (of recruits for the US Army, 1910s) according to their average intelligence . . . The left-hand scale reads in units of the combined scale. The right-hand scale reads in units of 'mental age' representing what would be the approximately equivalent scores on the Stanford revision of the Binet-Simon scale". Picture from the book *A Study of American Intelligence* authored by Carl Brigham, who was then the chief of Division of Psychology, Office of the Surgeon General of the US Army from 1923.

Source: Brigham, 1923

needed to solve some of the tests (tests had a time limit!), this did not change his conclusion that Beta was a clear measure of inborn intelligence, free from language and culture. He also stated that even if the test indeed created a situation that was "typically American", this was also valid, as the inability to respond adequately to such a situation was an undesirable trait (Brigham, 1923). The fact that nonverbal tests are not, nor can they be, culture-free, even though they do not require knowledge of the spoken language is a fact that has become known and accepted decades later. The same goes for the modern attitude that a psychological test does not have psychometric properties per se, but rather that it is something that needs to be empirically documented for every population the test is intended for. This is the understanding that validity and reliability refer to conclusions that can be brought about by a certain group in a specific situation, and that they are valid only for that specific instance of test application on that specific group, and not for the test per se or for all possible groups. At the time his analysis was done, Brigham took for granted the belief that results of a nonverbal test speak about clear, inborn intelligence. He believed that they speak not only about the intelligence of a person, but of intelligence that is inborn, i.e., caused by genetics. With the same confidence, he concluded that the validity of the test was good enough to make conclusions about respondents. With these beliefs, he noted how average values of groups tested with Alpha and Beta change with an increasing number of years of residence in the US and concluded that there was an increase in "intelligence"[1] with the number of years of residence in the US on both tests. He concluded that it was clear that the increase in "intelligence" was not a consequence of Americanization, nor of better proficiency in language, because if it were so, the increase would be only Alpha.

From this he derived that there was only one remaining explanation – as this was a cross-sectional study, not a longitudinal one, data do not really show an increase in intelligence with years of living in the US, but it showed differences in intelligence between immigrants that were arriving before and those that were arriving then. He then divided the recruits born abroad from the sample according to their country of origin and concluded that the highest average achievement have respondents from England, and after it Scotland, the Netherlands, Germany, Canada, Sweden and Norway. On the other hand, he found that the lowest average scores were obtained by respondents from Poland, and just slightly above them were respondents from Italy and Russia. He compared them with the proportion of immigrants by nationality in the decades before testing and concluded that in the decades before testing, English immigrants and members of groups with better scores had been a larger part of the immigrant population, and that in time the ratio changed in favor of people from countries with low achievement, with years immediately before the testing having a much larger proportion of immigrants from low-achievement countries. He concluded that people of low intelligence had started coming to America! In other words, in groups coming to the US in the decades before testing, there were more Englishmen and Germans – people whose test scores are similar to "whites" born in the US. During the time of the testing, more Italians, Russian, Poles and other ethnic groups were emigrating. He made some further analyses to compare achievement of recruits of various ethnic backgrounds with different other groups: he calculated the percentage of members of each ethnic group that had a higher score than the average of "white" officers, the percentage of people in each group whose performance received the three worst grades, the percentage of people in each group with scores higher than the average of "black" recruits, and the percentage of people in each group below the "mental age" of seven, etc. He presented an array of ethnic groups sorted by these criteria into on ordinal order, with English at the top and "blacks" clearly at the bottom, with results much lower than results of Poles, Italians and Russians.

Convinced of the capacity of the nonverbal Beta to measure intelligence independent of language or any other environmental or variable factor, Brigham failed to notice that the same reasoning works in the other direction as well. Namely, as much as it could be concluded that the average intelligence of immigrants coming to the US was decreasing, it could equally be concluded that these ethnic groups constituting "new immigrants" had less time to fit into the American culture, thus leading to a lower score, because the English from his sample was mainly people who had been living in the US for a long time, while Poles, Russians and Italians were mainly "fresh" immigrants. And, aside from this, there was also the fact that they originated from cultures that differed from the US culture much more than was the case with England, the Netherlands or Germany.

Instead, he devoted the last two chapters to interpreting the situation in line with racist theories of the time, writing about the superior "Nordic" group vs the inferior "Mediterranean" and "Alpine" groups, and about the danger posed by the increased inflow of "inferior people or inferior representatives of this people into the country". He wrote about how future Americans would be less intelligent than people from his time if the mixture of races was to occur, which he considered unavoidable. He wrote about the inferiority of the "Alpine Slav" versus the representatives of the "Nordic" race and about the "undesirable results that would ensue from a cross between the Nordic in this country with the Alpine Slav, with the degenerated hybrid Mediterranean or with the negro or from the promiscuous intermingling of all four types." (Brigham, 1923, p. 208). He finished with a call for revision of immigration laws to make immigration highly selective, but stated that such change would only "afford a slight relief from our present difficulty" (Brigham, 1923, p. 210). He stated that the "really important" steps would be those that would be "looking toward the prevention of the continued propagation of defective strains in the present population" (Brigham, 1923, p. 210).

The echo of the conclusions of this book were huge, especially when we take into account the fact that similar conclusions were also derived by other authors in their papers, first of all Robert Yerkes, the president of the American Psychological Association and the person who headed the recruit testing system (Snyderman & Herrnstein, 1983). Critical voices that existed at that time, were not particularly influential. Findings and conclusions presented by these authors were in line with the fear the American public of that time had from the "new immigration", as well

210 AMERICAN INTELLIGENCE

impossible to predict at the present time that the rate of infiltration of white blood into the negro will be checked by the declining rate of increase in the negro blood itself. The essential point is that there are 10,000,000 negroes here now and that the proportion of mulattoes to a thousand blacks has increased with alarming rapidity since 1850.

According to all evidence available, then, American intelligence is declining, and will proceed with an accelerating rate as the racial admixture becomes more and more extensive. The decline of American intelligence will be more rapid than the decline of the intelligence of European national groups, owing to the presence here of the negro. These are the plain, if somewhat ugly, facts that our study shows. The deterioration of American intelligence is not inevitable, however, if public action can be aroused to prevent it. There is no reason why legal steps should not be taken which would insure a continuously progressive upward evolution.

The steps that should be taken to preserve or increase our present intellectual capacity must of course be dictated by science and not by political expediency. Immigration should not only be restrictive but highly selective. And the revision of the immigration and naturalization laws will only afford a slight relief from our present difficulty. The really important steps are those looking toward the prevention of the continued propagation of defective strains in the present population. If all immigration were stopped now, the decline of American intelligence would still be inevitable. This is the problem which must be met, and our manner of meeting it will determine the future course of our national life.

FIGURE 3.2 Conclusion of the book *A Study of American Intelligence* authored by Carl Brigham, who was then the chief of Division of Psychology, Office of the Surgeon General of the US Army (1923) (Brigham, 1923), in which, based on the results of testing soldiers with intelligence tests of the time, he warns of the alleged rapid decline of "American intelligence" due to mixing of races, and calls for taking decisive action toward "prevention of the continued propagation of defective strains in the present population". Recommendations such as these were applied several decades later by Nazi Germany and its allies and satellites in the form of death camps and policies of extermination of "lower" and unwanted "races", ethnic groups and individuals.

as with the existing system of segregation of African Americans, confirming the beliefs that were already dominant in the public.

However, only a few decades later World War II began. The racist theory, widely popular in science up to that point, saw its grotesque zenith in the form of the Nazi ideology in Germany, and to a lesser extent, in the fascist ideologies of allies and satellites of Nazi Germany. Recommendations such as those given by Brigham, Madison and others about the need to take decisive steps that would "prevent the continued propagation of defective strains in the current population", about the need to "defend" from the propagation of the "Alpine race" and other "genetically defective" people, the Nazis applied in practice. They established death camps and death squads for perpetrating genocide over "inferior" races, mobile units for murdering "genetically defective", "crazy" and "feebleminded" individuals, and killed tens of millions of people in Europe, Africa and Asia until the end of the war. However, this path led the Nazi Germany and its allies into war with the Western Allies, Soviet Union and the US. Fascist and racist political organizations that based their ideologies on racist theory and which were, in spite of the increasing resistance, still widely popular in the UK and the US, were quickly suppressed after the war started.

In psychology, behaviorism, that started its development in 1913 with the article "Psychology as the behaviorist views it" (Watson, 1913), reaches its peak in the years around the Second World War. After decades of belief in natural, innate differences in abilities between people, in the power of psychological tests to identify those differences and in the interpretations of these results in the scope of racist theories, a complete loss of faith in the powers of psychological tests occured. How much this change was influenced by the war with the Nazi and fascist regimes in Europe can probably not be accurately assessed, but the rejection of the theoretical views that the Nazi and fascist ideologies were based on happened in parallel with the development of the situation that led to war. And a key postulate of these theories is the postulate about innate psychological characteristics. In the new world, behaviorist views that all behaviors are learned and that a man is born as an empty slate, "tabula rasa", that is only to be filled by learning, became dominant. And when nothing is innate, but everything has to be acquired by learning, there is no longer room for tests that measure innate characteristics. From the unfaltering belief that everything is innate and that very little depends on the living conditions, the psychological community in the US shifted to equally unfaltering belief that nothing is innate, that all are born equal, and that all individual differences happen as a consequence of learning – an attitude that was in total opposition with the belief in the "hierarchy of races" on which the Nazi ideology stood.

This spirit led to a strong reexamination of psychological tests and the conclusions of previous authors. In this manner, Cattell started his famous 1940 paper with the following words:

> Psychologists dealing with the application of intelligence tests seem to pass through alternating phases of uncritical overconfidence and cynical despair with regard to the validity of their measurements. To judge by recent

> utterances the fashionable phase at the moment is disillusionment; the tests do not measure any constant characteristic of the individual, and no two tests measure the same thing.
>
> *(Cattell, 1940, p. 161)*

He also relayed the words of Neff, whom he cited as saying, "Most authorities [in the area of psychological tests] are now agreed that a test standardized on one racial or national group cannot be applied to a group of differing culture and background"(Cattell, 1940, p. 161), but for whom Cattell claimed that he also "joins absurdly in the current panic stampede" when he concluded that all differences in IQ can be completely accounted for in environmental terms.

Even though this stance, that tests need to be separately standardized for different groups of people, is a huge step forward from the testing practice of earlier decades in which tests created for one culture and one population were used to assess characteristics of people from other cultures, Cattell criticized it, stating that it points to the powerlessness of psychology and that its acceptance would lead to differences between groups of different social status, race and other properties remaining completely unexplored.

Instead of that, he proposed that tests free of culture be created by identifying areas of common knowledge in different cultures, i.e., what is necessarily known to members of different cultures. He proposed some objects and processes that were necessarily known to different cultures like human body parts, animals, natural phenomena, life processes such as breathing, coughing, sleeping, eating, drinking, etc. This approach proposed by Cattell corresponds to a large extent to the strategy of reasoning employed today in what is called test decentering, which is an important procedure in preparing a test for cross-cultural adaptation.

In the remainder of the paper he considers various factors that could be problematic in creating a test based on the principles he proposed – from how that would narrow the domain of behaviors included in the test, thereby compromising content validity, through stating that common topics still need to be explored by using test items that need to be expressed in some way, thus introducing into play different contextual meanings of the same notions in various cultures, to the question of the form in which these common elements could be included in a test. As a better solution he proposed a test based on items that represent perceptual tasks, but with elements, that, according to him, due to their geometrical (instead of pictorial) nature, have only a "perceptive" meaning and are independent of "apperceptive associations". He presented parts of his test and stated that there was enough data that such tasks are loaded with the "G" factor (general intelligence factor) and that the fact that all tasks in the test were exclusively from one small area of behavior was not a problem if they were valid indicators of the construct being measured. We can recognize that, in his reasoning, Cattell is relying on the model of parallel indicators that postulates that all indicators are more or less equivalent, as long as they are loaded with the true score (the construct that is being measured).

At the end of the paper, Cattell discussed the problem of how validity may be compromised due to differing testing conditions and differences in the motivation of respondents from different groups and cultures being tested. He stated the opinion that this is something that is best solved ad hoc by an interviewer in the field who is best able to assess "which adequate motives he may stimulate in various groups"(Cattell, 1940, pp. 178–179). He supported this with opinions of some previous authors who claimed that a tactful experimenter may "induce a proper test attitude in even the most barbarous peoples, by studying their incentive systems" (Cattell, 1940, p. 179). He also proposed exercise and individual testing as additional methods to improve testing conditions.

Although written in a situation of a great loss of faith of the psychological public in the power of psychological tests, this work of Cattell's introduces some new elements and concepts important for the practice of cross-cultural testing that remain valid today. Those are concepts like test decentering, basing the test on contents that are common for the cultures the test is created for, taking into account differences in connotative meanings of words and notions, loading of test items with the measured construct and also the importance of equalizing test conditions, attitude of test-takers toward the test and motivations of test-takers from various social groups. Although it is now quite easy to demonstrate that the expectation that perception tasks based on geometrical shapes are free of culture is not valid, ideas presented here by Cattell remain important components of the practice of cross-cultural adaptation of tests and cross-cultural testing.

However, at that time and in several decades after, except for Cattell and maybe a just a few other authors, there was no other work in the area of psychological testing of any greater or lasting prominence, at least in the English-speaking world. A couple decades after, psychology will be dominated by behaviorism and the belief that people are all born equal (not in legal rights, but in psychological properties), that all behaviors are a product of learning and dependent exclusively on the context, past and current. However, some new concepts enter the psychological vocabulary of that time – concepts such as "test bias", referring to a situation that a test is "biased" toward some groups; the idea that psychometric characteristics of a test can vary between samples and between testing situations; and that tests need to be standardized separately for different cultural, ethnic, linguistic and other groups. Also, the science of psychology is spreading through the world, it is established outside Western Europe and the US, and in the scope of research on learning processes and perception, knowledge about various other phenomena relevant for the functioning of tests is obtained.

In the early 1960s, attitudes of psychologists started to shift once again. In 1959, Noam Chomsky published his criticism of Skinner's behaviorism (Chomsky, 1959), and in that text he brings the concept of innate capacities back into play by using the example of imprinting as a most obvious manifestation of the innate capacities. Other authors, aside from Chomsky, also brought forth ideas that disputed postulates of behaviorism, particularly the one about the empty slate. The cognitive revolution in psychology starts its full swing! The empty slate metaphor stopped being an undisputable psychological concept. In the same year, in the organizational psychology, John Holland published his theory of vocational interest types

(Holland, 1959) and the concept of dispositions started to again gain the right of citizenship. However, statistical analyses were still done by hand, and doing calculations on anything but very small datasets was very hard and prone to errors. Except for a few mathematically oriented psychologists (like Cattell), most psychologists restricted themselves to only the simplest analysis. Only with the appearance of personal computers in the end of the 1970s and the beginning of the 1980s did the application of psychological tests in research truly pick up. Somewhere in those years the digital revolution also started, communication between countries became easier and the world scientific production started to increase ever faster. In psychology, the Big Five personality model was created and there were ever more new theories proposing various psychological dispositions, both cognitive and conative. Psychological testing is back in the play! Globalization based on information technologies started leading to the ever-greater unification of the world science and the standardization of the psychological profession. International exchange of tests increased, creating a need to adapt tests to languages of foreign countries. Experiences from the first half of the 20th century, about the need for test standardization were still there, but there were still no clear guidelines nor unified methodology on how to do that. Due to this, what followed was a period of very uneven practice in test adaptations – tests were translated into new languages, with translations being sometimes better, and sometimes worse, depending on the methodological knowledge and assessments of adaptation's authors and it often happened that new language versions that do not work at all or were known to have a factor structure different from the original entered practical use. Interest for cross-cultural research increased fast, often even faster than methodology was developed. Google Scholar search, for example, about studies presenting the functioning of a new language version of a test will hardly produce any results for the period between 1960 and 1980, but the same literature search for the period after 1980 will produce an abundance of results. The increase in the number of studies was particularly visible in those done on the Chinese population. China was opening toward the world, developing economically, and ever more authors conducted studies aiming to examine how the well-known Western tests and constructs functioned on China's huge population. More and more papers about the functioning of psychological tests and constructs in different cultures were published throughout the world (e.g., Annor & Amponsah-Tawiah, 2017; Darcy, 2005; De Raad, Smederevac, Čolović, & Mitrović, 2018; Elosua, 2007; Hedrih, 2008; Hedrih, Stošić, Simić, & Ilieva, 2016; Saucier, Georgiades, Tsaousis, & Goldberg, 2005; Sinclair & Wallston, 2004; Tak, 2004; Tošić Radev & Hedrih, 2017; Yang, Lance, & Hui, 2006; Želeskov Đorić, Pedović, & Hedrih, 2009). There were ever more papers and studies about factors different from the measured construct that influence achievement of people and certain groups on tests, like illiteracy (Reis & Castro-Caldas, 1997), "stereotype threat" (Steele & Aronson, 1995), general factor of interests (Hedrih, 2008), socially desirable responding (Pauls & Stemmler, 2003) and many others.

Globalization led to a sharp increase in the number of organizations that function in multiple countries (multinational enterprises and institutions) and to the ever-greater interconnection between economies of world countries. In Europe, connections between countries become tighter, primarily due to strengthening of institutions of the European Union. This created ever more standardized exams and similar procedures that resulted in internationally recognized certificates and increased the need to assess and compare psychological properties of people from various countries and cultures.

Test adaptation standards today

Today, at the time this book was written in 2019, test adaptation is obligatory. Responding to the needs of psychologists and test users, in 1985 the American Psychological Association (APA), American Educational Research Association (AERA) and the National Council for Measurement in Education created new Standards for Educational and Psychological testing (AERA, APA, & NCME, 2006), that also mention requirements for new language versions of a test. These standards have had numerous revisions – the latest before the writing of this book was in 2014 – create a certain "golden standard" for a good practice of psychological testing by proscribing rules and conditions that psychological tests and testing procedures need to observe. Although standards for psychological practice are proscribed by national associations of psychologists in each country, standards of these associations in most cases follow the standards proscribed by APA.

Among other thing, these standards also state that:

- "When a test user makes a substantial change in test format, mode of administration, instructions, language or content, the user should revalidate the use of the test for the changed conditions or have a rationale supporting the claim that additional validation is not necessary or possible".
- "When a test is translated from one language or dialect to another, its reliability and validity for the uses intended in the linguistic groups to be tested should be established".
- "When it is intended that the two versions of dual-language test be comparable, evidence of test comparability should be reported" (Hambleton, 2005, p. 5).

What do these three standards mean? When a test is translated into another language, the fact that we are convinced that we translated it well does not mean anything. What is needed is that the two language versions be psychologically equivalent and this means that test items should cause reactions influenced by the same psychological trait and this must be the trait we intend to measure. However, this psychological equivalence between the two versions is not something that may be taken for granted or just assumed. Equivalence of two language versions of a test is something that needs to be empirically verified on each group separately. It is possible that a test measures one psychological trait in one group and something else entirely in the other.

The same situation happens when we adapt the test for some other group, even when we do not change the language. If we changed test items or instructions, or any part of the test, to adapt it for some special group, even though it is still a test in the same language, the equivalence of these two versions may not be taken for granted, but must be empirically established.

Finally, even if it turns out that different language test versions are equally reliable and valid, and that they assess the object of measurement in the same way, it is still possible that one language version is harder or easier than the other. This can lead to a situation in which groups taking the two test versions obtain different scores even though their trait levels are the same, or that they obtain the same scores, even though their trait levels differ. If two test versions are equally valid and reliable, that still does not mean that all the items have the same difficulty in both languages. Correlations, which most reliability and validity testing procedures are based on, are not sensitive to differences in trait levels, but only to positions of test-takers in distributions. This is the reason why difficulties of the two versions must also be empirically examined and validity of the method of comparing scores on the two tests supported by evidence.

Another set of standards, and one directly referring to cross-cultural or cross-language adaptation of tests was proposed by **the International Test Commission**, a non-government organization representing an "Association of national psychological associations, test commissions, publishers and other organizations committed to promoting effective testing and assessment policies and to the proper development, evaluation and uses of educational and psychological instruments" (www.intestcom.org). Standards that they proposed, entitled **ITC Guidelines for Translating and Adapting Tests** in their first version, consisted of 22 guidelines organized in four sections – Context Guidelines, Test Development and Adaptation Guidelines, Administration Guidelines and Documentation/Score Interpretation Guidelines (International Test Comission, 2005).

The second edition of these guidelines was published in 2017 (International Test Comission, 2017) and it consists of 18 guidelines organized in six sections.

Three **Pre-condition Guidelines** specify that before starting any adaptation procedure, legal rights for creating the adaptation need to be obtained from the test copyright holder and that the level of overlap in the two populations in the construct to be measured needs to be established. Effects of cultural differences that are not relevant for assessment goals need to be minimized. Compared to the first edition of the guidelines, it is visible that these guidelines more or less correspond with the Context Guidelines from the first version with the addition of the guideline about copyright, which did not exist in the first edition.

Five **Test Development Guidelines** state that test creators/adapters need to:

- **Take into account linguistic, psychological and cultural differences** between target populations during translation and adaptation, and this should be done through the choice of experts with appropriate expertise;

- **Use appropriate test translation designs and procedures** to maximize appropriateness of the adapted version of the test for all populations this test version is intended for;
- Provide evidence that **test instructions and item contents have similar meanings** in all populations for which the test is intended;
- Provide evidence that **item formats, rating scales, scoring categories, testing conventions, administration methods and other procedures are appropriate** for all populations the test is intended for; and
- Collect **pilot evidence about the adapted test** that would allow for item analysis, reliability assessment and small-scale validity studies, so that changes to the test can be made before conducting a large study of test functioning.

Confirmation Guidelines require the author of the adaptation to:

- Select a **sample with properties relevant for the planned test use** and of sufficient size are relevance for empirical analyses;
- Provide **relevant statistical evidence about construct, method and item equivalence** between test versions in all intended populations;
- Provide **evidence to support norms, reliability and validity of the adapted version** in all intended populations; and
- Use **appropriate equating and data processing methods** when linking test scores from different language versions.

Two **Administration Guidelines** require the adaptation author to:

- Prepare the administration material and instructions in such a way that **they minimize possible culture or language-related problems** that might be caused by test administration procedures or answering methods and that could influence the validity of conclusions derived from test scores;
- List **testing conditions** that need to be strictly satisfied in all intended populations.

Score Scales and Interpretation Guidelines require the adaptation author to:

- Interpret any **differences in group scores based on all relevant available information**;
- **Make population score comparisons only when the highest level of measurement invariance has been established** between the scale scores. In other words, scores of members of different populations may be compared only when appropriate statistical procedures have shown that scores are comparable.

Documentation Guidelines require the adaptation author to:

- Provide **technical documentation** about any changes made to the test and detailed evidence supporting the equivalence of different test versions after the test adaptation is created;

- Provide **documentation for all test users** that will help with appropriate use of the adapted version in the new population.

If we summarize these guidelines, several important stances become prominent:

- **Cultural differences must be taken into account** and test adaptation has meaning only to the extent to which the measured construct exists in all intended populations, i.e., has loading on test items in all intended populations. If two test versions do not load on the same construct, the two tests should not be considered to be versions of the same test;
- **Equivalence of different test versions is something that needs to be supported by evidence**, and not automatically assumed. This evidence needs to be empirical, derived using statistical methods from data obtained by administering the test to test-takers, but also through judgement about accuracy and adequacy of the translation. The same goes for the validity of every single test version on its intended population;
- **Comparison between populations, members of different population or scores of test-takers who completed different test version may be done only to the extent to which the scales and scores are comparable**. This must be done while having in mind that differences in test scores should not be the only indicator that differences in construct levels exist, but conclusions about differences in construct levels need to be supported by data showing sufficient levels of measurement invariance between the compared groups (will be discussed in a later chapter) and also supported by other evidence whenever possible;
- There are **other important issues aside from test items**! Characteristics of the language used in the test, test instructions, familiarity with item content, answering method, administration procedure and all other elements of the test and the testing situation are important elements that can secure or compromise equivalence of test functioning on different groups and thus must be taken into account. It is not enough to standardize testing conditions, but the context in which testing is done must also be considered. This must be thought of in advance and procedures necessary to solve possible problems should be planned; and
- **Acquiring legal rights to create the test adaptation** from the copyright holder is the first thing that should be done before starting the work on the adaptation.

Still, in spite of these guidelines proposed by these two organizations and many scientific papers dealing with particular aspects of cross-cultural test adaptation methodology, this methodology is still working its way to being completely accepted by psychologists throughout the world. At the moment this book is written, one can still find psychologists, researchers and published scientific papers, even in very prestigious journals, that use inadequate translations from a foreign language, even in spite of evidence of their nonequivalence with the original, or those that compare populations based on raw test scores of the language versions, without any evidence of validity of such a comparison or even in spite of evidence rejecting validity. One can also find situations in which researchers administer tests in a language test-takers do not understand sufficiently or without evidence that the test functions adequately on the population it is administered to (for example, giving tests in the local language to foreign students or language minorities), where researchers use norms obtained on one test version on members of a different population who took a different language version of the test, etc. There are also situations where one can hear, even from psychologists with adequate methodological knowledge in other areas, an explicit or implicit opinion that cross-cultural adaptation refers only to situations where a test is to be administered to members of primitive tribes in faraway countries or people from some faraway, less developed countries, and not for people from the developed world for whom equivalence is something to be assumed and that needs no exploration. This is often also accompanied with an opinion that adaptation to these languages is not really cross-cultural adaptation, and that for this reason, the above-mentioned guidelines can be neglected!

One part of the reason for this state of affairs certainly lies in the fact that the area of cross-cultural test adaptation is still new, that standards and procedures are still being developed and that there are almost no publications that cover this whole area in the way, for example, research methodology textbooks exist.

Another reason is that topics related to testing in a multicultural context are still very modestly, and very often not at all, included in university psychology curricula, and there also seems to be a distinct lack of open-access publications on the area. A notable exception from this situation are the ITC guidelines that are freely available on the internet and can be viewed and downloaded by everyone.

In order to quickly improve the situation in the area of cross-cultural adaptation of tests it would be very helpful if topics on cross-cultural adaptation of tests and use of tests in multicultural contexts were studied in more detail at universities and if the psychological public had easier access to resources on the cross-cultural adaptation and test use methodology.

Why is a translation not enough? Factors influencing the equivalent functioning of tests

Why is a translation not enough? With most of the other materials translated into other languages, it is enough for the translation to be accurate in order for the meaning to be conveyed and thus the goal of communication achieved. With nonverbal tests this is even easier because, apparently, there is nothing to translate, as these tests do not use the spoken language or its written representation. While it is true that some complex items of nonverbal tests may require some specific knowledge in order to be interpreted, is this also the case with simple pictures? For example, back in 1940, Cattell was convinced that it does not apply to simple shapes, that they are culture-free (Cattell, 1940). However, many studies conducted during the history of psychology showed this to not be true (e.g., Serpell, 1979). Also, there are ample studies in scientific literature showing that tests do not function as intended, although it is beyond reasonable doubt that adaptation authors secured an adequate translation of the tests they used (e.g., Du Toit & De Bruin, 2002; Elosua, 2007; Želeskov Đorić et al., 2009). Why is this so?

Psychological tests are not like other types of texts. If we look at it from the perspective of the S-O-R[2] model of psychological tests, we can see that neither test items, nor the test as a whole, are simply text the symbolic meaning of which needs to be conveyed, but stimuli that need to cause certain reactions. We call these reactions answers of test-takers. And these reactions should be precisely caused by psychological traits we intended the test to measure. This means that stimuli included in the test need to activate very specific internal factors – O variables from the S-O-R model – that correspond to the construct the test is intended to measure. These internal factors need to produce exactly the reactions we need. All this needs to happen although we effectively replaced all the stimuli from the original test with a different set of stimuli during the process of translation. The stimuli in the new language version of the test are not the same stimuli that are in the original version. Of course, our language knowledge tells us that these new stimuli have the same meaning as the original ones, that words from one language version, according to linguistic and grammar rules, correspond to stimuli from the other language version, but in spite of this, the material fact remains that this is one completely different set of stimuli! And given that it is a new set of stimuli, we need to verify whether this new set has the same properties as the old. This means empirical verification. It sometimes happens that this empirical verification shows that this new set of stimuli does not cause reactions influenced by the same psychological trait as the original set. How is this possible? From the S-O-R perspective, there are two possibilities:

- **That stimuli do not activate the correct O variables**, but some wrong ones. This could happen either because they are not good stimuli for the desired variables in the population or because the desired O variable does not exist in the new population; or
- That **O variables that are activated**, even if they are correct ones, **do not activate the expected reactions**, but some others. This may happen because the O variable incited by the new test stimuli have different behavioral manifestations in the new population.

It should be taken into account that test items are never the only factor influencing responses of test-takers, but that the test-taker always responds to the test as a whole and to the entirety of the testing situation. Hambleton (2005) organizes possible sources of the compromised validity of results of adapted tests in comparison to the original into cultural differences and technical issues, and there are also factors that may influence the validity of results interpretation.

Cultural differences as a factor of equal functioning of two test versions comes in the form of **equivalence of constructs, testing conditions, culturally influenced attitudes of test-takers** towards the test contest and testing, **test format** and **required work speed.**

Construct equivalence

When considering cultural differences, the first question that arises is, does the psychological construct measured by the test also exist in the culture for which the test is being adapted? In a previous chapter, concepts of emic and etic were presented. While some psychological constructs might really be universal for all human populations and cultures (etics), there are also constructs that are not universal (emics). If a psychological construct that the test intends to measure does not exist in the culture for which the test is adapted, then the adapted version will not function equally as the original version, no matter how the translation is done.

The other possibility is that the construct exists, but that it does not have equal behavioral manifestations in the two cultures. From the S-O-R perspective, it is possible that the O variable is the same in both cultures, but that the S variables needed to activate it differ. For example, in a society that allows free speech on topics of interest to society, it is often sufficient to ask people what they think about a political or socially important topic (S) in order to obtain a response (R) that adequately expresses their opinion (O). In a repressive society, a society in which members expect punishment if they express an opinion that is not in line with attitudes supported by those in power, the same question (S) will not incite a response (R) which is a result of what a person really thinks (O). In order to find out what a person thinks on the topic in this case, a different approach is needed. In a society in which there are taboos about a certain topic, or in which certain topics are considered private, posing a direct question about those topics (S) will typically not results in answers (R) equal to those that could be expected in a society that considers these same topics to be something that may be discussed in public, even when the actual factual situation (O) is the same. These differences may also exist between different social categories of the same society. For example, in many parts of the world, sexual activity of males is considered to be a form of achievement making males more prone to answer questions about this activity (S) in a way that represents them as being more sexually active than they really are (R). On the other hand, in these same societies female sexuality tends to be considered as a type of resource, something that is spent and, due to this, females that are highly sexually active are seen as less valuable. This then creates a tendency of females in these societies to answer the same questions in a way that presents their sexual activity as very small or even nonexistent. Moreover, these answers in both groups sometimes have little to do with the real level of sexual activity (O).

It is also possible that reactions incited by the same psychological construct differ. For example, in Western countries, it can be expected that extraverted[3] young people will often visit discotheques, but the same cannot be expected from older extraverted people in some of the conservative countries of, for example, North Africa. In Serbia in Europe, a quick downward motion with the head (a nod) is used to express assent, while moving one's head in the left-right direction expresses the rejection of the idea proposed. Just 100km eastward, in Bulgaria, the same left-right motion is used to express assent, while a nod expresses disagreement. A long practice of psychological testing showed that the ability to solve mathematical problems, like those given to children in school, is closely correlated with intelligence. However, a study by three Brazilian authors (Carraher, Carraher, & Schliemann, 1985) showed that Brazilian street children, who are forced by the nature of their position to start a form of "street business" they can earn a living from, are successful from a very young age in solving mathematical problems related to the functioning of their street business, while at the same time being very poor in solving problems of the school type that require the same mathematical operations.

Testing conditions

Cultural differences may lead to different testing conditions and it is possible that researchers might not even be aware of that, i.e., these differences might go unnoticed, especially if researchers are not personally administering tests, but are delegating this work to others. The instruction that test-takers receive is essentially not only the text that is read to them by the experimenter, but effectively also includes all the other instructions, directives, suggestions and information that test-takers received about testing and completing the test, and which are not documented. For example, among Western schoolchildren, a basic expectation in a testing situation is that everyone should work for him/herself, because that is the usual way testing in school is performed. Even when there are attempts at cooperation during testing, students try to do this covertly, knowing that this is not allowed. In contrast to this, among the Zinakantekan Maya girls from Mexico, as reported by Patricia Greenfield (1997), the work is done cooperatively, while the idea that everyone responds for him/herself is foreign to them. Girls that participated in this study even expected that the questions that were posed to them be answered by their mothers, who know more, and the idea that information is split among individuals was in complete discord with their view of the world.

Sometimes the physical conditions in which testing is done may be completely different in two cultures or two groups to which a test is administered. While children in European schools typically do tests in classrooms that have normal temperature and are adequately aired, Sternberg (2004) describes his experience with a situation of testing children in a childcare center in India, where the testing was done at the temperature of 45 degrees Celsius in shade and under the conditions of a very strong stench of garbage and rot coming from places near this center. It may sometimes happen that test-takers are ordered by the authority (for example, students are ordered by their teachers or the school principal) to do the test the best they can or in a certain way. It may also happen that these same authority figures conveyed to students that the testing is not particularly important and that they need not put too much effort into it. These differences in testing conditions may lead to unequal functioning of two test versions, regardless of translation quality. And if, on top of that, the fact that testing conditions differed remains unnoticed, adaptation creators might reach a wrong conclusion that tests do not function equally, even though this might not have been the case had the testing conditions been equal. It may also happen that although tests function equally, the achievement of one group is lower, and that this difference is caused by differences in testing conditions and not by true differences between groups. Or, that achievements are equal, even though the achievement of one of the groups would be better if the testing conditions were equal.

Attitudes towards the test content

When they come in contact with the test, test-takers will form an impression about it and thus obtain a certain attitude toward it. This might be both toward the test as a whole and toward its specific parts. They may also form an opinion on which parts of the test are more important, which tasks should they pay more attention to, which should be solved and which may not be, and if one should complete the test at all. These attitudes might be essentially different in two groups doing two versions of a test. For example, Sternberg (2004) cites the famous Soviet neuropsychologist Alexander Luria, who found that villagers from the Asian part of what was then the Soviet Union had lower achievement on cognitive tests because they refused to accept test tasks in the way they are presented. Unlike Europeans and North Americans who perceive abstract taxonomic sorting tasks like those in cognitive tests as worthy mental problems, members of Kpele people from Africa see that sort of thinking as unsophisticated, while they attach much greater value to sorting tasks that are based on challenges of everyday life (Sternberg, 2004).

Test format

It might also happen that groups taking the test are unequally familiar with the method of responding the test requires. For example, when administering tests based on Likert-type scales to people in some more remote areas in Serbia, one can still find people who have never encountered the concept of stating a level of agreement with a statement and who will, even after being given an explanation of the concept, still try to circle whole items they agree with, while ignoring those they disagree with, instead of marking their level of agreement with every item on a Likert-type scale. Such situations happened during the field collection of data for the "Study of diversity of work-family relations at the beginning of the 21st century" (Hedrih, Todorović, & Ristić, 2013), and after talking to participants who answered the test in this way it was discovered that the concept of grading one's level of agreement and reporting it by circling numbers was new to them, foreign and non-understandable.

A classic study by Robert Serpel showed that children from Zambia participating in his study were better at recognizing patterns than British children in situation when answers were given by folding wire models. On the other hand, British children were more successful than Zambian in solving these tasks when patterns were represented by drawings on a paper (Serpell, 1979). Serpel explained his results by the fact that British children are much more familiar with paper drawings as they encounter them both in school and in everyday life, while Zambian children are more skillful in folding three-dimensional models, because manipulation with such objects is something they have much experience with in everyday life.

We should also mention here the **Flynn effect** – a phenomenon that the performance of people from Western Europe and North America on cognitive tests rose steadily throughout the 20th century. The cause of this phenomenon, as Flynn himself proposed in his book (Flynn, 2007), is the fact that during that period, tasks like those found in cognitive tests became ever more widely available and more familiar to the general population. Such tasks can now be found in school textbooks, popular magazines, on the internet and in different media. Better familiarity of the population with these tests improved the test-taking skills of the population leading to an improved performance of whole populations on these types of tests (R), although the measured constructs like intelligence (O), most probably remained the same.

When considering test format, it may also happen that people from different groups have **different response styles** to certain item formats or generally different response styles regardless of item format. For example, in a study of vocational interests (Tracey & Robbins, 2005), researchers found that Native American participants showed a general tendency to rate their preferences and competencies for activities and vocations included in the inventory of vocational interests used in the study low. This is a response style known as disacquiescence or rejecting test response style. A style opposite to this one is the accepting test response style, reported in some German and British test-takers, and even more frequently in test-takers from Malesia, especially members of the Malayan ethnic group (Harzing, 2006). Similar to this, an affinity for extreme response styles was reported in residents of Mexico, in residents of countries of South America, but also Turkey and Greece (Harzing, 2006). In the same study, that included participants from 26 countries, a correlation was reported between the response style of the participant and the culture of his/her country in the scope of Hofstede's dimensions, thus indicating deeper relations between the response style of a person and his/her cultural origin.

Required work speed

The ability of test-takers to focus exclusively on the test and to work as fast as possible is a skill that not all test-takers have and that is not present in all cultures. This is the reason why it cannot be taken for granted that test-takers will work as fast as they can, even if they are taking a speed test.[4] In many groups/cultures, and especially in those closer to the polychronic then to the monochronic pole side of this dimension of cultural differences, people are not very familiar with quick test solving, nor do they have the skills necessary to adequately solve a speed test. This leads to such people having worse results on these tests irrespective of the real level of the measured traits. If a process study[5] is conducted in such cases, it can often be observed that test-takers like this, in a situation of limited time which demands fast work, are not able to focus on the test and that they are wasting time, for example by asking unnecessary questions and sometimes even that, unable to adapt to the required method of work, they answer randomly and then report that they have finished the test, even much before the time is up, only to be able to get out of this situation that is unpleasant and unnatural for them.

******

Technical aspects that can influence the equivalence of two language versions of a test can be grouped into those that have to do with **test contents**, those that have to do with the **translator** and those having to do with the **translation process**.

Test contents

Not all tests are equally easy to adapt for another culture. Some tests contain idioms and phrases that are unique for their language. Such tests are much harder to adapt to another language than tests that only contain expressions that are directly translatable. For example, items like "I will visit there again when the pigs fly", "I often think that this whole affair is a wild goose chase", "I often cut corners" and "I like people who can hit a nail on the head" are generally harder to translate to another language. These sentences use **idioms**, sets of words that have a meaning that is different from the literal meaning of the words. A valid translation of these sentences into another language would require finding equivalent idioms in this other language or finding an adequate way to express the same meaning directly with appropriate words, which is often quite hard. In the same way, we will easily agree that an item translated from, for example Serbian, that goes, "I often have a feeling that I picked all the watermelons" ("Često imam utisak da sam obrao bostan") sounds quite baffling in English, and might make a reader think that it really has something to do with watermelons, which is not the case.

Aside from phrases and idioms, tests may sometimes include **contents that are specifically familiar to a certain social group or culture**, but not to the other. All items that require test-takers to know geography, history, literature, public figures, social contents and customs, media contents, social system and most other cultural contents might be adequate for one, but inadequate for another group. Even for some contents that may seem to us as being known to everyone, cultures may be found where such contents are completely inadequate. For example, we can expect that most test-takers from Europe and the US could recognize the correct answer to the question "When did the World War Two begin?", but the same would probably not be the case in Pakistan, where WW2 is hardly even mentioned in the school curricula. Another example would be an item from a general information subscale of an intelligence test used in the former Yugoslavia. This item asked the test-taker to name the president of Yugoslavia. During the 1950s, 1960s and 1970s, when Yugoslavia was ruled by the then president-for-life Josip Broz Tito and when there was a strong cult of his personality, this used to be a very easy question. Everyone in their right mind knew the answer perfectly. Due to this, a failure to answer this question correctly was a simple, yet valid, indicator of some deeper clinical-level psychopathological processes in the respondent. However, in the 1990s during the dissolution of Yugoslavia and quick sequences of often quite little-known presidents, this question lost its psychometric value. Clinically normal people who just did not follow politics could easily be uncertain who was president at that particular moment, and even how the country they live in was named at the moment.

On this same point, there is little doubt that it would have little sense to include in an intelligence test a question that would ask residents of, for example, some Asian country to name the current governor of Alaska, or the largest river in Scotland or to name an actor of a TV series that is exclusively popular in Great Britain, but not in their country. However, this does not apply exclusively to verbal content, but also to nonverbal tests, and even includes perceptual habits. For example, attention tests used in Europe and North America often use a format in which the test-taker is asked to recognize certain target symbols in a thick mass of symbols. But, although not explicitely written in instructions, it is taken for granted that test-takers will approach the tast by "reading" the symbols from left to right, the way one reads text in European lanuages. But this is not the way the same test would be approached by people from cultures where reading is from right to left, or from cultures that use different writing and reading systems, for example people accustomed to the Chinese writing system.

The test content and its appropriateness for adaptation for other cultures is something that should be taken care of from the start. **Test decentration** – the procedure in which contents of the test that are inappropriate for cross-cultural adaptation are replaced with more appropriate contents – is one way in which the problem of hard-to-adapt content could be mitigated. However, more and more authors point to the need to have adaptation for multiple cultures in mind from the start when constructing a test.

In his presidential address to members of the American Psychological Association, Robert Sternberg (Sternberg, 2004) stated that **studies that have only a single culture in focus** may cause their conclusions to be implicitly or even explicitly generalized to other cultures, causing multifaceted damage to psychology in this way. He states that such studies may:

> (a) introduce limited definitions of psychological phenomena and problems, (b) engender risks of unwarranted assumptions about the phenomena under investigation, (c) raise questions about the cultural generalizability of findings, (d) engender risks of cultural imperialism, and (e) represent lost opportunities to collaborate and develop psychology around the world.
>
> *(Sternberg, 2004, p. 328)*

The same is the situation with psychological tests developed with only a single culture in mind, and then adapted for use in other countries. Approaching test creation from the start with an explicit intent that the test be used in multiple cultures might greatly mitigate all these problems.

Translator

To maximize the probability that different language versions of a test function equally it is not sufficient that the translator be proficient in only the target language of the translation, but it is also necessary:

- That **the translator knows the target culture** very well. A translator that has no knowledge of the target culture might not be able to notice contents that are inadequate for that culture and the character of which would be changed in the process of translation;
- That **at least two translators are always used**. Aside from the fact that this is a minimum number of translators required for the two most widely accepted test adaptation procedures (that will pre presented in a later part of this book), having two translators prevents the individual perspective of a specific translator, i.e., the way he/she understood things, to be built into the translation thus potentially changing the target version of the test; and
- That translators **know and understand at least the basic concepts of test constructions**, so they can pay attention that some of the important properties of items do not get altered in the process of translation (for example, properties such as difficulty which can easily be changed if the adapted version of the test uses words that do not have the same usage frequency[6] as words from the original language).

In practice, it is often easy to spot situations in which the translation process is taken lightly, with people doing test adaptations by simply using as a translator any available person that knows the target language. It may sometimes be the test creator him/herself or a friend, a relative or the closest available person that knows the language sufficiently to make the translation. Conducting the whole formal adaptation procedure (to be described later) might, at first glance, look like just a cumbersome formality. This is not done for most other translations, but is required for tests. Tests seem like content that is easy to translate, however, unlike other translations, the goal of test translation is not for the translation to be "accurate", but for the **adapted version to be psychologically equivalent to the original version**. This means that, instead of aiming for the translation to reflect the meaning of words of the original test as accurately as possible, a translator doing the adaptation needs to aim at finding stimuli that will cause the same reactions in the new population as those caused by the original stimuli in the original test version. For this to be possible, it is necessary that the translator have sufficient understanding of how psychological tests are constructed. This is necessary so he/she would understand that the goal of the translation is psychological equivalence and not accurate translation. It is also necessary that the translator be familiar enough with both cultures to be able to recognize situations and items for which a direct translation would be inadequate and that he/she is also able to come up with and propose alternative items that would be psychologically equivalent to the original item in the culture for which the test is adapted, even when such item has a different meaning that the original item.

It should be noted that this is often not an easy task. Studies of philology that educate professional translators typically have no contents at all about psychological tests or psychological testing. Translators are trained to convey meaning as accurately as possible from one language to another while making as few changes to the meaning as possible in that process. The idea of sentences being stimuli intended to cause reactions influenced by a certain psychological trait might seem quite foreign to translators who did not have previous contact with psychological tests. The author of this text had a personal experience of hiring a translator who felt insulted upon hearing that there would be another translator involved. This translator stuck to her belief that another translator would be there because we did not trust her enough and refused to accept explanations that this was a standard and necessary methodological procedure that has nothing to do with her or our evaluation of her translation skills!

And this is not the end, as there are additional issues to be considered. If the researcher managing the adaptation process is not him/herself sufficiently familiar with both cultures, he/she will be in a difficult position to assess which translator is really sufficiently familiar with both cultures to be able to do the adaptation adequately. This means that, in practice, we will usually have to rely on indirect criteria for selecting a translator, like his/her reputation, reputation of the agency for which the translator works, personal acquaintance with the work of the translator, translator's own statements about his/her competencies and the like. As such criteria are often not sufficient for valid assessment, test functioning problems caused by inadequate translation or by some inadequately translated test elements are far from being rare.

Translation process

When considering the translation process itself, the first decision that needs to be made is the one about the dialect to which the test will be adapted. While it might, initially, seem only logical that a test be adapted into a standard language, a standard language is not always the option of choice. Sometimes the social dynamics within a culture are such that there are very emotionally charged attitudes toward certain dialects or toward the standard language. For example, when adapting tests for the language spoken in Croatia, Bosnia-Herzegovina and Serbia, and which is formally recognized in these countries as three different languages, with marginally different standards, asking a test-taker that acknowledges one language standard as their own to complete a test that is in another language standard of the same language might sometimes result in very negative reactions. Although they perfectly understand the language of the test, some test-takers might refuse to take the test and even show a hostile attitude toward the test administrator. It may also sometimes happen that test-takers do not know the official language standard well enough and this is particularly possible in those countries that apply a proscriptive language policy, i.e., proscribe standard language rules that might even be different from the language really used by the people living in that territory. For example, the current official standard version of the Montenegrin language proscribes the use of certain letters that are not used in everyday written language used in that country and so it is not rare to find fully literate people that do not understand those letters. And while the use of these letters would probably not make the test unintelligible for such test-takers, it might lead to certain differences in test functioning, if nowhere else, then maybe in an increased time test-takers would need to understand the meaning of words using such letters. Another possibility is that the language in question is one where there are dialects that are very different from the standard language, sometimes even so different that the dialect or the standard language are very hard to understand to a person that knows one of these, but not the other.

For this reason, the question of **dialect** that will be used in the adaptation is an important one to consider and it should never be neglected. Psychologists doing the test adaptation need to be aware of who their intended population is, i.e., who are the people for whom the adapted version is intended and thus make a decision about the dialect to which the test will be adapted. Even when the adaptation is planned to be in the official standard language, there should be awareness of the existence of dialects and a formal decision should be made that the adaptation is done in the standard language and not in one of the dialects. This should then be explicitly included in the formal plan for test adaptation and in communication and possible contracts with translators and other stakeholders. This decision should never be neglected nor should it be assumed that everyone involved will by default think of the same language version or dialect when doing the adaptation. The author of this text had a situation like this in his personal experience (Hedrih et al., 2016). When hiring a translator for an adaptation of a Serbian version of a vocational interest inventory into Bulgarian, we did not explicitly state that we wanted the test adapted to the standard Bulgarian language. We received a translation from a translator who assured us that he knew Bulgarian language perfectly and that the translation was fine. However, when we gave the translation to the second translator (it was mentioned earlier that a methodologically correct test adaptation requires at least two independent translators!), she informed us that our translation was not in the standard Bulgarian language at all, but in some "strange language that combines Serbian and Bulgarian words and sentence constructions". It turned out later that our test was translated to a dialect that is spoken in a number of settlements near the Serbian-Bulgarian border instead of the standard Bulgarian. Of course, the work of the first translator had to be done again, thus creating additional translation costs and postponing the rest of the study for some days. For this reason, one should always explicitly state the exact dialect/language standard he/she wishes the test to be adapted into.

An equally important topic to consider when creating an adaptation is also the **frequency of the words in the language of the adaptation**, i.e., how often words from two test versions are used in everyday communication. Some words are used in communication more often, and some rarely. In other words, some words have a higher frequency and some have a lower one. For example, all English-speakers will probably know the meaning of the word "healthy", but it can be reasonably expected that a much smaller number of them will know that the word "salubrious" means more or less the same. The word "talkative" will be known to most, but a significant number of people might be baffled if the word "garrulous" was used instead. Some psychological tests are based on this – it can be expected that low-frequency words will probably be unknown to people with a smaller number of words in their vocabulary, so these tests use items with low-frequency words as indicators of cognitive abilities or language knowledge. If a translator is not aware of the role frequencies of words play in the functioning of such tests, he/she might replace low-frequency words from the original test with high-frequency synonyms in the adapted version and thus make the whole item easier, creating a situation in which that item does not function equally in the original and the adapted version of the test.

In a similar fashion, a translator that does not know the language he/she is translating to well enough, and needs to rely heavily on the dictionary, will often also not be able to recognize which of the synonyms offered in the dictionary is an adequate replacement for a word in the original language and which is a word of a different frequency than the original word, as these data are usually not included in dictionaries. In this way it may happen that he/she replaces a high-frequency word from the original with a low-frequency word in the adapted version or vice versa. This would than make the adapted version harder (or easier) to understand for the test-takers causing a difference in functioning. It might also happen that the translator knows the language to which the test is being adapted very well, but does not know the language of the original version well enough and then relies heavily on a dictionary and from it draws a wrong conclusion about frequencies of words he/she is translating. It might also happen that the translator perceives a word of the original version language that he/she does not know as a low-frequency one and then replaces it with a low-frequency one, even though it might be just an average frequency word. From the fact that one personally does not know a word it is easy to reach a conclusion that this is because that word is not used often. These are the reasons why careful attention should be paid to frequencies of words in the process of translation. Translators should be reminded of the importance of this and translators should be selected who know both languages well enough to be conscious of frequencies of words used in the test in both languages.

If test functioning is directly dependent on frequencies of words that are used in the test, it is good to consult so-called **frequency dictionaries** of both languages if such dictionaries exist and are available. Frequency dictionaries are dictionaries that list words of a language and their frequencies of use. They are usually created by counting the frequency of each word in a sample of texts or other materials in that language and reporting these counts in a dictionary form.

In the process of adaptation, it is sometimes convenient to also conduct **the decentering of the original test**. If the translator concludes that items, parts of items or certain parts of the test cannot be translated adequately to the language of the adaptation or that they cannot be translated in a way that would result in reactions caused by the same psychological trait as in the original, it is possible that, in cooperation with the psychologist heading the adaptation process, the translator proposes that some parts of the original test be changed and replacements created that would be easier to adapt. This is sometimes not necessary because the change may be done in the adapted version only. But if test adaptations are done in multiple foreign languages, i.e., for multiple other cultures, and it turns out that the same revision of the original test would be adequate everywhere, then it is often better to also make that revision in the original test, than have an item with one meaning in the original and an item of a completely different meaning in all other test versions. This should particularly be done when it is obvious that revision of the item is necessary, but adaptations for different languages are done by different teams of researchers. In this case, if decentering was not done, i.e., if the problematic item was not replaced, it could happen that the problematic item is replaced in all adaptations, but in a different way in each adaptation, as each adaptation is done by a different team. This way, the item would have different content in every version (although, hopefully, all those versions would be psychologically equal), thus increasing the divergence of test versions and this is something that might create additional complications in later use. However, it should not be neglected that when items of the original test are changed, that is no longer the same test, which means that a new verification of its psychometric properties and its functioning on the original population is required. This should be done both for the new items and for the test as a whole, and it might also include an update of all the accompanying materials of the test, including procedures for interpreting individual results and especially numeric values used in these procedures.

Finally, the process of test adaptation itself, as well as the later process of examining metric invariance of different test versions, should be done by applying **a methodologically valid adaptation design**. Designs that are not valid do not allow for valid conclusions about functional equivalence – metric invariance of the two tests. It is very important that the adaptation process be adequately documented in all steps, because if empirical data later showed that test versions do not function equally, good documentation of the adaptation process can be precious for discovering possible causes of inequality between test versions.

Factors influencing the validity of interpretation of results

Aside from the listed factors that might cause psychological nonequivalence, it is sometimes possible that, in spite of an adequate adaptation, the process of administering the test to test-takers with the two (or multiple) versions is such that results can neither be treated as valid indicators of equivalence of the two versions nor of the functioning of the test in the two cultures.

A factor that probably quite often compromises the validity of comparison of functioning of two test versions, i.e., of the test on different social groups, is the **motivation of test-takers**. Motivation is a particularly powerful factor with achievement tests, as it can cause large differences in achievements of compared groups, even if the real average levels of the measured trait in the two groups are not different at all. To make matters worse, differences in the motivation of test-takers are a factor that psychologists are prone to neglect relatively easily and a factor that only relatively recently started drawing the deserved attention of researchers in the scientific literature and psychometric studies (e.g., Chan, Schmitt, Deshon, Clause, & Delbridge, 1997; Eklöf, 2007). For example, the author of this book was recently offered to be a reviewer of an adaptation procedure of a cognitive test in which the validity of the original version was tested on people who applied for a job in a factory during the selection procedure, while the adapted version was tested on secondary school and university students, test-takers who had little incentive to put extra effort into the test aside from their internal motivation to help the researchers. The first situation is a classic example of what is called **high-stakes testing**, while the other situation is a clear example of so-called **low-stakes testing** or it might be even justified to say no-stakes testing. If this situation, for example, showed that test-takers who completed the adapted version have lower achievement, would that mean that the adapted version is harder or that assessed abilities are lower with the second group or just that test-takers who completed the original version were more motivated, and put more effort into the test because of that? While these data alone cannot give us a valid answer about which if any of the three options is correct, taking care that the motivation levels of groups that are to be compared are roughly equal can at least exclude the third possibility.

Similarity of test contents to contents test-takers are exposed to in their everyday life is another factor influencing the validity of results interpretation. Test-takers generally perceive familiar contents faster. They already know how such contents should be approached and how familiar problems are to be solved. If test-takers are asked to assess some behavior that they find close and familiar, as can be the case with tests of typical behavior, they will do it much more easily, quickly and accurately than if they are asked to assess some behavior that is unfamiliar, that they need to imagine and that they might not even be able to imagine adequately as they do not have all the necessary elements for this, as these are not specified in the test because authors of the text believed that they are implied.

For example, in the classic task where children are asked to determine in which direction a bus drawn on a road moves, the bus on the picture has only windows, but no doors, as children are expected to conclude that doors must be on the other side of the bus, the side that is not on the drawing. And as doors must be on the side of the bus that is closer to the sidewalk, so that passengers would not disembark in the middle of the road, and with knowledge that traffic rules say that a bus drives on the right, children are supposed to conclude that the front side of the drawn bus is the one on the left side of the picture. Although to every city dweller that encounters and applies traffic rules every day this task will appear easy, it still requires the person to be acquainted with how buses look on both sides and with traffic rules. This is no problem at all for children from a modern city, but might represent a hard task for children from remote or undeveloped places where motor vehicles are rare and the traffic infrastructure in their surroundings is not such that these traffic rules are applied, or that they make sense at all.

In a similar fashion, if materials used in the test are not equally familiar to both groups, this may compromise the validity of results interpretation. We already mentioned the example of Serpell's finding that Zambian children from his study scored worse than British children when tasks were given on paper, but scored better when same tasks were given in the form of wire models (Serpell, 1979). There is also an anecdotal example of a famous Serbian psychologist from the first half of the 20th century, Borislav Stevanović,[7] who found that differences in achievement between city and village children on his adaptation of the Binet-Simon scale were caused by a difference in familiarity of the test contents to these two groups of children. While the test contents were very familiar to children from the cities, children living in villages had much less experience with contents similar to those in the test. When he calculated scores only based on items which could be assumed to be equally familiar to both groups, differences in achievement between these two groups disappeared.

When considering similarity of contents to which test-takers from different groups are exposed it is also necessary to pay attention to **similarities between school systems and school curricula of these groups**. It is justified to assume that, for most people, contents of a psychological test are most similar to contents that are encountered in schools (especially when cognitive tests are considered), and there are also findings showing that exposure to similar education systems may lead to greater similarities in the way two groups of people think (e.g., Sternberg, 2004).

Sociopolitical factors

Finally, one should also take into account the wider social, economic and physical conditions in which test-takers live and work, and which could influence the behavior during testing. **Are test-takers permitted to answer the test sincerely or are they afraid of consequences that would occur if they gave a certain type of answer**s? In my own personal experience, I witnessed that soldiers who participated in combat during war, and who themselves state that this experience left serious psychological consequences on them, refrain from expressing this in a psychological test or in an official conversation with a psychologist due to fear that they will be receive a diagnosis of a psychological disorder and thus be considered no longer capable for military service and discharged or transferred to a position that is less paid or does not lead to promotions. In countries that are governed by authoritarian regimes, in which human rights are violated, test-takers may often be afraid to say or write their sincere opinion for fear of being arrested, punished or murdered by those in power. Alternatively, it is also possible that test-takers in such environments **work under threat of punishment** or harm to life, liberty or health should they not score in a certain way on the test.

Do test-takers from both groups have **enough food, water, housing, freedom of movement**? What about their family members? As proposed by Maslow's theory of motivation, higher-order needs, which include the motivation to help the development of science through participating in psychological testing, will not have much importance when basic life needs are not met. People who are chronically hungry might apply to participate in psychological testing only due to hope that they will receive some food that researchers distribute to test-takers. Or they might apply motivated by better accommodations and living conditions given to study participants, for example in a refugee camp. Sometimes only an opportunity to take a nap in peace and quiet at the place the testing is done can be a motive. But in all these cases, these people will hardly be able to really focus on test contents, so comparing their results with results of their well-fed and well-slept peers who completed the other test version and who live in freedom and safety will be very problematic.

All these factors should be carefully considered when planning test adaptation and a study to test if different versions function equivalently. Researchers should always be aware of their existence and of the possible effects they can have on test results and conclusions about equivalence or non-equivalence of different language versions of a test.

Basic procedures for adapting tests

Terms

In the following text, the test version which is to be adapted into another language will be called "the original version of the test" or just "**the original version**". The population on which functioning of the original version was examined will be called the "**original population**". Language the original version is in will be called the "**original language**".

The language version of the test that is to be created through the adaptation process will be called "the target version of the test" or just "**the target version**". Populations for which the target version is intended will be called "**target populations**". Language of the target version will be called "**target language**".

Persons who speak only one language will be called "**monolingual**". Persons speaking two languages will be called **bilingual** persons. Persons speaking multiple languages will be called "**multilingual**". When talking about bilingual persons in the context of cross-cultural adaptation of tests, this word will be used to describe **persons who speak both the original and the target language**, regardless of whether they speak any other language as well. The term "**monolingual persons**" or "**monolinguals**" will be used to refer to people who speak either the original or the target language, but not both of them, regardless of whether they speak any other additional language that is not relevant for the specific test adaptation situation.

The term "**psychological equivalence**" of two test versions, two stimuli or two test-taker responses will be taken to mean that these are under the influence of the same psychological construct or that they cause reactions influenced by the same psychological construct, regardless of their content or linguistic equivalence.

Content overlap between the original and the target version of the test

We mentioned earlier that the idea of test adaptation is not to simply replace items in one language with items of the same meaning in the other language, although most psychological tests currently used are obtained in precisely such a way. We know that the goal of test adaptation is to achieve psychological equivalence, i.e., that stimuli in the target version of the test cause in test-takers reactions influenced by the same psychological trait as in the original, and not content equivalence between the two versions of the test (which is the goal of text translations). Due to this, it is sometimes necessary and useful, when creating an adaptation, to abstain from the idea that all items of the target version have the exact same meaning as their counterparts in the original version. Van De Vijver and Poortinga (2005) propose three levels of content overlap between the original and the target version of a test:

- **Application**
- **Adaptation**
- **Assembly**

According to these authors, **a situation of application of a test in another culture** occurs when contents of the original and the target version of a test are completely identical, i.e., when translation of the original version into the target language was the only thing that was done. Before the appearance of the methodological guidelines and standards for test adaptation, meaning roughly up until the 1990s, practically all test adaptations into another language fell in this category. Although the way tests function has been known to psychologists for a very long time, the idea that a construct might manifest differently in different cultures and the application of this idea in practice is relatively fresh. Even today, most existing test adaptations, both those used in psychological research and those used in psychological practice, are cases of test application in another culture, according to this classification. A great advantage of this approach to test adaptation is its simplicity – test contents are just translated from one language into another and that is it. Sometimes this approach to test adaptation is a consequence of culturological closeness of two human populations that really results in tests with identical content also being psychologically equivalent. In such cases, this approach is the method of choice. But much more often, this approach is a consequence of insufficient familiarity or incomplete knowledge of problems of cross-cultural adaptation of tests by people doing the adaptation. And with this comes a lack of awareness of the fact that direct translation and direct content equivalence is neither the only nor always the best option for test adaptation. Specifically due to this lack of awareness, it is still not rare to encounter research papers, sometimes even published in very prestigious scientific journals, in which authors, even after stating that factor structures of the original and the target versions of the test are not even similar, let alone identical, still continue their "research" of the factor structure of the test and (wrongly!) conclude that the target version is "usable" although its factor structure is nowhere near what is theoretically expected or what is obtained with the original version.

A situation of **test adaptation for another language or another population** happens when a certain proportion of items is just translated into the target language, while other items are replaced with new items that do not have equivalent meaning to their counterparts from the original. This is a method of choice when there is reason to believe that some items will not be psychologically equivalent to originals when translated into the target language. In this case, new items are created for the target version with different content that the originals, but hopefully items that will cause reactions in members of the target culture that are influenced by the same construct that influences responses to their counterpart items from the original version. For example, in the process of adaptation of the Personal Globe Inventory, an inventory of vocational interests from American English into Croatian, the author of the Croatian adaptation, Iva Šverko, replaced the item asking the test-taker how much he/she would like to work as a personal shopper with a question asking the test-taker how much he/she would like to work as a taxi driver. Unlike the vocation of personal shopper, which is well known in the US, but completely unknown in Croatia, the vocation of taxi driver is well known (Šverko, 2008a, 2008b). For this same reason, this change in item content was also done in Serbian (Hedrih, 2008), Bulgarian (Hedrih et al., 2016) and North Macedonian (Hedrih, Šverko, & Pedović, 2018) versions of this inventory.

Assembly: Construction of a test for another culture or assembly is a method of choice when the test is hard to translate and when it can be reasonably expected that the adaptation of the test into the target language would not be adequate – that the target version would not be psychologically equivalent with the original and that the problem of nonequivalence could not be solved by simply replacing some items (as is the case with adaptation). In the assembly option, a test is created anew for another culture, but still with the intent to assess the same psychological construct or the same group of psychological constructs. It should be noted that this option should not be considered to be the same as the emic approach to test construction, even though the authors of this categorization (Van De Vijver & Poortinga, 2005) include a study that actually used the emic approach to test construction as an example for this approach (Cheung et al., 2011).

Creating the target version of a test

The process of adapting a test starts with a phase in which the target version is created. There are two main approaches for achieving this goal:

- **Forward translation**
- **Backtranslation**

A common feature of both of these approaches is that they require the participation of at least two translators working separately.

Forward translation

To create a test adaptation through a procedure of forward translation, one translator needs to translate the original version of the test into the target language (thus creating the target version of the test) and then the other translator, working independently, compares the original and the target version and gives his/her assessment of the equality of every test element.

There are various ways in which this procedure can be performed and documented, but probably the **two most popular** are the following:

- **Textual parts of both the original and target version are broken down into small parts**, for example individual sentences or items, and individual corresponding elements from the two version are pasted in Excel or some similar program next to each other in two parallel columns. Then, in the third column, the other translator marks if he/she considers elements in each corresponding pair to be equal or not, and also writes his/her comments if he/she considers them unequal. In the fourth parallel column the psychologist heading the adaptation process or the translator, or both translators, together consider the situation and write down the decision they made on how to resolve that exact situation. An advantage of this approach is that this partitioning of the test into small elements ensures that the translator will pay due attention to every pair of sentences/items and judge their equivalence. A disadvantage is the fact that tabular representation is not the real format of the test and it is possible that the translator would note some additional issues if he/she looked at the real test format. Looking at the real test format might also enable the translator to note some possible interactions between items, readability problems and the like. It should also be noted that it might sometimes be a problem to partition test instructions into small elements, as one can often find test versions that function equally, but have instruction texts that are psychologically equivalent, but not sentence-for-sentence identical. An example of this are various language versions of the HEXACO inventory – http://hexaco.org/hexaco-inventory (Ashton & Lee, 2009). When this is the case, it might be hard to find a way to meaningfully partition test instruction text into small parts. In this case, a valid option is to just compare whole versions of instruction texts without partitioning them.

- To give the second translator **both versions formatted exactly like they would be applied** and then ask him/her to write his/her comments about the equivalence of the compared versions into the target version or into a separate document. In this way, the second translator has insight into the final version of the test, can look at the test as a whole, and not only item-by-item, but this approach also makes it easier for the translator to miss some of the needed comparison.

After the second translator gives his/her comments then he/she should, together with the psychologist doing the adaptation and sometimes also with the first translator, consider these comments and find a solution for each of them. When needed, other experts can also be included in this activity, and this phase may also be entrusted to a third translator, who would work independently. For example, when doing the adaptation of the work-family conflict scales (Netemeyer, Boles, & Mcmurrian, 1996) from English into Serbian, we found that the first translator translated the English word "strain" into Serbian as "umor", a word meaning tiredness or exhaustion. After consulting a dictionary and the other translator and determining that there is no word in the Serbian language that is completely synonymous to strain, this translation was accepted.

It is very important that all documents about this assessment of equivalence of the two test versions be diligently kept, with all comments, dilemmas and alternatives that were considered, both those that were adopted as final and those that were just considered but not adopted. If it should turn out later, during the empirical testing of equivalence, that items that do not function equivalently in the two versions are those that were identified as potentially problematic during the adaptation, this might point to a possibility that differences in functioning might be resolved by adopting some of the alternatives that were previously considered, but not accepted, or by making some other easy change in the translation.

A big **advantage of the forward translation procedure** is that a **direct comparison between the two versions is made** and this assessment is given by an independent person, one who did not participate in making the translation. This person gives his/her direct evaluation of whether the two versions are equivalent or not. An **important disadvantage** is that **the evaluation is based solely on the conclusions of the translator** about the equivalence. If the researcher does not know both the target and the original language, he/she cannot evaluate the equivalence him/herself, but must completely rely on the translator. This is not a problem if we are sure that the translator will do the job adequately, that he/she will be conscientious, thorough and diligent, and that he/she also possess enough knowledge to make the assessment correctly and notice problematic and unequal translations. However, this is not something that can always be taken for granted. People hired to do the translation may sometimes do it carelessly, they may not really know one of the languages or the dialects of the translation well enough, and they may even sometimes count on the first translator doing the job adequately and then believe that their comments would just be a humiliation for the colleague who did the translation and then claim that everything is in order, even though they did not even look at the test. The trouble with these situations is that the psychologist will often not be able to recognize them with enough confidence should they arise and identifying places in the test that should be reconsidered relies solely on this second translator. If he/she states that there are no problematic places, then there is also no material to be considered.

Another weakness of this procedure is that **translators are bilingual people**, and for this reason they may find acceptable and understandable a lot of materials that monolingual persons would not understand. For example, one can often find translations from English into a number of world languages that involve ad hoc created Anglicisms – words that have English origin, but are integrated into the language. These Anglicisms are sometimes used instead of the already existing words of the other language. This may also happen with other languages, especially in situations when the first translator does not really know the target language well enough, and then inadvertently creates new words based on the original language, but adopts them into the grammatical construction of the target language, creating an ad hoc neologism. While such words might be perfectly understandable to people who speak both languages, like translators, they can easily be completely unintelligible to monolingual test-takers. Also, given that translators know the grammatical rules of both languages, it is possible that they do not notice when a sentence in one language is constructed following grammatical rules of the other language. This is again something bilingual persons will have no problem with, but might be very confusing for monolinguals. Translators also **have an above-average education**, usually having a university degree and those working with psychological tests also often have scientific qualifications in the area of philology and additional knowledge of scientific methodology and psychological testing. This means that they have a vocabulary that is much wider that the vocabulary of an average person, making it possible that they completely miss low-frequency words or very complicated sentence constructions in the translation that would be unintelligible to a typical test-taker. Finally, it is possible that translators **know one language better than the other**, creating situations where they are not able to notice some clear mistakes in the translation. This is particularly possible if they do not know the target language well enough. They might then be able to recognize that correct words were used or that grammar rules were observed, but will not be able to detect unusual sentence constructions, or use of words that would not be applied in that way by native speakers. It might also happen that they do not notice **literal translations**, i.e., situations when words from the original language are just replaced by words from the target language, without any changes to the sentence construction that is completely retained from the original language, and as such probably inadequate in the target language.

Backtranslation

Backtranslation procedure is performed by having one translator translate the original version into the target language, and then another translator, working independently, translates the target version back into the original language. The translation obtained by translating the target version back into the original language is called the backtranslation.

When the second translator completes the backtranslation, the psychologist leading the adaptation process does the comparison between the original version and the backtranslation. As with the forward translation this can be done by:

- **Partitioning the whole textual content** of the test into separate sentences, elements or items and pasting this into a tabulation program like Excel in two columns – one for the original version, the other for the backtranslation and then a third column for writing comments and conclusions about the equivalence of translations.
- **Comparing formatted versions** of the original test and the backtranslation, and then writing comments and conclusions about equivalence of translations in the backtranslation or in a separate document.

It should be noted that, when comparing the original version and the backtranslation, the default expectation should not be that the two versions be perfectly identical, but that they be similar enough, i.e., that the meaning of the compared elements is the same. It will sometimes happen that the sentence in the original version and the backtranslation are perfectly identical, but it should not be expected that this happens too often. When a translation from one language into another is done adequately, the sentence construction also changes because different languages have different rules for composing sentences. And a sentence can typically be composed in several ways. This might then cause the backtranslation, although it is a good backtranslation, to have a different order of words in a sentence compared to the original. This happens because the second translator does not know which of the multiple valid word orders were used in the original, so he/she may choose a different, albeit completely valid, word order.

Words of two languages are also not complete synonyms, i.e., identical terms that completely replace one another, so it will typically happen that scopes of their meaning are more or less different. Because of this, it may happen that the translator doing the backtranslation chooses some of the synonyms, and not the exact word used in the original version. And if the scope of the meaning of the word from the target language is wider than the scope of the meaning of the word from the original or with incomplete meaning overlap, it is possible that the translator comprehends the sentence in a somewhat different way than intended, and then chose, in the backtranslation, a word that is not really a synonym of the original.

Two languages may also differ in tenses available in each language, and this may cause a sentence in a backtranslation to be in a different tense than the original.

While all the mentioned discrepancies between the original and the backtranslation are normal, the main issue that needs to be looked out for is whether there was an **essential shift of the psychological meaning** of elements in the backtranslation compared to the original. Are there items in the backtranslation that, without intention, have a different meaning than their corresponding items from the original version? Are there items the meaning of which are essentially changed and thus it can be reasonably expected that the item will not cause responses in test-takers that are driven by the construct test is intended to measure, but by something else? If there happen to be such items in the backtranslation, then the psychologist must, together with both translators, carefully explore how this shift in meaning came to be and try to find a translation of the item or the test element into the target language that will not result in shifted meaning. That the new translation of the item no longer results in meaning shift is, of course, something that has to be verified again. But, as both translators have now been included into this consideration and are thus prone to simply confirm that everything is now in order with the new translation, it is good to consult a third translator, independent of the previous two, and ask him/her to translate the new translations of the problematic items or test elements back into the original language (but do not mention to him/her that there already exists a backtranslation, just ask him/her to do the translation!). There is also an option to include only the first translator into the discussion about shifted meanings between the original and the backtranslation, so we can have the second translator available to independently verify that a meaning shift no longer occurs, but we then run the risk of the first translator simply claiming that his/her translation into the target language is good, but that the meaning shift was caused by the other translator. As the psychologist, aside from being a translator him/herself, has no way of determining if such a statement is true or not, if the translator reacts like this it will not help to resolve the problem of shifted meaning adequately. Because of this, it is better to rely on a third translator that did not participate in the process of adaptation before this stage to resolve such situations. This discussion, of course, refers to situations in which the meaning of the item in the adapted version changed unintendedly. It does not refer to situations in which an item was intentionally replaced with an item of different meaning in order to maintain psychological equivalence between the two versions.

What happens if **the original version and the backtranslation are completely identical**? While this is theoretically not an impossibility, it is not a situation that happens often. Possible options are:

- That the **translation** from the original into the target language **was literal**; that words of one language were simply replaced with words from the other language, but with no changes in sentence construction or order of words, even though these changes are typically necessary to create naturally sounding sentences in the other language. This is a method of translation often practiced by people who do not know the target language well enough – they know it sufficiently to understand words, but have not mastered sentence composition or the more complex grammar rules and hence refrained from using them. If the translation from the original into the target language was like this, then the translator doing the backtranslation needs only to retain the existing sentence composition (which is already appropriate for the original language) and replace words in the target language with words of the original language, thus obtaining a translation that is identical to the original. Such an outcome may also happen when translation is done by using some of the lower-quality translation software tools that just replace the words, but do not alter sentence composition. If both the initial translation and the backtranslation are done in this way, obtaining a backtranslation that is identical to the original is even more probable.

- That it is **not a backtranslation at all, but just a copied version of the original** that the translator doing the backtranslation somehow acquired. It might not even be an attempt to cheat the researcher, but simply a desire to do the job as well as possible, while not understanding the idea behind the backtranslation procedure. Recognizing that he/she is translating a psychological test that has its name, and wishing to do the backtranslation as well as possible, the second translator might find the original version on the internet or somewhere else and then copy it completely or use it as a reference to check his/her translation (if for example, he/she is not confident enough in his/her translation skills). If the translator who was doing the backtranslation had access to the original test, and this is often something that the psychologist cannot prevent, especially when the test being translated is a more famous or publicly available one, it is very probable that the original and the backtranslation will be more similar than they should be, if not completely identical.
- That **everything is in order**, but **random chance** and properties of the specific test being translated led to the two versions being completely identical.

In a situation when backtranslation and the original are identical, one should always be aware of these three possibilities. While it is the easiest in such a case to assume the third option to be the explanation for what happened, this should never be done automatically and a thorough examination of the possibility that it was the other two reasons should be done. If needed, an additional translator should be hired to verify this, and the last option should be accepted only after the possibility that the other situations in question have been eliminated.

A great **advantage** of this procedure of test adaptation is that the **researcher** leading the adaptation process **is included in the assessment of equivalence** of the two versions and she/he can directly evaluate if the two versions are equivalent or not by comparing the original and the backtranslation. Unlike the forward translation, where it is up to one of the translators to warn the researcher when he/she notices a pair of items that do not match, in this procedure, that is done by the researcher, who understands how tests function and can be more sensitive to differences between items and more readily recognize when they are not equivalent.

The main weakness of this procedure is that it does not compare the two versions that are really important – the original and the target version, but compares two versions in the original language. So, while this process is useful for discovering pairs of items in which the meaning shifted, it does not really provide a guarantee that the original and the target version are equivalent. As noted earlier, a bad, literal translation into the target language might also result in an equivalent backtranslation, and then it is up to the individual experience and "feel" of the researcher to recognize that the original version and the backtranslation are too similar, that something is not right, and then to take steps to resolve the problem. This is something than may not easily happen, as there are no precise and objective criteria for deciding when the two versions are "similar enough" and when their similarity is "suspiciously high".

Combining the forward translation and the backtranslation

Another option for a procedure for adapting a test is to combine the two previously mentioned procedures. One translator would first translate the test into the target language, another translator would do the backtranslation (translate the target version back into the original language) and a third translator would compare the original and the target version, while the researcher would compare the original version and the backtranslation. In the next phase, the researcher would compare elements that were marked as problematic in the forward translation and in the backtranslation procedure and note if these elements are the same or not.

In the tabular document about the translation process, there would be elements of the original version in one column, elements of the target version in another, comments of the translator about the equivalence of these two in the third column, backtranslation in the fourth column, and comments of the researcher about the equivalence of the backtranslation and the original in the fifth column. One more column would contain data on whether the element was marked as problematic in both procedures, in just one or nowhere; the next column would contain proposed solutions and the final column would contain the final adopted version of the translation of that element.

While this combined approach has obvious advantages because it largely alleviates the disadvantages of both the forward translation and the backtranslation procedure, it does make the process of adaptation and its documentation somewhat more tedious and expensive, as it requires at least one more translator. Although one can imagine cases in which this combined procedure would be clearly more useful than just forward translation or backtranslation alone, this is not really necessary in most cases, because the obvious issues with version equivalence can be detected very effectively with only one of these procedures. On the other hand, when the additional expenses for a translator and additional work on documenting the adaptation process are not a big item in the budget, applying this combined approach can be useful.

TABLE 3.1 An example of a tabular record of the process of adaptation using a combination of forward translation and backtranslation methods. Part of the tabular record of the adaptation of the Work-Family Conflict scale (Netemeyer et al., 1996) into Serbian language is presented in the table. Original, backtranslation and translation were placed in rows; a decision was made about their equality, and when it was negative, a new translation was proposed and then the authors decided on the final translation and wrote what the issue was and how it was resolved (Resolution column).

Original	*Backtranslation*	*Translation*	*Equality?*	*Resolution*	*New translation*	*Final translation*
1. The demands of my work interfere with my home and family life.	1. Job/work-related requirements hinder/ interfere with my private and family life.	1. Zahtevi mog posla ometaju moj privatni i porodični život.	Y			1. Zahtevi mog posla ometaju moj privatni i porodični život.
2. The amount of time my job takes up makes it difficult to fulfill family responsibilities.	2. The amount of time that my job requires makes it difficult for me to meet my family responsibilities.	2. Zbog količine vremena koju posao zahteva teško mi je da ispunim porodične obaveze.	N	Rephrased	Zbog količine vremena koju moj posao zauzima teško mi je da ispunim porodične obaveze.	2. Zbog količine vremena koju moj posao zauzima teško mi je da ispunim porodične obaveze.
3. Things I want to do at home do not get done because of the demands my job puts on me.	3. Because of the demands of my job I cannot do things around the house even though I want to (do them).	3. Zbog obaveza u vezi s poslom ne uspevam da završim stvari koje bih želeo kod kuće.	N	Backtranslation not good. Translation kept.		3. Zbog obaveza u vezi s poslom ne uspevam da završim stvari koje bih želeo kod kuće.
4. My job produces strain that makes it difficult to fulfill family duties.	4. My job exhausts me so much that it makes it hard for me to meet my family responsibilities.	4. Moje posao me toliko umori da mi je zbog toga teško da ispunim porodične obaveze.	N	No word for strain in Serbian language. Replaced with exhaustion, tiredness		4. Moje posao me toliko umori da mi je zbog toga teško da ispunim porodične obaveze.
5. Due to work-related duties, I have to make changes to my plans for family activities.	5. I have to rearrange plans for family activities because of my job demands.	5. Zbog obaveza u vezi s poslom moram da menjam planove porodičnih aktivnosti.	N	Rephrased	Zbog obaveza na poslu moram da menjam planove porodičnih aktivnosti.	5. Zbog obaveza na poslu moram da menjam planove porodičnih aktivnosti.

Simultaneous construction

Although most tests that currently exist in multiple language versions arrived at that situation by being initially in only one language and created for one culture, and then adapted to other languages and for other cultures afterward, more and more authors believe that tests should be simultaneously constructed in multiple languages and in multiple cultures. Theoretically, this would enable us to avoid a large number of problems that appear after the test content has already been fixed in one language and then needs to be adapted into another.

There is a clear and concrete need in modern society for simultaneous construction of parallel versions of a test in multiple languages due to the following:

- An important proportion of test users are organizations that operate in multiple countries and with people of diverse linguistic and ethnic background, and thus have a need for results of psychological tests they use to be comparable. At the moment, this problem is often resolved by administering tests to everyone in a single, usually English language, even though this solution is often methodologically inadequate.
- The increasing international mobility of people leads to the creation of ever more multicultural environments in which psychologists in their practice work with people of diverse ethnic and linguistic backgrounds, and thus require appropriate tests to use in their work.
- In some parts of the world, the market for psychological tests in just a single language is too small to make the creation, examination of psychometric characteristics and sale of tests in just one language profitable. For example, in the Balkans region of Europe, after the dissolution of Yugoslavia, the region was divided into a number of small countries with a small and declining number of inhabitants. Due to this, test publication, adaptation and distribution for only one of these countries is a business that is at best only marginally profitable and sometimes completely unprofitable, even for the most popular tests. Simultaneous construction of multiple language versions and their simultaneous empirical validation can be a solution in such a situation, because the part of doing the adaptation and planning validation studies can thus be centralized and made cheaper. It can be organized so that all language versions are validated in the scope of a single validation study done in multiple countries, and in such a case collecting empirical data from multiple countries/multiple language groups boils down to having a more complex sampling procedure.

Whichever of these reasons might be the motive for simultaneous construction of multiple cultural/language versions of a test, the fact remains that the multicultural approach overcomes one of the great weaknesses of modern psychology, and that is the centering of theories and instruments of psychology on one culture, usually the one the psychologist belongs to. That is the approach that created psychology as it is today, with all its weaknesses, a science sometimes called "the science about the behavior of rich, white people from the West" or even "the science about the behavior of psychology students and their peers".

As generalizability is an important goal of science in general, and also of psychology in particular, the creation of psychological measurement instruments applicable to a larger number of human populations represents a scientific value per se, independent of the fact that such a general approach puts additional assessment options into the hands of psychologists, options that are particularly useful in multicultural environments.

When we opt for the simultaneous construction, the first decision that needs to be made is the one about which approach to take. Two options exist:

- That we opt for **the etic approach**, i.e., that we construct an instrument that measures psychological traits that exist in all cultures/linguistic groups we intend to create the test for; or
- That we opt for a **combination of the etic and the emic approach**, i.e., that we construct an instrument that will measure some constructs that are common for all intended cultures of the test, but also some constructs that are specific for a particular group. These specific measured constructs need not exist in all language/cultural versions of the test, but if they exist in at least some of those groups, we speak of combination of the emic and the etic approach.

An exclusive emic approach is, of course, **not an option here**, because, if the test measured completely different constructs in each group, we would be speaking of a construction of a number of different instruments and not about a simultaneous construction of multiple language versions of the same instrument.

The etic approach

If we opt for the etic approach, constructs the test is intended to measure must be such that it can be reasonably expected that they exist in an identical form in all intended populations of the test. Such an assessment can, of course, not be made by an individual psychologist, unless he/she possesses very detailed data from previous research studies in all target populations, so it is typically necessary to consult experts for each of the target populations/cultures. After reasonable expectations that the construct functions in an identical way in all target populations is established, the next phase is deriving indicators for each construct that the test is intended to measure. In the scope of this, we can either only choose indicators that can be reasonably expected to be valid in all target populations or we may permit that a certain proportion of indicators differs between populations. The first option provides for a greater uniformity of future test versions, but at the expense of lower content validity. The second option provides for better content validity, but at the expense of lower uniformity and possibly also lower levels of measurement invariance between future test versions.

After forming a list of indicators, those that are to be included in the test are selected (mainly verbal indicators, i.e., those that can be expressed in the form of items) and items are created based on them. If indicators are the same in all populations, then items should also be created so that they are the same in all versions, i.e., in an ideal case, items would just be translations of the same content to different languages. In cases where this is not possible, when there is a need that some items differ substantially between various versions, these items should be created so that their psychometric properties are as similar as possible between the versions if the content cannot be the same.

Equivalence of translations of the test and of items are also evaluated here through the processes of backtranslation or forward translation with a due notice that, given that multiple language versions are created, it is often convenient to have one language version be a central version and then compare all other versions with that version. If needed, a control can be done again in a later phase, when preliminary test versions are finished, by repeating the translation equivalence evaluation process by treating some other language versions as a central version or by making random pairings, but it should be noted that such a control procedure requires additional translators that need to know the exact combination of languages that is selected for comparison.

Most of the time, researchers do not really have a free hand in choosing which language they will make the "central" language when constructing multiple parallel language versions, because it is typically easy to find translators who can translate from a "small" language to some of the "bigger" languages (meaning more popular or with more speakers), but it is quite a problem to find translators who can translate from one "small" language into another "small" language. For example, it is quite easy to find translators who can translate from any other language into English or from English (of course, not one translator that can translate from English into all those various languages, but a separate translator for translations between each language and English). Translators who can translate from Serbian into English, Turkish into English, Arabic into English, Georgian into English or any other language into English are very easy to find. Most people of good education, even when that education is not in the area of philology can, to a certain extent, translate between their first language and English. On the other hand, it is very difficult to find a person that could translate Slovenian into Georgian or Thai into Somali directly. This is even harder if we take into account that test adaptation cannot be done by any translator, but that this person needs to fulfill additional criteria to do the job effectively. Due to this, these additional control comparisons will be limited to only those combinations of language versions for which qualified translators are available.

Combination of etic and emic approaches

A combination of etic and emic approaches is a good option when there are good theoretical reasons to believe that cultures, i.e., human populations for which the test is intended differ to a sufficient extent that in at least some of them there are psychological traits that do not exist in other cultures for which the test is intended. It is good if such an expectation could be backed by previous research studies in which these specific traits or constructs have been identified and confirmed in these cultures. When this is the case, the task of test construction is approached so that, for those traits that have the etic status, construction is conducted in the way that is described under the etic approach, while for those constructs that are emics, indicators and items are developed only for the population in which these traits exist, in a way that this would be done for regular, monolingual tests. A similar approach was used in the construction of the Chinese Personality Inventory (Cheung et al., 2011), but it should be noted that this specific study was not a case of simultaneous construction for multiple cultures, but only of inclusion of the emic approach in creating a personality inventory for one (Chinese) culture.

A combination of etic and emic approaches enables better coverage of the psychological domain by the test through inclusion of psychological traits that are culture-specific, but at the expense of comparability of persons tested with this test. In cases like this, meaningful comparisons between test-takers from different cultures can be done only in regard to constructs that are etics. On the other hand, if the purpose of the test is to predict some criterion behavior, then it is beyond doubt that emic measures may improve the predictive power of all test versions that include them.

It must be noted that the decision on whether to use etic or a combined etic-emic approach should always be based on valid theoretical reasons. Psychologists doing simultaneous construction of multiple language versions of a test must be very attentive to avoid falling into the trap of "cultural imperialism" in which they would, without a valid reason, just assume that there are no cultural differences and thus no reason to use any approach aside from the etic approach. The psychologist must also pay careful attention to avoid falling into the reverse trap of "chauvinism of small differences" in which he/she would, again without valid reason, decide that some of the cultures included are so specific that an emic approach is necessary, all done with a wish to show that a certain culture or culture group is different and special. This author believes that the trap of "cultural imperialism" illustrates quite adequately the situation in which the science of psychology, albeit unintentionally, currently resides.

When considering the application of the strategy of simultaneous construction of multiple language versions of a test, it should be noted that although there are currently still not many examples of this approach either in test construction or in theory building, those few that do exist are very influential and famous. Maybe the most famous example of tests made simultaneously for a large number of linguistic groups are tests created in the scope of the OECD-supported Program for International Student Assessment (PISA) – www.oecd.org/pisa/test/other-languages/xandar-82-languages.htm. At the moment this book is written, PISA tests exist in 82 different languages.

Notes

1 The word "intelligence" as reference to the construct measured by Alfa and Beta is given in quotes because it is very disputable if what these tests measured in these situations is indeed intelligence or a conglomerate of factors, intelligence is only one of. The stance of the author of this book is that these measures should not be treated as clear and exclusive measures of intelligence, hence the quotes.

2 S-O-R model views tests as sets of stimuli (S) that cause reactions of test-takers (R), and these reactions will vary between test-takers in accordance with their differences in internal psychological characteristics (O). According to this concept, we influence test-takers by using stimuli-test items (S), to which they react differently, and since stimuli are the same, we conclude that differences in reaction must be caused by differences in internal psychological properties of test-takers.

3 Extraversion is a personality trait proposed by the Big Five model. Persons with high extraversion are social, prone to seeking stimulation and interaction with others, talkative, etc.

4 A type of cognitive test where tasks are deliberately easy so almost every test-taker would be able to solve them if he/she had enough time, but the test is administered with strict time limit, generally insufficient to complete all tasks.

5 A process study is a method of assessing construct validity of a test or a testing situation in which the researcher observes test-takers while they work or analyzes their errors, or asks the test-takers to think aloud in order to analyze their mental processes during work. Conclusions about validity are then made by comparing the observed behavior of test-takers and with the behavior that should be theoretically expected having in mind test contents, characteristics and constructs the test is intended to measure.

6 Usage frequency refers to how often a word is used in speech or in texts. This is also related to the percentage of the population that will know the meaning of the word or have it in their vocabulary.

7 Borislav Stevanović was born in 1891, and defended his doctoral dissertation in psychology at the King's College in London in front of a committee that included Charles Spearman. He worked as a professor of psychology at the University of Belgrade.

References

AERA, APA, & NCME. (2006). *Standardi za pedagoško i psihološko testiranje*. Zagreb: Naklada Slap.

Annor, F., & Amponsah-Tawiah, K. (2017). Evaluation of the psychometric properties of two scales of work – family conflict among Ghanaian employees. *The Social Science Journal*. https://doi.org/10.1016/j.soscij.2017.04.006

Ashton, M. C., & Lee, K. (2009). The HEXACO – 60: A short measure of the major dimensions of personality. *Journal of Personality Assessment, 91*(4), 340–345. https://doi.org/10.1080/00223890902935878

Boake, C. (2002). From the Binet±Simon to the Wechsler±Bellevue: Tracing the history of intelligence testing. *Journal of Clinical and Experimental Neuropsychology, 24*(3), 383–405.

Brigham, C. C. (1923). *A study of American intelligence*. Princeton: Princeton University Press.

Carraher, T. N., Carraher, D. W., & Schliemann, A. D. (1985). Mathematics in the streets and in schools. *British Journal of Developmental Psychology, 3*, 21–29. https://doi.org/10.1111/j.2044-835X.1985.tb00951.x

Cattell, R. B. (1940). A culture-free intelligence test. *The Journal of Educational Psychology, 331*(3), 161–179. Retrieved from http://psycnet.apa.org.proxy.kobson.nb.rs:2048/fulltext/1940-04768-001.pdf

Chan, D., Schmitt, N., Deshon, R. P., Clause, C. S., & Delbridge, K. (1997). Reactions to cognitive ability tests: The relationships between race, test performance, face validity perceptions, and test-taking motivation. *Journal of Applied Psychology, 82*(2), 300–310. Retrieved from http://psycnet.apa.org.proxy.kobson.nb.rs:2048/fulltext/1997-03393-010.pdf

Cheung, F. M., Van De Vijver, F. J. R., Leong, F. T. L., Cheung, C., Van De Vijver, F. M., & Leong, F. J. R. (2011). Toward a new approach to the study of personality in culture. *American Psychologist, 66*(7), 593–603. https://doi.org/10.1037/a0022389

Chomsky, N. (1959). A review of B. F. Skinner's verbal behavior. *Language, 35*(1), 26–58. Retrieved from http://cogprints.org/1148/1/chomsky.htm

Darcy, M. (2005). Examination of the structure of Irish students' vocational interests and competence perceptions. *Journal of Vocational Behavior, 67*, 321–333. https://doi.org/10.1016/j.jvb.2004.08.007

De Raad, B., Smederevac, S., Čolović, P., & Mitrović, D. (2018). Personality traits in the Serbian language: Structure and procedural effects. *Journal of Research in Personality, 73*, 93–110. https://doi.org/10.1016/j.jrp.2017.11.008

Du Toit, R., & De Bruin, G. P. (2002). The structural validity of Holland's R-I-A-S-E-C model of vocational personality types for young Black South African men and women, *Journal of Career Assessment 10*(1), 62–77. https://doi.org/10.1177/1069072702010001004

Eklöf, H. (2007). Test-taking motivation and mathematics performance in TIMSS 2003. *International Journal of Testing*, 7(3), 311–326. https://doi.org/10.1080/15305050701438074

Elosua, P. (2007). Assessing vocational interests in the Basque country using paired comparison design. *Journal of Vocational Behavior, 71*(1), 135–145. https://doi.org/10.1016/j.jvb.2007.04.001

Flynn, J. (2007). *What is intelligence? Beyond the Flynn effect.* Cambridge: Cambridge University Press.

Grant, M. (1916). The passing of the great race. *Geographical Review, 2*(5), 354–360.

Greenfield, P. (1997). You can't take it with you: Why ability assessments don't cross cultures. *American Psychologist, 52*(10), 1115–1124.

Hambleton, R. (2005). Issues, desings, and technical guidelines for adapting tests into multiple languages and cultures. In R. Hambleton, P. Merenda, & C. Spielberger (Eds.), *Adapting educational and psychological tests for cross-cultural assessment* (pp. 3–38). Mahwah, NJ and London: Lawrence Erlbaum Associates.

Harzing, A.-W. (2006). Response styles in cross-national survey research. *International Journal of Cross Cultural Management, 6*(2), 243–266. https://doi.org/10.1177/1470595806066332

Hedrih, V. (2008). Structure of vocational interests in Serbia: Evaluation of the spherical model. *Journal of Vocational Behavior, 73*(1), 13–23. https://doi.org/10.1016/j.jvb.2007.12.004

Hedrih, V., Stošić, M., Simić, I., & Ilieva, S. (2016). Evaluation of the hexagonal and spherical model of vocational interests in the young people in Serbia and Bulgaria. *Psihologija, 49*(2), 199–210. https://doi.org/10.2298/PSI1602199H

Hedrih, V., Šverko, I., & Pedović, I. (2018). Structure of vocational interests in Macedonia and Croatia – evaluation of the spherical model. *Facta Universitatis, Series: Philosophy, Sociology, Psychology and History, 17*(1), 19–36. https://doi.org/10.22190/FUPSPH1801019H

Hedrih, V., Todorović, J., & Ristić, M. (Eds.). (2013). *Odnosi na poslu i u porodici u srbiji početkom 21. veka.* Niš: Filozofski fakultet, Srbija.

Holland, J. L. (1959). A theory of vocational choice. *Journal of Counseling Psychology, 6*(1).

International Test Comission. (2005). *ITC guidelines for translating and adapting tests.* Retrieved from www.intestcom.org/files/guideline_test_adaptation.pdf

International Test Comission. (2017). *ITC guidelines for translating and adapting tests* (2nd ed.). https://doi.org/10.1027/1901-2276.61.2.29

Kamin, L. (1974). *The science and politics of I. Q.* New York and London: Routledge, Taylor & Francis Group.

Kamin, L. (1982). Mental testing and imigration. *American Psychologist, 37*(1), 97–98. http://dx.doi.org/10.1037/0003-066X.37.1.97.b

Knox, H. (1914). A scale, based on the work at Ellis Island, for estimating mental defect. *Journal of American Medical Association, 62*, 741–747.

Netemeyer, R. G., Boles, J. S., & Mcmurrian, R. (1996). Development and validation of work-family conflict and family-work conflict scales. *Journal of Applied Psychology, 81*.

Pauls, C. A., & Stemmler, G. (2003). Substance and bias in social desirability responding. *Personality and Individual Differences, 35*, 263–275.

Reis, A., & Castro-Caldas, A. (1997). Illiteracy: A cause for biased cognitive development. *Journal of International Neuropsychological Society, 3*, 444–450.

Saucier, G., Georgiades, S., Tsaousis, I., & Goldberg, L.-R. (2005). The factor structure of Greek personality adjectives. *Journal of Personality and Social Psychology, 88*(5), 856–875. https://doi.org/10.1037/0022-3514.88.5.856

Serpell, R. (1979). How specific are perceptual skills? A cross-cultural study of pattern reproduction*. *British Journal of Psychology, 70*(3), 365–380. https://doi.org/10.1111/j.2044-8295.1979.tb01706.x

Sinclair, V. G., & Wallston, K. A. (2004). The development and psychometric evaluation of the brief resilient coping scale. *Assessment, 11*(1), 94–101. https://doi.org/10.1177/1073191103258144

Snyderman, M., & Herrnstein, R. J. (1983). Intelligence tests and the immigration act of 1924. *American Psychologist, 38*(9), 986–995. http://dx.doi.org/10.1037/0003-066X.38.9.986

Steele, C., & Aronson, J. (1995). Stereotype threat and the intellectual test performance of African Americans. *Journal of Personality and Social Psychology, 69*(5), 797–811.

Sternberg, R. J. (2004). Culture and intelligence. *American Psychologist, 59*(5), 325–338. https://doi.org/10.1037/0003-066X.59.5.325

Šverko, I. (2008a). *Profesionanlni interesi u funkciji dobi i spola: Evaluacija sfernog modela (Vocational interests as a function of age and gender: Evaluation of the spherical model)*. University of Zagreb, Zagreb, Croatia.

Šverko, I. (2008b). Spherical model of interests in Croatia. *Journal of Vocational Behavior, 72*, 14–24. https://doi.org/10.1016/j.jvb.2007.10.001

Tak, J. (2004). Structure of vocational interests for Korean college students. *Journal of Career Assessment, 12*(3), 298–311. https://doi.org/10.1177/1069072703261555

Tošić Radev, M., & Hedrih, V. (2017). Psychometric properties of the multidimensional jealousy scale (MJS) on a Serbian sample. *Psihologija, 50*(4), 521–534. https://doi.org/10.2298/PSI170121012T

Tracey, T. J. G., & Robbins, S. B. (2005). Stability of interests across ethnicity and gender: A longitudinal examination of grades 8 through 12. *Journal of Vocational Behavior, 67*(3), 335–364. https://doi.org/10.1016/j.jvb.2004.11.003

Van De Vijver, F., & Poortinga, Y. H. (2005). Conceptual and methodological issues in adapting tests. In R. Hambleton, P. Merenda, & C. Spielberger (Eds.), *Adapting educational and psychological tests for cross-cultural assessment* (pp. 39–64). Mahwah, NJ and London: Lawrence Erlbaum Associates.

Watson, J. (1913). Psychology as the behaviorist views it. *Psychological Review, 20*, 158–177. Retrieved from http://psychclassics.yorku.ca/Watson/views.htm

Yang, W., Lance, C. E., & Hui, H. C. (2006). Psychometric properties of the Chinese self-directed search (1994 ed.). *Journal of Vocational Behavior, 68*(3), 560–576. https://doi.org/10.1016/j.jvb.2005.12.003

Želeskov Đorić, J., Pedović, I., & Hedrih, V. (2009). Friendship functions and personality traits. *Psihologija, 42*(3). https://doi.org/10.2298/PSI0903341Z

4

ASSESSING EQUIVALENCE OF DIFFERENT LANGUAGE VERSIONS OF A TEST

Differential test and item functioning and measurement invariance

In previous chapters, we mentioned the S-O-R concept of psychological testing that represents psychological testing as a process in which test-takers are exposed to stimuli (S) that cause them to give responses (R) that will be influenced by internal psychological variables (O). This implicitly assumes that even though test-takers will give different responses, all those responses will be influenced by the same O variable, and their variability will be a consequence of different intensities of this O variable in different test-takers. This concept also implies that the researcher/test administrator knows which O variable precisely influences test-takers' responses and that this O variable will be the same for all test-takers.

If it turns out that test-taker responses are caused by some variable different from the O variable the researcher expects, then we have a situation of compromised validity of the test or of the testing situation, irrespective of whether it is another internal psychological variable or an external factor that influenced the responses. However, if it turns out that responses of some test-takers are influenced by the O variable that the test constructor or the researcher counted on (the one that should influence responses), while responses of other participants are influenced by some other variable, we have a situation of differential test or item functioning. When it happens that the same O variable influences responses of all test-takers, but test-takers with the same intensity of the measured trait, belonging to different groups, give different responses, this is again a situation of differential item functioning. An example of this case is the situation when an item is harder for test-takers from one group then test-takers from another group with the same trait intensity. In general, differential item and test functioning happens whenever a test or some element of a test function differently on two groups of test-takers.

When psychometric properties of an item are different for two groups of test-takers, we have a case of **differential item functioning, DIF** for short. When psychometric properties of a test measure – or a group of test measures – are different for different groups of test-takers, this represents a case of **differential test functioning**.

Differential test functioning is a phenomenon that was noticed by psychologists in the relatively early days of psychological testing. Soon after the first massive application of psychological tests began, first on immigrants at Ellis Island in the US, and then in the process of recruitment for World War I in the US (see Chapter 3 about history), it was noticed that the psychometric properties of a test may change from sample to sample, i.e., be different on different samples. For example, Raymond Cattell's (Cattell, 1940) classic attempt to create a culture-free test was motivated by his desire to solve the problem of differential functioning. In the same paper, Cattell speaks of a disappointment in psychological tests that became dominant in the psychological community of the time, and which was, according to Cattell, caused by the realization that psychometric properties of a test can change between samples, i.e., between different groups of people.

In the beginning, differential functioning was called **bias**, a term stemming from an initial idea that a test, as a measurement instrument has its fixed, real psychometric properties, but that it may happen that in some applications it does not display these psychometric properties, but displays some different, usually worse properties instead. It was then believed that the test is biased toward those groups, meaning that it does not assess their characteristics correctly. An implicit assumption ingrained in the term "bias" is that bias is a rare, unusual occurrence. A test was seen as generally unbiased, but it might just so happen that it functions in a biased way with some groups, causing them to have lower achievement. Only relatively recently, after many, many findings related to many different tests showing that changing psychometric properties between groups and between testing situations are for many tests more often a rule than an exception, do we see an increasing use of the term differential functioning instead of bias. Ellis (1989), for example, notes that the term differential item functioning is "less value-laden, more accurate" (Ellis, 1989, p. 912) and is slowly replacing the term item bias.

It should be noted that this view – that differential functioning and bias are synonyms – is not shared by all authors. For example, in their classic text on statistical procedures for identifying differential item functioning, Clauser and Mazor claim that differential item functioning and item bias are not synonymous. They state "differential item functioning is present when examinees from different groups have differing probabilities or likelihoods of success on an item, after they have been matched of the ability of interest." (Clauser & Mazor, 1998, p. 31). The same authors also state that an

> item is considered biased against examinees of a particular group if members of that group are less likely to answer that item correctly than examinees of

> another group because of some aspect of the test item or the testing situation which is not relevant to the purpose of testing.
>
> *(Clauser & Mazor, 1998, p. 40)*

It can be noticed that these two definitions are really definitions of the same concept. If examinees from different groups have different probabilities of success on an item, this means, at the same time, that at least one of the considered groups will necessarily have a lower probability of success on that item. The only way for this not to be the case is if members of all groups with equal levels of the trait have the exact same probabilities of answering the item correctly, but if that was the case, there would be neither bias nor differential functioning. Still, these authors insist on the difference between the two concepts stating that DIF is necessary but not a sufficient condition for an item to be biased. However, in newer papers it can be seen that the terms differential item functioning and item bias are used as synonyms, although their relations are not explicitly discussed (e.g., Hidalgo & López-Pina, 2004; Kristjansson, Aylesworth, Mcdowell, & Zumbo, 2005) or that the term bias is not used at all.

In the mentioned classic paper, aside from differential functioning, Clauser and Mazor also define the following concepts (Clauser & Mazor, 1998):

- **DIF amplification** – a phenomenon that items from an observed set show no significant DIF individually, but when considered together, the total level of DIF becomes significant/substantial.
- **DIF cancellation** – happens when some individual items have substantial DIF, but when all these items are considered together, no group of examinees achieves an advantage. This happens because different items show differential functioning in different directions, effectively cancelling each other's DIF. DIF that makes one item easier for one group is cancelled by DIF of another item that makes that item harder for the same group; the result of both items observed together being that neither group has an advantage.
- **Item impact** – happens when examinees from different groups have different probabilities of giving a correct response to an item, but this is due to real differences in the ability measured by that item (Clauser & Mazor, 1998).

Differential functioning and test bias. The opinion of the author of this text and the rule that will be applied in the rest of this book is that test and item bias is synonymous to differential item of test functioning. It is also my opinion that differential functioning is a better term because it is not based on the assumption that a test has some "real" psychometric properties, but recognizes the fact that psychometric properties can be different on different populations and in different testing situations. In the remainder of this text, I will exclusively use the term differential functioning to describe all situations where a test shows different psychometric properties for different groups of test-takers, regardless of what kind of difference in psychometric properties is in question. I will use the same term to describe situations in which an individual item shows different properties of different groups of test-takers.

Types of differential functioning

What can differential functioning be like? Differential test functioning may appear in relation to any examined psychometric property. When an examined psychometric property is not the same in two examined groups, this is a situation of differential functioning of the test in those groups. Wherever some psychometric property is calculated, there exists a chance for differential functioning, either of an item or of the test, to appear.

When differential functioning is only observed on the item level, a classic division is between the **uniform and the nonuniform DIF**:

- **Uniform DIF** exists whenever an item is easier/harder for one group than for another on all levels of the measured variable. This means that in all subgroups that can be created by trait level from both groups taken together, the item will be harder for one group than for the other (e.g., Kristjansson et al., 2005).
- **Nonuniform DIF** exists when the difference in achievement between members of the two groups with the same trait level is not the same for all trait levels (e.g., Clauser & Mazor, 1998; Kristjansson et al., 2005).

For example, if a difference in achievement between members of two groups exists in test-takers whose trait level is high, but does not exist between test-takers from the two groups with medium or low trait levels, it is a case of **nonuniform DIF**. If the difference in achievement between the two groups remains the same in test-takers with the low level of the measured trait, in test-takers with the medium trait level and in test-takers with the high trait level, we have a case of **uniform DIF**.

From the perspective of the **item response theory (IRT)**, differential item functioning happens when item characteristic curves are not the same in all groups. In this perspective, we have a case of **uniform DIF** when item characteristic curves in two groups are parallel, but do not coincide, i.e., when item characteristic curve from one group is positioned left or right from the other on a graph. We have **nonuniform DIF** when item characteristic curves are not parallel. As item response theory defines item difficulty, discrimination, carelessness and guessing parameters, these are the characteristics in which differential item functioning can occur. In other words, an item may have different difficulty, different discrimination and/or different guessing and carelessness parameters on the two considered groups.

The differences in item difficulty mentioned above represent probably the easiest cases of differential functioning. If an item is just easier for one group than for the other, but responses are influenced by the same psychological trait in both groups, this is a much easier situation than the one in which item responses are influenced by one trait in one group and by something else entirely, including maybe also non-psychological factors, in the other group. If this happens, we have a case of differential item functioning that represents different dimensionality of the two samples. This type of DIF can typically be observed through drastically different factor loadings of same items in the two groups or through different fits of data from the two groups into the same confirmatory factor model (e.g., Stark, Chernyshenko, & Drasgow, 2006).

DIF may also manifest itself through **different inter-item correlations**, and at the test level through **different internal structure of the test** (Hedrih, Stošić, Simić, & Ilieva, 2016; Šverko & Hedrih, 2010), i.e., it can be detected in procedure other than factor analysis.

All types of differential functioning that have to do with psychometric properties of various components a test, or relations between various components of test, are called **internal differential functioning**. When relations between test measures and important external variables, like for example correlations between test scores and important variables that are not part of the test, are different in groups that completed different test versions, this is called **external differential functioning** (Fajgelj, 2003).

A concept that is very closely related to differential functioning is the concept of **measurement equivalence**. Measurement equivalence is "obtained when the relations between observed test scores and the latent attribute measured by the test are identical across subpopulations." (Drasgow, 1984, p. 134). Measurement equivalence, defined like this, represents an **absence of differential functioning**. When there is no differential functioning, there is measurement equivalence. The same author also states that for measurements to be equivalent, it is necessary that the test has equivalent relations with external variables, i.e., relations with important external variables should be equivalent in all subpopulations for which the test is intended. This means that if sets of measures obtained on different groups are to be considered equivalent it is necessary to determine that there is neither internal nor external differential functioning.

Another term with the same meaning is **measurement invariance**. A score is

> said to be measurement invariant if a person's probability of an observed score does not depend on his/her group membership, conditional on the true score. That is, respondents from different groups, but with the same true score, will have the same observed score.
>
> *(Wu, Li, & Zumbo, 2007, p. 2)*

Equivalent functioning and differential functioning of different language versions of a test

Although DIF primarily refers to the functioning of the same test on two different groups of people, everything said about differential functioning equally refers to situations in which two language versions of a test are applied to two different language groups of people. In an ideal case, different language versions of a test should have a status of strictly parallel forms between each other and should psychometrically be the same test. Data on whether there is differential functioning or not represents, for this reason, a central topic when evaluating different test versions.

However, as with other parallel forms of a test, different language versions of a test represent completely new sets of stimuli (the S from the S-O-R concept) and this situation is not altered by the fact that the new set of stimuli was obtained through translation, resulting in more or less identical meaning of corresponding stimuli from the two sets. A new language version of a test is a new set of stimuli, and for these two versions to be considered alternative versions of the same test, it is necessary to have empirical evidence showing that the original and the target version of the test provide equivalent measurements, i.e., that there is no differential functioning, as is required by modern standards for adapting tests (International Test Comission, 2017). If there is no such evidence or if evidence shows differential functioning between the two versions i.e., measurement inequivalence, these two language versions of a test should be treated as different tests if a decision is made to use them at all after these results.

Assessing sources of compromised measurement equivalence before starting the empirical collection of data on the equivalence

The main method of collecting evidence of measurement equivalence of two language versions of a test includes, of course, the collection of empirical data on the functioning of different versions on real test-takers. However, before starting the process of collection of empirical evidence, i.e., of administering the test to real test-takers, and after the creation of the target version has been finished, when possible, it is a good idea to obtain an assessment of the equivalence of the two language versions from experts for the culture for which the new language version is intended.

In a process that looks a lot like the process **of assessing content validity, an expert or a group of experts for cultures involved are asked to evaluate the test** as a whole as well as individual items in regard to the equivalence of:

- **The measured constructs**. Experts are asked to give their evaluation of whether the measured construct is equivalent in both cultures and whether it has the same manifestations in both cultures.
- **The measurement method**. Should differences in testing conditions be expected? Is item format equally familiar in both cultures? Are samples that test versions will be administered to comparable? Should any examiner-related effects that could change testing results be expected?
- **Items**. Are translations of items adequate? Are item contents equally relevant for the measured construct in both cultures? Are there other factors that could lead to differential functioning of certain items in the two cultures?

This can be practically executed by creating a short questionnaire with all these questions and asking the experts to answer it. The first part of the questionnaire could consist of pairs of items from the two language versions being compared, similar to how it is done in the forward translation procedure, and then ask the experts to **evaluate similarity of meanings** of corresponding items. Of course, such approach requires the experts to not only know the two cultures but also the two languages well enough to complete. After that, experts could be asked to evaluate the similarity in the difficulty of items within each pair of corresponding items. Next, the experts may be asked to evaluate the similarity of test instructions in the two languages, and then the familiarity of formal properties of the test, such as **the item presentation method** and the **method of responding** for the members of the two cultures, After providing evaluations for individual pairs of items, the experts could be asked to give **global evaluations** on all the questions on the equivalence of the measurement method and equivalence of constructs.

Experts

An important question when conducting the evaluation procedure is who could be the experts that could provide these assessments? It is clear that they should be people well acquainted with both the original and the target culture, but also very familiar with both the target and the original language. But where can such people be found? What formal qualifications do they need to have?

The answer to these questions is that there are **no strict conditions in this regard**. A researcher should **take the most adequate people available**. Sometimes these people will be other psychologists who are, through various circumstances, acquainted with both cultures. At other occasions, experts will simply be educated people of some other profession. At times, available experts will neither be familiar with both languages nor with both cultures, so it will not be possible to obtain answers from them on all the questions, but only on those that do not require knowledge of both languages, and these will primarily be the questions about the test as a whole. Experts will sometimes not be able to assess the equivalence of items or instructions in the two languages, but may well be able to assess familiarity of people from the target culture with formal properties of the test and also answer other questions in the area of construct and measurement method equivalence.

It is important to have in mind that a final expert assessment, conducted before the collection of empirical evidence on measurement equivalence of test versions has begun, is a simple step that may be taken to make a final evaluation of the test adaptation, and the last chance to notice any large mistakes in adaptation in the phase before the empirical data collection, when these mistakes can still be corrected cheaply. This procedure represents at the same time a final prediction of the equivalence of the measured construct and other factors relevant for test functioning in the two populations, which can be very useful if empirical evidence later shows that the two versions do not function equivalently. If it turns out that the experts predicted that there might be a possibility of differential functioning of certain test elements or in a certain way, and the empirical evidence shows that is what really happened, this expert evaluation can then be precious in resolving the issues that led to differential functioning. An evaluation of possible sources of nonequivalence obtained before such nonequivalence was evidenced by empirical results has a much greater epistemological value that an explanation created after the empirical results are already known.

Pilot testing

Current guidelines for test adaptation (International Test Comission, 2017) recommend that a pilot study be conducted before the main empirical data collection in the study of equivalence of different language versions of a test. This pilot study should be conducted on a more modest sample (for example, some hundred participants) from the target population, consisting of participants that are easy to obtain, even if it is a convenience sample. Data collected in this way still allows various psychometric analysis to be conducted, including item-analysis. Although these data cannot yield a firm evaluation of the equivalence of the two versions, this testing may help to remove any bigger mistakes or item functionality problems, if such exist, before the main study and at comparatively little cost. This enables the researchers to be more confident that the much more expensive and time-consuming main study will not "fail" because some obvious, but big, flaw went unnoticed because the adapted version does not function at all or due to some other problem that is big enough to be recognized in the pilot study.

Data collection designs for the empirical evaluation of the equivalence of two language versions of a test

After the test adaptation, i.e., after the target version of the test is created, the next step is to empirically evaluate whether the two versions function equivalently. As was noted before, the fact that two tests are just different language versions of the same test does not automatically mean that they can be treated as parallel versions of the same test or treated like versions of the same test at all. Such treatment needs to be supported by empirical evidence. The term "empirical evidence" refers to a need to verify that compared language versions of a test function equivalently on their intended populations. To fulfill this purpose there are three basic categories of research/data collection designs:

- The original version and the backtranslation are administered to a group of monolingual test-takers, speaking the original language.
- The original version and the target version of the test are administered to a group of bilingual test-takers, speaking both the original and the target language.

- The original version is administered to a group of monolingual test-takers speaking the original language and the target version is administered to a group of monolingual test-takers speaking the target language.

The original version and the backtranslation are administered to a group of monolingual test-takers, speaking the original language

In this design, the researcher still does not do anything with the target versions of the test. The original versions and the backtranslation are administered to a group of monolingual test-takers from the original population, and then the functioning of these two versions on these groups is compared. If everything is in order, it is expected that no differences in functioning between the two versions show up, particularly because these are the same language versions of the test. Even if we take into account that some differences between the original and the backtranslated version, such as differences in tenses, formulations and some minor things, will exist when everything is done correctly, these are all differences for which it was concluded (in the previous phase) that they would not impact test functioning. This is the reason why a conclusion from this study stating that the original version and the backtranslation function equivalently is not really a find of particular significance. This is also the reason why this design itself does not represent a real comparison of the two different language versions of the test – the target version is not examined here at all. However, for these same reasons, a negative result of a study of this type – a result showing that the original version and its backtranslation do not function equivalently on a sample from the original monolingual population is a result with great epistemological value. If this study shows that two insignificantly different versions of the test in the same language do not function equivalently in the original population, there is little purpose in engaging in further data collection and examining the functioning of the two versions on different populations.

If a study of this type yields a negative result, finding that the original version and the backtranslation do not function equivalently, researchers should return to the planning phase and look for the cause of the problem. Is it possible that the original test is bad? Maybe the theory it is based on is invalid? If the original version of the test does not function, if it is based on an invalid theory or if some of its basic postulates are not good, there is little point in adapting it for another language or another culture. Is it possible that there was some big fault with the translation that went unnoticed? Maybe there was an error in the testing procedure or the testing standards were not observed?

A big advantage of this type of research design is that it provides answers to these questions with relative ease because numerous possibilities can be excluded – test-takers for both versions are the same, meaning that differences between groups as cause of differential functioning are automatically excluded. These are monolingual test-takers from the same culture, so cultural differences are also excluded. These are two versions of the same test in the same language, so differences between languages are also excluded. And, when these three important factors are excluded, among factors that remain it is much easier to identify those causing differential functioning. It should be noted that another important advantage of this research design is that it is also relatively cheap to perform. Only test-takers from the original culture participate and these test-takers are usually easy to find for the researcher if he/she him/herself is from the same culture (or is located at a place where members of that culture live). For this reason, even if this design does not test the target version and is hence not a real test of functional equivalence of the two versions, it can be an easy-to-perform advance step that can be done before the main study in which samples from the original and the target population will be compared, especially if samples from the target population are harder or more expensive to obtain, and also if a very large main study is planned.

The main deficiency of this design is that it does not compare the original with the target version. While a negative outcome of a study using this design has high epistemological value, a positive outcome of such study is epistemologically almost worthless. It is completely possible that the original version and the backtranslation function equivalently, that they are almost identical and that, in spite of this, the target version turns out to be invalid or completely psychologically different from the original. Functioning of a test on monolingual test-takers from the original population does not tell anything about the functioning of the test in the target population, because these two populations may differ in important properties, first in cultural characteristics, and possibly also in other important psychological properties.

An additional problem that can arise with this design is that a test learning effect may occur. If two test versions are administered to test-takers in immediate succession or with a small time difference, it is probable that test-takers will memorize the test, so with the second version they will answer from memory instead of really considering answers to items, resulting in the study showing a falsely high level of functional equivalence of the two versions.

However, this problem can easily be solved by making the research design a bit more complex. For example, test-takers can be randomly allocated into two equal groups of which one would complete the original version and the other the backtranslation. The randomization procedure secures equality between the two groups. Taking into account that the two test versions are almost identical, it is probable that the procedure of creating the groups would hardly be noticeable for the test-takers.

The original version and the target version of the test are administered to a group of bilingual test-takers, speaking both the original and the target language

With this research design, the study is conducted on a group of test-takers speaking both languages – the original and the target language. All participants complete both test versions. The idea behind this design is that, since both versions are administered to the same test-takers, all obtained differences in functioning of the two versions will be consequences of "real" differences in the functioning of the two versions. Additionally, unlike the previously described research design, test-takers here really complete the two different language versions that need to be compared, and thus results about the functioning of these two versions – the target and the original version – are really obtained on the same group of test-takers. Aside from this, given that it is the same group of test-takers that completes both tests, i.e., that it is a case of repeated measures, this design allows comparisons that would be impossible with two independent groups of test-takers, i.e., with two independent samples.

While this design might look perfect at the first glance, the first problem that arises in practice is the nature and other properties of bilingual test-takers. Different language versions of a test are usually not created with an intention to be administered to bilingual test-takers, but are intended for monolinguals. In this sense, bilingual test-takers have many properties that make them very unrepresentative for the monolingual population. And also, the idea behind having two language versions of a test is not only that they will function equally in the two languages, but it is also expected that each of these versions functions adequately in the culture related to the language the version is in. Having this in mind, which culture do bilingual test-takers belong to?

To better understand this issue, it is important to consider who the bilingual test-takers taking part in a study like this can really be. The following possibilities are typically found in research studies:

- **Bilingual test-takers are immigrants**. A situation often found in psychological literature is that bilingual test-takers are immigrants from the target culture, living in the original culture, who are then participating in a test adaptation to the target language and it is assumed, for the target culture. Much less frequently, the situation can be found where a test is adapted for the culture in which bilingual immigrants live, while it is originally in the first language of these test-takers. In this category, we often see studies done on people living in some of the Western countries (typically the US), but who originate from the country where the target language is spoken. Taking into account findings that with time spent living in another country people adapt to it, and especially finding that their understanding of the culture they currently live in improves, a question of whether we can really obtain a valid evaluation of the functioning of the test on people from the target culture by administering the test to immigrants living in the original culture becomes highly justified. The answer to this question is most often no. Immigrants of foreign origin, even from the start, are a selected group of people, and with years of living in another country on top of that, they cannot really be considered to be representative of the population of their country of origin.

- **Bilingual test-takers are foreign students or domestic students of foreign origin**. Very often, they are students of psychology or social sciences studying in the country in which the language of the original version is spoken (typically English). The situation with foreign students as bilingual test-takers is similar to the situation with immigrants as test-takers, with the addition that validity of evaluation of test functioning in the target culture obtained on these students is additionally compromised because they are more educated than a typical member of the general population (they are all university students) and this increases their ability to understand or solve a test that would likely cause trouble for "average" monolingual test-takers. The situation is even worse when bilingual test-takers are domestic students of foreign origin, children of first- or second-generation immigrants. While these students might have learned the language of the country of origin of their ancestors, their connection to the culture of that country is problematic at best and often non-existant.
- **Bilingual test-takers are a national minority, residents of a border area or of a multiethnic community in which both languages are spoken**. These very descriptions are reasons why such test-takers cannot be considered to be representative of the general monolingual population of either culture/language. While it is very much possible that their contact with both cultures enables them to understand psychological aspects of both the original and the target cultures, it is more probable that such test-takers belong to a culture of their own or to a subculture that is at least somewhat different from the original and the target culture of the test. For example, it is quite obvious that residents of Quebec, although mostly bilingual in English and French, could hardly be considered representative for the population of France or the population of the United Kingdom for that matter. In the same manner, residents of New Mexico, who are bilingual in Spanish and English could hardly be taken to be representative of the population of modern Spain (or Mexico, for that matter).
- **Bilingual test-takers are people who studied the original or the target language in school or in the scope of some other education program**. This includes situations when tests are administered to test-takers who are native speakers of one of the languages of the test, and learned the other language through formal education. Bilinguals from this category typically have very little or no experience with the culture of native speakers of the other language, although they may speak that other language very proficiently, sometimes even having better knowledge of grammar and formal aspects of the language as well as a richer vocabulary than a typical native speaker. This is the reason why, when working with this type of bilinguals, it is easy for the researcher to mislead him/herself into believing that these people are very well acquainted with the culture of the population whose language they speak, although in reality they are not. It might often happen that bilinguals of this type themselves believe that, given their language proficiency, they are also very familiar with the culture of native speakers of the language, even when

this is not the case. An additional source of compromised validity of conclusions about equivalence of two test versions based on test-takers of this type lies in the fact that people who acquired good knowledge of a foreign language through schooling also happen to be, on average, more educated than an average member of intended populations of the test.

- **Bilingual test-takers who learned the original or the target language through contact and exposure to cultural contents in that language, sometimes without any formal language learning support**. This category includes persons who acquired their language knowledge through exposure to and interaction with cultural products in that language. A characteristic of people in this category is that, even when they had some formal language training, they acquired their main language competencies through interaction with cultural contents in that language – movies, computer games, TV series, etc. It should be noted that currently, this category almost exclusively includes young people with different native languages, who acquired knowledge of English through interaction with various contents in English such as movies, videos, computer games, etc. Thanks to the current almost total domination of English-language products on the global cultural market, there are many people worldwide who speak perfect English and are very familiar with cultural contents in English in their area of interests, even though they themselves are not native speakers of English. Aside from English, throughout the world, there are also people who learned certain aspects of some other languages through interaction with cultural contents in that language, but such people are much rarer and their acquired language proficiency is usually much lower than in persons who acquired English language knowledge in this way. Although this category of people may be an excellent and easily available source of bilingual test-takers, especially when one of the languages in English, cultural knowledge of this group is based solely on internationally available cultural contents, meaning that they usually have little experience with the culture of monolingual English speakers (or speakers of the language they acquired in this way), although they may be strongly convinced of the contrary. These are the reasons why this group can also not be considered representative for the monolingual population.

It should be noted that bilingual persons found in practice will often be combinations of these categories or will belong to different categories at different points in time. For example, a person who became proficient in a foreign language through schooling or through interaction with cultural products may easily become a foreign student in the country that language is spoken. Also, a person who is proficient in the language of a country or who studied in that country might, if a good opportunity arises, easily start a business or immigrate to that country.

Aside from these five categories, researchers will sometimes encounter other categories of bilingual respondents – persons whose parents come from the two cultures of the test versions or who, due to close business cooperation, acquired knowledge of the other language or culture, but these types of people will rarely be available in any greater numbers, meaning that there will hardly be a chance to base a study on them. Large enough research samples of bilingual test-takers will usually consist of people belonging to the above-described categories.

What can be concluded from all of this? A great challenge in researching the equivalence between different test versions is controlling various factors that are neither part of culture, nor the test, but that can lead to an invalid conclusion that test versions function inequivalently. In this context, bilingual test-takers look like a good solution at first glance – they speak both languages, can take both test versions, they allow repeated measures designs and the problem of intergroup differences is eliminated. All indicators of differential functioning can confidently be attributed to differences in functioning of compared test versions. However, the fact remains that bilingual test-takers, by their very nature, are non-representative for the monolingual population. Bilinguals are rarely equally familiar with both cultures and both languages. It is most often the case that only one of the languages will be the first, native language of the bilinguals, while they know the other much less that the first. Bilinguals may also have very little familiarity with one of the two cultures, or even not be familiar with any of the two cultures for which the test versions are intended because they belong to a separate subculture, like in the case of members of separate bilingual communities (e.g., Quebec bilinguals for modern populations of France and England). Bilinguals will often also be more educated than the average of the general population. It might also happen that their first language is neither of the languages of the two test versions, but some mixture of the two languages characteristic for the group that they belong to, but that is often not formalized as a separate language. Such language mixtures may use constructions from one language, but with many loan words from the other. Or, they use specific sentence constructions from one language with words from the other language. This can all cause the results obtained on a sample of bilinguals to differ substantially from results that would be obtained on monolinguals. The most common wrong conclusion this design may lead to is the conclusion that test versions function equivalently in a situation when these test versions would not function equivalently on monolinguals.

Due to their specific background and language skills, it is often much harder for bilinguals to detect items that were translated in way that is psychologically inadequate. For these same reasons, bilinguals will also have much less trouble with poor grammar. Because they speak both languages, it will be easier for bilinguals to understand badly or inadequately translated items, as they can combine knowledge of the two languages when interpreting the translation. It might also be possible that some bilinguals do not recognize words from one of the languages that are used by monolinguals because these bilinguals use loan words from the other language in their place. Finally, due to their typically better education, it will be easier for bilinguals to understand the test requirements, main idea of the test and what is required of the test-takers compared to monolinguals.

Finally, the question of psychological equivalence of responses test-takers give in different languages remains. Studies have indicated that behavior of test-takers depends on whether they are responding in their first, native language or in a language they learned letter in life. These studies showed that examinees make more rational and better-quality decision when responding in a foreign language than when they think in their first language (Costa, Foucart, Arnon, Aparici, & Apesteguia, 2014; Keysar, Hayakawa, & An, 2012). Findings like this also bring into question the equivalence of responses of test-takers and the meaning of the finding of equivalence, as they indicate that if a person responds once in a foreign language, and the other time in his/her native language, this might not be two equivalent situations of psychological testing.

This all points to the need to also take care about which of the two languages is the first language of bilingual test-takers included in the study, and this piece of data should be included in the design as a separate variable. This should be done in addition to making the design more complex (through, for example, group randomization or counterbalancing) when it is necessary to neutralize the effect of learning of the test or eliminate some similar problems.

Although results of administering the test to a group of bilingual test-takers can surely be useful when collecting evidence on functional equivalence between two language versions, the final conclusion about equivalence should not be based on them, especially if that conclusion is positive. Even if two versions are shown to function equivalently on bilingual test takers, this should not still be taken as final evidence that the compared versions will function equivalently when applied on monolinguals.

The original version is administered to a group of monolingual test-takers speaking the original language and the target version is administered to a group of monolingual test-takers speaking the target language

Of the three presented data collection designs, only this design includes the one crucial comparison for evaluating functional equivalence between two language versions of a test. In this design, each test version is administered to a sample from a population for which that version is intended and a sample representing the category of population for which it is intended. From the point of validity, this is the best type of design – each version is evaluated on a sample from the very population it is intended for and conclusions about functional equivalence are made based on comparing samples from intended populations.

However, unlike the previous two designs, with this design, the study is not conducted on a single sample, nor on two paired samples, but on two completely different samples taken from two different populations. Because of this, the first question that arises is which of the obtained differences are caused by the test itself, which are due to differences between populations from which the samples are taken and which are due to differences between samples that do not reflect differences between populations. Closely related to this question is the question of how to choose the two samples. Generally, there are two options:

- **Choose samples that are as representative of the intended populations as possible; or**
- **Choose samples from the two populations that are as similar to each other as possible**, and in this way reduce differences between the two samples that cannot be reduced to language and culture to a minimum.

Samples as representative of the intended populations as possible

The approach in which we choose samples that are as representative of the intended populations as possible is more or less a classic approach in psychological research. We choose here as representative a sample as can be obtained, and this allows us to confidently conclude that the way the test functions on the sample corresponds to how it would function on the whole population. But what happens if we want to determine whether the test functions equivalently on two populations or not? If a study like this results in finding huge differences in functioning, such as having different latent structures in the two populations, the issue is more or less clear, but what happens if only minor differential functioning is found? For example, what if test-takers from one of the samples are more successful on the test that test-takers from the other sample? Or if they are more successful on some items? Or if DIF is found that does not bring into question the existence of the construct in the two population, but has to do with some minor aspects of test functioning? Is this difference really caused by some items being easier/harder for one population then the other, or is it, maybe, caused by differences between populations in the level of expression of the measured construct by the phenomenon called item impact (Clauser & Mazor, 1998). Unfortunately, this approach cannot provide a good answer to this question. Given that the comparison is made between two independent samples taken from two different populations, populations the relations of which in regard to the measured construct are unknown, there is no way to determine if differences in mean achievement of respondents from the two samples on the test are a product of differential functioning or of item impact, i.e., true differences between populations.

Samples as similar to each other as possible

This approach to cross-cultural data collection was popularized by Geert Hofstede and associates through their famous IBM study (Hofstede, 2011; Hofstede, Neuijen, Ohayv, & Sanders, 1990). In this study they analyzed answers of employees in a number of IBM branches throughout the world with an intention to explore cultural differences between these groups. The idea of this approach is that, if we choose samples from populations that are as similar to each other as possible in properties that are not directly relevant for the comparison, but can influence the results, then these differences will be eliminated as possible causes of differences in results on compared groups. For example, when exploring the functional equivalence of two language versions of a test, primary factors of interests are language and culture of the two populations (factors of interest in the sense of how and if they alter test functioning). In line with this, the aim of a study would be to explore whether two language versions of a test function equivalently in the two cultures connected to these languages. This also means that, in such a study, researchers are not interested in differences in test behavior that are consequences of other factors on which the original and the target population might differ, such as average education level, age, vocational interests, personality traits and other traits two populations might differ in. The choice of groups that are as similar to each other as possible is done with an aim to remove all other differences between groups except language and the general culture of groups using the two languages. Following this line of reasoning, the assumption the IBM study was based on was that people in different national branches of IBM work on similar jobs, have passed through similar education and selection processes, and work in similar job environments. Due to this, it can be expected that they are also similar in many other important psychological properties, while being obvious that they differ in their ethnic origin and their first/native language and consequently in the general culture they belong to.

Unlike researchers who try to obtain a sample that is as representative of the general population as possible, a goal for which there are traditional and well-known sampling procedures, researchers who intend to use pairs of samples from the original and the target population that are as similar as possible face two problems that they need to solve:

- The first problem is the identification of groups from the two populations that are similar enough to be used in a comparison like this;
- The second problem is that these chosen groups, although maybe not representative for the general population, need to be similar enough to the population for which the test is intended to allow valid generalizations of results obtained on the sample to that population.

So far, there are no fixed procedures that could guarantee that the two groups the researcher chooses for comparing test versions will be adequate solutions for the two problems described previously. Evaluations of their adequacy for this task will necessarily rely on the judgement of researchers based on the available data and on various heuristics.

Groups that can be conveniently examined for these purposes are those that are selected on certain properties, allowing for a reasonable expectation that these groups will be similar to each other in as many psychological and demographic traits as possible, but that they are also not too different from it (as in living separated from the general population or there being marked cultural differences, etc.).

For example, if we had access to members of some small religious organization that exists in both countries, even though their members would have many similar characteristics, if they live separately from the dominant culture and with little communication with them (i.e., Salafists, Jehovah's Witnesses), they would not make a good sample for this purpose.

So, groups we are looking for in the two populations are those that are identical or were similar to each other in as many properties as possible, but are at the same time parts of that population – meaning that they live among the general population, have daily interactions with other members of the general population, consider themselves to be a part of that general population and have other properties by which they are similar to it. Additionally, if the test is not intended for the general population, but for some more specific subpopulation, members of the groups from which the sample is taken need to be a part of that subpopulation. For example, there would be little sense to examine a test intended for children on groups of adults, no matter how much the available group of adults fulfills other conditions. On the same basis, there would be little point in evaluating a clinical differential-diagnostics test intended only for people with a certain type of psychopathological disorder on a sample without those psychopathological disorders.

Ideal groups for this approach to data collection are those for which it is certain that their members live among other members of the general population (or the subpopulation for which the test is intended), in constant contact with them, but which are known to be selected by certain properties. Such groups may be, as was the case in the IBM study, employees in various national branches of the same company, if it is a company for which it can be expected, based on their business model and personnel selection procedures, that they hire people of similar characteristics in all the countries they operate in. Another potentially convenient group are people who work in a certain vocation or students of high schools or universities with similar programs or who are studying for the same vocation in both countries of the test versions. High school students of higher years and university students may be particularly convenient groups if the test which is being evaluated is primarily intended for people of their age or if it is firmly established that age is not a significant factor of test functioning. However, all these recommendations for potentially convenient groups need to be taken as heuristics only and not as definitive or firm guidelines for practice, because in each individual case the researcher needs to consider the entire situation and concrete populations that are to be compared and then decide, based on all information available, which solution is the best.

When considering this type of design for comparing equivalence of two language or cultural versions of a test – the design in which original version is administered to test-takers from the original population, and the target version to test-takers from the target population, it should be taken into account that a great advantage of this design, in comparison to the two previously described, is that testing is done in real conditions – the test is administered to test-takers from real intended populations of the test, making the results more or less generalizable to those populations. We should have in mind that neither the design utilizing monolinguals from the original population nor the design utilizing bilinguals have this advantage, and that their main weakness is that with them there is little or no justification for generalizing results to the general population. Even though in this type of design many factors important for test functioning may remain uncontrolled and even unknown, thus complicating the interpretation of results, the fact that test functioning is examined on test-takers from the real intended populations gives this design a great advantage.

A problem of interpretation of results remains. While interpretation of positive results –those supporting equivalence of test versions – is only faced with the question of their generalizability to the general population or the intended population of the test, negative results create a much more ambiguous situation for the researcher, forcing him/her try to decide if the results are a case of differential functioning or of real differences between the compared samples. In such a case, it is typically difficult to decide on why such results were obtained without additional analyses and data. This is especially the case in situations when results show different test achievements of members of compared groups, with little or no difference in latent structures of compared test versions.

Making inferences about test equivalence based on empirical data – equivalence levels

After collecting data on the equivalence of test versions using one of the designs described in the previous section, the next phase is statistical analysis of the data and making inferences based on them about whether the compared test versions function equivalently or not. In general, inferring about equivalent functioning of compared test versions comes down to examining and comparing their psychometric properties. Both properties of the test as a whole and of individual items are examined and inferences made on whether they are equal in both versions or not. This decision about equivalence is typically not binary (as in just declaring compared versions to function equivalently or not), but includes the examination of various degrees of equivalence. For example, Van De Vijver and Poortinga (2005) propose four equivalence levels:

- Construct inequivalence
- Structural or functional equivalence
- Measurement unit equivalence
- Scalar equivalence/full score equivalence

These four levels form a hierarchy with each following level representing a higher level of equivalence. The first level represents a total lack of equivalence and the fourth represents the level of equivalence in which scores from the two versions can be compared.

Level one – construct inequivalence – refers to situations in which results show that compared tests are completely inequivalent and thus incomparable. Compared tests measure different constructs in the two groups. Latent structures of the two test versions do not resemble each other sufficiently for even the lowest level of equivalence. A result like this can be obtained when the construct that exists in the original culture does not exist in the target culture and can, hence, not be measured, but a result like this may also be a consequence of an inadequately adapted test. For example, it is possible that a translation of items was done without regard for psychological equivalence of two versions and this resulted in translated items being psychologically inequivalent to the original. It might have been possible to create a test composed of different items that would be psychologically equivalent to the originals and thus able to successfully measure the construct in the target culture, but this was not done.

One particular "trap" into which researchers sometimes fall when they examine the functioning of the target test version happens when they do not use results from the original culture as a reference, but rely on deductions from the theory the test is based on. There are many tests in psychological literature that do not function at all or do not function any longer, tests that are based on refuted theories or theories that were never confirmed; tests that never had theoretically expected psychometric properties even in the original culture. Sometimes there are no published papers describing empirical examination of their properties in the original culture at all. This sometimes happens because authors who created the test did not do an empirical study of its functioning or did a sloppy study, publishing little data. It also happens that authors explored the functioning of their test on the original population, but results showed that the test does not work and the authors then fell victim to a publication bias favoring positive results by either concluding themselves that their results are worthless or by being rejected by editors of scientific journal who believed that authors "did not obtain anything". Then the word about the test not functioning spreads among researchers in the local area where the authors work, but it does not reach researchers in other countries. These researchers may then "discover" the test, find it interesting and decide to do an adaptation to their language, not knowing that the test did not work on the original population. When they complete the adaptation, they realize that they have no data on the functioning of the original version, and eager to find any replacement for the data, decide to rely on the theory, i.e., compare their empirical data to the propositions of the theory. Based on this, they then come to a wrong conclusion that there is construct inequivalence between the original and the adapted version, when the correct conclusion would be that the test or the theory behind it are bad and that they do not function on either population. From a practical standpoint, these two conclusions might look the same – both of them are conclusions that the test does not work. However, from a theoretical standpoint, there is a huge difference between a situation in which a test measures a construct successfully in one culture, but the adapted version does not work in another culture and the situations in which a test does not measure anything in the original nor in the target culture.

Another incorrect procedure that can sometimes be encountered in scientific texts about adaptation of psychological tests is one where authors conclude that the adapted version does not measure the constructs it was supposed to measure, but then set forth, using explorative factor analysis or some similar statistical procedure, to explore the "real" latent structure of the adapted test version. They obtain a latent solution that fits the data and then give names to these factors, although these factors have no basis in any theory. Sometimes they even conclude that the test works well, but that it "only" has a different latent structure. A procedure like this is plain wrong. As we all know, a psychological test is not a natural phenomenon, nor do answers to a test represent a naturally correlated set of behaviors that could be meaningfully explored in order to discover latent variables behind them. A psychological test is a set of a limited number of purposefully selected stimuli that were selected with a goal of inciting responses influenced by a strictly specific latent variable (or a set of latent variables). So, stimuli were intentionally selected based on an expectation that they will be able to cause a strictly limited set of desired behaviors. If they cannot do that, it is then incorrect to declare them a measure of some other, ad-hoc made-up construct, and then use that to declare that the test is valid. While it is perfectly valid to conduct exploratory procedures to show that the latent structure of a test is better described by some model different from the theoretical model the test is based on, such a latent structure can only evidence that the test does not function as intended and not evidence that the test is valid, but measuring some other ad-hoc invented constructs instead of those it is intended to measure. The only valid conclusion in such a situation is that the test does not function as intended.

Level two – structural or functional equivalence – exists when the two test versions just measure the same construct or constructs that are similar enough, but nothing more than that. This level corresponds to what some other authors name **configural measurement invariance** (e.g., Chen, 2007). This type of equivalence is typically examined through various procedures based on correlations between items or test elements, mainly factor analysis, but also through studies of internal structure and through examining the equivalence of nomological networks of two versions, i.e., through examining their external validity. Exploring the equivalence of nomological networks[1] is especially a method of choice if more substantial changes were done in the target version during the adaptation or construction process (thus making comparison of factor structures more complex or impossible) and the test is based on a theory that does not provide for any more precise hypothesis about relations between test elements.

Examination of structural equivalence of two test versions usually starts from examining the equivalence of their factor structures. This can be done by confirmatory factor analysis and exploring if both versions fit the same factor model. For structural equivalence to be confirmed, results need to show that same items associate with same factors in both groups, but their factor loadings may differ (Chen, 2007). A more classic approach is to use exploratory factor analysis on both versions and then compare patterns of factor loading obtained on the two groups.

This comparison may be done by calculating Tucker's congruence coefficients. Tucker's coefficients are calculated between patterns of loading of items on each factor obtained on the sample from the target population, and patterns of loading of items on each factor obtained on the sample from the original population (each factor from one group is compared to each factor from the other group). There is a long debate about how high a Tucker's congruence coefficient between loading patterns of two factors needs to be for the two factors to be declared similar enough. While the author of this text considered coefficients higher than .82 to be marginal, and those over .92 to indicate good congruence, Lorenzo-Seva and ten Berge (2006) propose that factors with congruence coefficients between .85 and .94 should be considered similar, and factors with congruence coefficient above .95. The same authors state that congruence coefficients lower than .82 should not be interpreted as showing any similarity between factors.

Tests are sometimes based on theories that give precise predictions of relations between various theoretical constructs the test is intended to measure. In such situations, it is possible to evaluate structural equivalence by conducting a study of internal structure of the test that would examine if interrelations between measures of constructs within each test version are in accordance with theoretical predictions. For example, Holland's theory of vocational interests proposes the existence of six types of vocational interests that form a hexagon in a two-dimensional latent space (Holland, 1959). According to this theory, when following the edges of the hexagon defined by these six types, the closest types will be in the strongest correlations and correlations will decrease with increasing distance between types. To test this, in studies examining the equivalence of different language versions of tests intended to measure Holland's types, a factor analysis of interest types is conducted first (it should be noted that this is not factor analysis of items – test scores

TABLE 4.1 Tucker's coefficients of congruence calculated between four factors extracted from two language versions of the PGI inventory of vocational interests (Hedrih et al., 2016). One was administered to a sample from Bulgaria, and the other to a sample from Serbia. F1–F4 are factors in the order of extraction from one and the other sample. Numbers in the table are Tucker's coefficients of congruence showing the level of congruence between each pair of factors from the two samples. Coefficients indicating that factors are similar (congruent) are bolded. Negative congruence coefficients that are bolded indicate that factors are congruent, but that directions of their loadings are reversed.

		Serbian sample			
		F1	*F2*	*F3*	*F4*
	F1	**1.00**	0.03	0.05	-0.01
Bulgarian sample	F2	-0.03	**0.98**	0.14	0.14
	F3	0.04	0.16	**-0.97**	-0.13
	F4	0.02	-0.12	-0.15	**0.97**

are entered as manifest variables in this procedure, not individual items) in order to test the hypothesis about the latent dimensions of vocational interests (Prediger, 1982), and after that specific tests are used to test hypotheses about correlation sizes between different interest types. Results obtained on different language versions are then compared (e.g., Hedrih, 2008; Hedrih et al., 2016, 2018; Hedrih & Šverko, 2007; Šverko & Hedrih, 2010).

As the next step, researchers may examine **the equivalence of nomological networks** of the two test versions, i.e., their relations with various external variables, which can be theoretically expected to be related in a certain way to measured constructs. This procedure is particularly important when there are significant differences between item contents in the two versions – for example, when assembly (Van De Vijver & Poortinga, 2005) was the procedure applied in the adaptation phase. In this situation, it is hard to make meaningful comparisons between factor structures, because individual items cannot really be expected to be equivalent and matching items from the two versions might be problematic given their different contents. If the theory behind the test also does not provide hypothesis that could be used for a study of internal structure, the option that remains is the comparison of nomological networks.

Structural equivalence of two test versions means that constructs measured by two test versions are equivalent or similar enough. Conclusion that the target version is structurally equivalent to the original version means that two persons who completed the target version may be meaningfully compared and their results interpreted as referring to the same constructs that were measured in the original version. Structural equivalence, however, does not allow for the comparison between scores obtained on different test versions. For example, if the two test versions are only structurally equivalent, and then by applying them we find that a certain group A has higher scores than a certain group B, while scores of the same two groups from the other population are equivalent, we can validly accept such a result (provided there is also sufficient level of measurement invariance between the two groups within the same test version). However, if we obtain that group A from one population, tested with the test version for that population, has higher means than group B from the other population, tested with the test version for that population, this cannot be interpreted as meaning that the measured construct is more expressed in group A than in group B. When there is only structural equivalence between two test versions, then we do not know anything about the score size and level of expression of the measured construct in the two compared populations, and for this reason we can also not compare scores meaningfully.

Level three – measurement unit equivalence – exists when two test versions can be considered to have equal measurement units, but it is unknown if they have the same intercepts. In other words, their measurement units are equal, but the same test score might not correspond to the same level of the measured trait in both samples. Due to this, raw test scores of the two versions are not comparable because the same test score might indicate a different level of measured trait in different versions. In a case like this, it remains unknown to the researcher which test scores correspond to which trait level in each version. If this was known, and if we also knew that measurement units are equal in both versions, equating scores of one version with scores of the other would be a simple matter of adding or subtracting a constant from scores of one or the other test. Thus, it would be easy to convert equivalence of this level to full test score equivalence. However, what is often encountered in practice is that, although measurement units of the two versions can be considered equal, the relationship between test scores and trait levels remains unknown.

In a confirmatory factor analysis approach, this level of equivalence is typically tested by making a multi-group confirmatory factor analysis and constraining factor loadings to be equal on the two groups. Measurement unit equivalence would be achieved if it was found that the model in which factor loadings of items are constrained to be the same in both samples fits the data as well as the unconstrained model – the one that was used to test for structural equivalence. While current statistics software packages often include chi-square-based tests of differences in fit between the unconstrained and constrained models, which are used to determine if these two models equally fit the data, researchers have noted that such tests easily become too sensitive as sample sizes increase. For this reason, researchers have proposed that differences in goodness of fit indicators be used to make inferences about whether different models fit the data equally. For example, it was proposed that the unconstrained and constrained model be considered to fit the data equally if differences in comparative fit index (CFI) between the two models is less than .01 and difference in root mean square error of approximation (RMSEA) is less than .015 (Chen, 2007; Cheung & Rensvold, 2002).

At this level of equivalence of two test versions, it is meaningful to compare sizes of individual differences between pairs of test-takers of which one pair completed one version and the other completed the other test version. For example, we can infer that test-takers A and B who completed the same test version differ more or less than test-takers C and D who completed the other test version. What we cannot compare is the trait level of test-takers who completed different test versions. In the current example, we cannot compare trait levels of test-takers A and D or of test-takers C and B, or of any other combination of test-takers who completed different test versions because we do not know which trait level corresponds to which test score in the two samples. On this equivalence level it is also not meaningful to compare mean scores of groups that completed different test versions – a higher mean score achieved by test-takers who completed one of the language versions does not mean that the measured construct has a higher level of expression in that group then in the group that completed the other language version of the test.

Level four – full scalar equivalence or full score equivalence – exists when measures obtained on two test versions have both the same measurement units and same intercepts. The relationship between the raw test score and the level of expression of the measured trait is the same in both tests, making their scores directly comparable. At this level, it is possible to directly compare scores of test-takers who completed different versions of the test, but also to make inferences about the level of expression of the measured construct in groups that completed different test versions. Two test versions that satisfy criteria for this level of equivalence can be considered to be parallel test versions and their scores to be directly comparable.

To be absolutely certain when establishing this type of equivalence, it would be necessary to have some elements that would be identical for test-takers of both test versions. There are discussions in the literature about using bilinguals for establishing this type of equivalence (a design where they complete both test versions). However, as was discussed in previous parts of this book, a big issue with such an approach is the fact that bilinguals are not representative of monolingual populations, and due to that, it may easily happen that results obtained on a sample of bilinguals show full score equivalence when results obtained on monolinguals would not show anything near that level of equivalence.

Nonetheless, within the confirmatory factor analysis approach to evaluating measurement invariance, full scalar equivalence is tested by comparing the fit of a multi-group confirmatory factor model where factor loadings and intercepts (and sometimes also residuals) are constrained to be equal on both (or on all) compared versions to the fit of a model where only factor loadings are constrained. If the results show that this additionally constrained model fits more or less the same (CFI not more than .01 and RMSEA not more than .015 lower) to the data as the model with factor loadings constrained, it is then concluded that full scalar invariance exists between the compared groups (Chen, 2007; Cheung & Rensvold, 2002).

Another possible alternative would be to find some external criterion – some recognized and valid measure of the trait the test aims to assess – that is such that it can be in an equal way used in both populations and can at the same time be considered equivalent or comparable in both populations. An example of such a criterion would be some external behavior, skill or achievement that is in a close and known relation with the construct or constructs the test is intended to measure. If it should then be shown that the relationship between the test score and this criterion is the same for both test versions, and the two test versions also pass all the other conditions for equivalence (satisfy conditions for lower equivalence levels), it could then be concluded that the two test versions are completely equivalent.

There is also an additional alternative in situations when the theory the test is based on provides ways in which score equivalence can be examined. A theory may contain specific expectations about relations between test elements – for example, it could specify that the score on one of its scales is a starting, zero point, and inferences could then be made about the equivalence of measurement units, for example, on the basis of relations between scores on other scales of the test and their relationship to this starting-point scale. A theory may also specify a certain relationship between the test scores and some easy-to-measure external criterion. The existence and properties of this relationship could then be easily tested.

Making inferences about test equivalence based on empirical data – statistical procedures

How can a procedure for evaluating the functioning of two language versions of a test be conducted? Such a procedure should start with three questions:

- **What kind of data do we have?** Do we have at our disposal empirical data collected in both the original and the target population, with both the original and the target version, or do we only have data collected with the target version of the test, and we know about the functioning of the original version from published results only?
- **What kind of theory is the test based on?** Is it a theory that simply proposes the existence of the measured psychological constructs, or a theory that, apart from this, proposes some precise relations between constructs the test measures, parts of the test or between constructs the test measures and some specific external variables?
- **Were the available data collected from monolingual test-takers from the original and the target population or was one of the other two data collection designs used (monolinguals from the original population doing the original and the backtranslation or a design using bilinguals)?**

If raw data obtained by using both test versions is at our disposal, our options are usually wider – it is possible to conduct all comparisons between the two versions that can be meaningfully established. On the other hand, if we do not have raw data for both test versions, but only for one of them, our options for evaluating functional equivalence of the two versions are reduced to those statistical analyses for which the data from the other test version – the one we do not have raw data from – is available to us. This second case typically happens when a researcher creates a test adaptation, usually in his/her own language, and then administers the test to a group of test-takers to explore its functioning, but he/she at the same time does not administer the original version, but obtains data on its functioning from available scientific publications – journal articles, monographs, etc., in which results of evaluation of psychometric properties of the original version on the original population are presented. Somewhat due to limited volumes of publications (like is the case with articles in scientific journals), somewhat due to author decisions, these publications often do not contain all the data necessary to examine test equivalence. Scientific publications will typically provide data for examining structural equivalence, but the data needed to establish higher levels of equivalence are often omitted as their presentation increases the length of the publication, especially when journal articles are in question. It should be noted that this situation seems to be improving, especially in papers following the confirmatory factor analysis approach to establishing measurement invariance. In situations like this, researchers who only have data from the target version of the test are limited to those comparisons for which they have data from both versions, meaning those analyses that were presented in the available publications on the psychometric properties of the original version of the test.

Raw data from both test versions are usually available when a design using bilingual test-takers was used and when the original version of the test and the backtranslation were administered to monolinguals from the original population. In practice, designs where the original version was administered to test-takers from the original population and the target version to test-takers from the target population are relatively less frequent and are usually encountered when researchers conducting the study are authors of both the original and the target version, or when authors of the target versions are close associates of authors of the original version, or they work in the same organization or on the same research project, so data is available to them.

When considering the theory that the test is based on, theories that provide precise hypotheses about relations allow specific statistical procedures to be conducted in which these hypotheses can be tested on data obtained on two different test versions. On the other hand, tests based on theories that provide no base for such hypotheses also offer no possibility to use such specific theory-derived hypotheses for equivalence evaluation, so the researchers are left only with general statistical procedures available for all tests. A special case are tests that do not measure latent constructs at all, but are constructed with an intention to predict a certain criterion behavior. With such tests, exploring if the target version of the test predicts the criterion as well as the original version is often the only meaningful comparison that can be made in order to evaluate the two test versions.

Properties of test-takers that completed the two test versions for the purposes of evaluating their equivalence are the key factor in deciding on the kind of inferences that can be made about equivalence between the compared versions. If the data was obtained on monolingual test-takers from the original population by asking them to complete the original version and the backtranslation, then the data about equivalence and nonequivalence can only be interpreted in the context of whether the translation was done adequately or not. If data are obtained on bilingual test-takers, conclusions can again only be made about the adequacy of the translation and only rarely about the quality of the adaptation, especially if changes in item content have been made in the target version in comparison to the original version. Only in the situation when the original version of the test was administered to test-takers from the original population and the target version to test-takers from the target population can results on equivalence of the two versions be interpreted in the context of psychological equivalence in the two populations and not only in the context of translation/adaptation quality.

A typical procedure for testing the equivalence of two language versions of a test typically starts with procedures to test for structural equivalence. The most common statistical procedure for this is **factor analysis**, but there are also other grouping analysis procedures or procedures for identification of latent variables that could serve the same purpose. Of course, for factor analysis and other similar procedures to be meaningful, it is necessary that the test in question measures latent traits and that good construct validity of the original test version on the original populations is to be expected. If this is not the case, if the test in question is invalid on the original population, the adaptation itself is rather pointless.

When factor analysis is used to examine the equivalence of two test versions, as was mentioned earlier, it is possible to use either confirmatory factor analysis or explorative factor analysis. With **confirmatory factor analysis** it is first considered if the data obtained on the target version of the test fit the same model specification as the data from the original version of the test. A very popular approach to this topic is based on procedures of **multi-group confirmatory factor analyses, MG-CFA**, in which multiple factor models are tested with increasing level of constraint of model parameters. Wu et al. (2007) summarize that these model constraints can consist of seven elements that could be constrained to be equal in both groups:

- The model specification (number of factors and factor loadings)
- Regression coefficients
- Regression intercept terms
- Regression residual variances
- Means of common factors
- Variances of the common factors
- Covariances among the common factors

These authors state that equality in the first four of these elements is a necessary condition for measurement invariance as these are elements of the measurement model, while the equivalence in the last three elements is not, as these are relationships between common factors and not between common factors – latent variables of the model and test items. However, according to these authors equality in the last three elements would suggest that compared groups belong to the same population regarding the construct of interest.

When using **explorative factor analysis**, as stated earlier, comparison is made by calculating congruence between structures of factor loadings on the two versions of the test. An exploratory factor analysis is performed on data from each version separately and congruence between patterns of loadings of possible pair of factors from the two analyses is calculated. To conclude that factors obtained on the two datasets are equal, Tucker's congruence coefficients (or some other measure of congruence that is used for this purpose) need to be over the critical threshold, while it is not necessary that corresponding factor have the same order of extraction. For example, correspondence between the pattern of loadings of the first factor extracted from the data from the first version and the pattern of loadings of the third factor extracted from the data from the second test version indicates an equal level of correspondence as if the same level of congruence was obtained between the first factors from the two groups or second-extracted factors as long as congruence coefficients are the same.

However, when using explorative factor analysis one should be careful – unlike confirmatory factor analysis, where the researcher inputs the key elements of the final factor structure in advance, with explorative factor analysis, the final factor structure depends solely on the fit of the data to mathematical conditions included in the procedure, and these conditions are general and have nothing to do with the theory the test is based on. Due to this it is possible that datasets that are structurally quite similar end up with different factor rotations, causing in this way patterns of factor loadings to be different, thus leading researchers to the wrong conclusions that factor structures obtained on two datasets have little similarity, when some other factor rotation would allow a certain level of similarity to be detected. To this point, it should be noted that factor solutions obtained through different rotations are all equal in regard to how well they account for the common variance in the data. It is good to know that, for this phenomenon to occur, it is necessary from the start that there be substantial differences in latent structures of compared versions. If latent structures of compared versions are identical, then the structures of covariances between items will also be identical in both version, and thus the results of explorative factor analysis will be identical, especially in the sense that in both cases the same solution will best conform to mathematical conditions required by the applied explorative factor analysis procedure. In other words, situations with factor rotations like the one described will not happen between versions that fulfill conditions for higher levels of measurement equivalence, but might happen with test versions that exhibit a detectable level of differential functioning.

Factor analysis, i.e., evaluating equivalence of latent structure of two test versions on samples from intended populations of the test is a typical first step in evaluating equivalence. Results of this evaluation may be a conclusion that latent structures of the two versions compared are similar or equivalent (to a certain level) or that they are not. If they are found to not be equivalent, this is typically the end of the equivalence evaluations. Latent structures of two test versions that do not show even the lowest level of equivalence – structural equivalence – show that these two test versions measure different constructs and any additional equivalence evaluation procedures are pointless.

Another possibility that exists when evaluation of the structural model is conducted using confirmatory factor analysis is that the theory-based factor model that fits the data from the original version does not fit the data from the target version, but there are minor revisions that can be introduced into the model that would make it fit the target population. This possibility is particularly to be expected when the test measures several connected constructs, all of which are subdimensions of a higher-order construct and thus in mutual correlations. In such cases, it often happens that some items that work fine as indicators of one subdimension on the original version obtain loadings on another subdimension in the target version (or obtain loadings on two subdimensions), and the model obtains a better fit if that item is specified to be an indicator of that other subdimension.

When this happens, the first thing to do is to check factor loadings and residual covariances (in confirmatory factor analysis) and compare them to records about the adaptation procedure to determine if it is possible that lack of equivalence of the two versions might be due to some inadequacy in the translation that was missed. Are there comments in these records that refer to items that manifested differential functioning in the factor analysis? Are items that function differently in the two language versions the same items that were already marked as potentially problematic during the adaptation procedure or in the preliminary expert assessment of the equivalence of the two versions? If the answer to these questions is positive, then the contents of these records may help conclude if the differential functioning that was detected was due to bad adaptation. If the final conclusion is that it indeed might be the case of inadequately adapted-translated items, then the solution should be sought in creating a better adaptation of these items and repeating the process of empirical evaluation of functional equivalence of two test versions later.

If the final conclusion is that differential functioning is not due to bad translation or adaptation, the researchers have two options – to keep the etic approach and conclude that the two versions are simply not equivalent, or decide to combine the etic and the emic approach and allow that there might be differences in manifestations of the measured constructs but that there is still some similarity between them in the two populations (if this is the case, of course). The difference between these two approaches is that with the first approach, all further activities about the target version stop, while the second approach allows the researcher to conclude that the test measures a similar construct in the target population, but not the same construct as in the original population. Such a test may potentially be further developed independently of the original version, but with broad basis on the same theory as the original test and be used for comparing test-takers within that population, although individual results from the two tests cannot be compared.

It should be taken into account that the procedure of factor analysis does not always require that there be a separate factor for each construct measured by the test, i.e., for each test score. Sometimes constructs measured by the test are neither theoretically nor empirically latent dimensions, but have a different status. For example, in tests based on the Holland's theory of vocational interests, the expected factor structure consists of three factors, the first of which is called the general factor (e.g., Hedrih et al., 2016, 2018), typically loading all items and two additional factors corresponding to basic dimensions of vocational interests – people-things and ideas-data (Prediger, 1982; Rounds & Tracey, 1993). It is important to notice that these basic dimensions are not objects of measurement of the test or are not primary objects of measurement of tests based on this theory. Tests based on Holland's theory typically measure six types of vocational interests (realistic, investigative, artistic, social, entrepreneurial and conventional) that are in theoretically defined relations with these basic dimensions-factors, but are not latent dimensions themselves. It should be noted that, with tests measuring Holland's types, factor analysis is conducted both on the item level and on the level of types and generally the same type of results is expected – the general factor + two factors corresponding to latent dimensions of vocational interests. The main difference between the results of these two procedures is that total communality is usually much higher when factor analysis is done on measures of vocational interest types than when it is done on test items.

Factor analysis is not the only option for evaluating structural equivalence of two test versions. When the test is based on a theory that specifies specific relations between test measures or test elements, structural equivalence may be evaluated by performing a study of internal structure, i.e., by examining whether the relations between these elements are in accordance with theoretical predictions. This is a procedure that is usually performed after factor analysis, but may also be performed instead of factor analysis, when factor analysis is not applicable. For example, the already mentioned Holland's theory of vocational interests (Hogan & Blake, 1999; Holland, 1959, 1994) predicts precise relations of correlations sizes between different combinations of vocational interests types that are measured by tests based on this theory. For this reason, when evaluating the structural equivalence of tests based on Holland's theory or one of the theories developed from Holland's theory, relations of correlations between various interest types are examined as the next step after factor analysis. For this purpose, researchers typically use specialized procedures like Hubert and Arabi's randomization test of hypothetical orders (Tracey, 1997), circular unidimensional scaling (Armstrong, Hubert, & Rounds, 2003), multidimensional scaling (Hedrih et al., 2016), circular stochastic process modeling (CSPF) (Browne, 1992; Fabrigar, Visser, & Browne, 1997; Nagy, Trautwein, & Lüdtke, 2010) and others.

There are situations in which factor analysis is completely inapplicable as a method for evaluating the structural equivalence of two tests. This typically happens when the adaptation process resulted in a target version of a test that is vastly or completely different from the original version and data were collected on independent samples. The difference is such that there is no correspondence between individual items, but only an expectation that two versions measure the same construct or the same set of constructs. The target version was created using the assembly approach, because authors of the adaptation concluded that translation of items of the original version would not be adequate, i.e., that translated items would not incite responses caused by intended constructs. Also, data were collected on independent samples, so there is also no way to pair responses on the two tests. Depending on the theory the test is based on, in such a situation it might be possible to use factor analysis to evaluate construct validity of each test version separately, but it is not possible to use it for evaluating their structural equivalence, because there is neither correspondence between individual items nor between individual test-takers. Unlike the situation when using the application approach to adaptation where each item from one version has a corresponding item from the other, in this situation, no relationship between items from the two versions exists that would allow the researcher to ascertain which item from one version corresponds to which item from the other version. In situations like this, the method of choice for evaluating structural equivalence becomes the analysis and comparison of nomological networks of the two tests. This is particularly the case when the theory the test is based on does not provide any specific expectations about relations between parts of the test that could be used as a basis for performing a study of internal structure. Comparison of nomological networks as a method of evaluating structural equivalence between two test versions is based on the expectation that both test versions measure the same or similar constructs, and that these constructs are in known relationship with certain variables that are not a part of the test. These relations have already been confirmed with the original version, so it should be expected that the target version will also be in the same relations with these variables if it measures the same constructs, no matter how much its content is different from the original test version.

Equivalence between tests when data have been collected on paired samples

It should be emphasized that inapplicability of factor analysis for examining structural equivalence of two test versions when there is no item-for-item correspondence between the two versions refers to situations when data on the functioning of the two versions have been obtained on two independent samples. When the samples are paired, i.e., when we are dealing with repeated measures, such as in a design using bilinguals, then joint factor analysis of items from the two versions also becomes an option.

The researchers do not always have the possibility to apply all the listed procedures. What they can apply depends on what data they have available, what kind of test they are working with and what the theory is like. If results of analyses show that two versions are structurally equivalent so that they can be considered to measure the same constructs, the next step is to assess if there are higher levels of equivalence between them. When data come from paired samples, evaluation of measurement unit equivalence or full scalar equivalence comes down to examining covariances between measures of same participants on the two versions and a search for nonuniform item-level differential functioning. High covariances support measurement unit equivalence between the two versions, but give no data about full scalar equivalence as these statistics are sensitive to joint variation but not to the intensity or expression level of the variable. Full scalar equivalence can be considered when test-takers achieve the same scores on both test versions, and this can be expressed as mean distance between test-takers (in the statistical space of measured constructs) or mean difference between scores and also when there is no uniform differential functioning on the item level. It should be taken into account that zero differences should not be expected here, but at most, the differences that would be obtained if this was a test-retest situation when the same test version was applied.

However, the main problem with evaluating the equivalence of two test versions using data from repeated measures obtained by administering both test versions to the same group of test-takers stems from the fact that such test-takers are bilinguals and, as such, as was explained in an earlier part of this book, they are almost never representative for the intended population of the test. Due to this, conclusions about the equivalence of two test versions and especially about higher levels of equivalence between two test versions made based on data obtained on such a sample can hardly be generalized to the general population (or such generalizations should be made with great restraint at best).

Another possible option for obtaining paired samples that would potentially be more representative for the general population than bilinguals is based on selecting monolingual samples that would be as similar to each other as possible (please see the chapter about designs for evaluating test version equivalence) with a sample created by pairing individual participants, and not just having samples as groups be similar. The idea behind this approach is to identify variables that are known to be related to constructs the test is intended to measure and that can be measured in a valid way in both groups. After this is done, pairs of test-takers from the two populations are created by matching them on values on these variables. As these variables are related to constructs the test is intended to measure, it can be expected that test-takers within each pair will also have roughly equal values of the construct(s) measured by the test. However, although this idea looks promising in theory, authors that have worked on this topic in practice believe that its practical usefulness is small and that this kind of sampling suffers from the same problem of the generalizability of conclusions about equivalence of the compared version as the results obtained using the design with bilingual test-takers (Cook & Schmitt-Cascallar, 2005).

Additional procedures for evaluating higher levels of equivalence between test versions with independent samples

At the time this book is written, there seems to be quite a broad agreement that procedures based on the multi group confirmatory factor analysis (MG-CFA) are a method of choice for establishing measurement invariance on all levels, and thus also for establishing equivalence between test versions. However, there are situations when these methods are not applicable or not adequate. Also, certain item impact effects can be imagined that could slip past MG-CFA procedures. Due to this, it is good to be aware of possible additional procedures for evaluating higher levels of equivalence with independent samples data.

When data on the equivalence of two test versions is obtained on samples of monolingual test-takers from the target and the original population, after establishing their structural equivalence, examining if there are higher levels of equivalence between the two versions requires that there be some way to link the values obtained on the two tests. One method how this can be done is to use an **anchor**, a set of items or another measure that can be considered identical and directly comparable (in the meaning of full score equivalence) and that are strongly linked to measures of both test versions. Such a set of items or a measure can then be used to examine the equivalence of the two test versions. Sometimes sets of items that are directly comparable because they are identical and are not translated, such as some nonverbal items, will be used for this purpose. Other times, researchers will make use of an external criterion, such as a visible behavior or some measurable achievement that is strongly related to the test scores (for example, the criterion the test was created to predict, and which will then serve as a link for establishing relations between two test versions). However, situations where researchers really have a valid external criterion that can be used to link the two test versions are relatively rare. Additionally, situations where a set of items can be used as an "anchor" for linking two groups that completed different test versions are far from ideal. In order to obtain an "anchor", it is necessary to declare a set of items to be equivalent, and there is usually little basis for that in a situation with independent samples and no external criterion. Declaring a set of items to be equivalent in two test versions, while lacking empirical evidence to support that, is based solely on the judgement of the researcher and theoretical reason, and such a situation is far from being ideal. So far there is ample evidence showing that nonverbal items may not be considered cross-culturally equivalent solely because they need not be translated (e.g., Serpell, 1979) and this very type of item will typically be what is available to a researcher who wants to create an "anchor" for linking two test versions. This will be discussed in more detail in the subchapter about equating tests.

Another option available to researchers is to explore the existence of item-level differential functioning by starting from an assumption that scores of the two test versions are equivalent. If such a procedure would yield findings of item-level differential functioning, i.e., that items have different difficulties in the compared samples, this can be taken as a clear indicator of nonequivalence. However, results obtained in this way should not be taken as final evidence that there is no differential functioning, but can be only taken as an argument supporting measurement unit equivalence of compared test versions.

Equating tests in the context of cross-cultural adaptation

The concept of test equating refers to the development of mathematical procedures for converting measures from a scale of one test to a scale of another test. When two tests are equated, their scores are completely convertible from one to the other, and from the standpoint of researcher, whether the test-taker completed one or the other is completely the same (Kolen, 2004).

A term similar to test equating is **test linkage**, but test linkage has a broader meaning. When we say that two tests are linked, this means that a certain relationship has been establishes between measures of the two tests, but it need not mean that scores from one test can be converted to scores of the other or vice versa, or that the two tests treated as full alternatives for each other.

The term **concordance** refers to linking scores on measures of similar, but not identical, constructs that are used as alternatives to each other for making a certain decision. An example would be two knowledge tests that can be used as basis for making a decision whether to enroll a candidate in a study program, but candidates can choose which of the two tests they will take (Kolen, 2004).

In psychological practice, test equating is important when it is necessary to find a way to use different test versions as parallel. Sometimes, parallel test versions are a solution when it is necessary to have repeated measures and the nature of the test is such that they can be learned (like with tests of cognitive abilities), so it is pointless to administer the same test to the same participant more than once. Other times, it is necessary to compare scores of test-takers who completed different tests and these test-takers are not available to all be tested again with the same test. Sometimes the psychologist switched to using another, newer test, but needs to be able to compare previous achievements of participants on the old test to new achievements on the new test. Sometimes regulations require that test-takers be able to choose which test they will take, but a certain decision about the same issue has to be made whatever they choose. In all these cases, but many others also, it is necessary to find a way to convert scores from one test to the scale of another or vice versa, or to have scores of different tests converted to a same standard scale. These are all situations when test equating is necessary.

In the second half of the 20th century and the beginning of the 21st, various authors proposed methods for equating tests or gave contributions to the methodology of test equating (Kolen, 2004). Test equating procedures include, but are not limited to:

- Mean-based equating
- Linear equating
- Nonlinear equating
- True score equating
- Equipercentile equating
- Alternative scoring-based equating
- Criterion-based equating

(Candell & Drasgow, 1988; Fajgelj, 2003; Kolen, 2004; Kolen & Brennan, 1995)

Mean-based equating can be performed when there is measurement unit equivalence, but there is a difference in difficulty between the two tests that can be adequately described by a constant. Therefore, the two tests differ in difficulty and that difference is a certain fixed number of measurement units. Test equating can then be performed by simply adding or subtracting that difference from one or the other score. Kolen and Brennan (1995), who describe this equating procedure, correctly noticed that in the condtion that the only difference between two tests is their difficulty and that that difference is fixed is too restrictive for real testing situations, but that this method of equating can serve to illustrate one important concept of test equating methodology – difference in difficulty. In practice, situations when this equating method is a method of choice are practically never encountered. Procedures similar to this one are those when laws and other types of regulations proscribe that scores of two groups of participants in certain testing situations are equated by adding a certain fixed value to scores of one of the groups, like for example, in some application of affirmative action measures in the area of educational testing. This lack of practical applicability is the main weakness of this test equating method.

Linear equating consists of performing a linear transformation of a scale of one test to a scale of another test. This is done using a procedure similar to the one used to convert raw scores to z scale with the difference that scores are converted to scale of some other test and not to M=0 and SD=1. The difference between this procedure and mean-based equating is that, aside from difference in means of the two tests, this procedure also allows differences in variability. Due to this, the mathematical transformation of scores equalizes both arithmetic means of the two tests and their standard deviations or variances. The assumption this procedure is based on is that the two tests differ only in the size of the measurement unit and in difficulty. Tests in this situation measure the same construct, are structurally equivalent, have distributions of the same shape, but only differ in the size of their measurement unit, and this size difference is constant throughout the test – for example, one test has a larger, and the other one a smaller measurement unit. The previously described mean-based equating procedure may be considered a special case of linear equating when variances of two tests are the same.

The basic procedure for performing linear equating, i.e., linear transformation of scores of one test to the scale of the other test requires that the mean of the test first be subtracted from raw score being converted and the result obtained in that way divided by the standard deviation of that test. In this way the raw score was converted to z scale. After that, the z score is multiplied by the standard deviation of the second test (the one to the scale of which scores are being converted) and the mean of that test is added. This is done for each raw score of the test. This is a **symmetric transformation**, meaning that an equivalent formula can be applied to convert the scores back to the scale of the first test by only replacing corresponding values in the equation.

The procedure of linear equating results in a distribution of transformed scores that is identical to the distribution of original scores. In other words, the process of linear transformation of scores from the scale of one test to the other changes the numbers, but does not change the shape of the distribution of scores. If the distribution of target scores is really the same or very similar to the distribution of the original scores, this is not a problem. However, if the distribution of original scores is different than the distribution of the target scores, the procedure of linear equating may yield unusual or inadequate results, such as target scores outside the theoretical range of the target scale or an inadequate concentration of scores in one part or certain parts of the target scale, or a reduced range of scores on the target scale compared to the range of scores calculated from the target test.

Nonlinear equating is a joint name for different procedures for converting scores from one scale to another that are based on some form of nonlinear conversion of scale scores. Scores from one scale are converted to another scale using some nonlinear function. The most well-known example of nonlinear equating of two scales are systems for calculating the equivalence of school grades, especially systems for establishing equivalence between grades obtained in different school systems in the process of recognition of exams/courses. Other examples of nonlinear equating, i.e., converting scores from one scale to another scale are conversions that include normalization of scores (conversion of raw scores from a distribution of unknown shape into normally distributed values using a mathematical transformation) or scale constructed with the intention to stabilize the variability of measurement error (Kolen & Brennan, 1995).

Equating of true scores (Fajgelj, 2003) is based on calculating the true score for every total score – either as a factor score of the first common factor, as a true score in the scope of some items response theory model or in some other way. When this is done, the relationship between the true and the total score is established in both tests, and these relations are then used to convert scores. The assumption is that true scores are equal in both tests, so it is possible to make a transformation of the total score of the first test to the true score, and then convert that true score to the total score of the second test. Fajgelj (2003) states that equating of true scores does not necessarily apply a linear relationship between the true and the total scores. In such cases, equating of true scores may be treated as a special case of nonlinear equating.

Equipercentile equating is probably the most well-known method for equating two tests. Equipercentile equating is based on pairing scores corresponding to same percentiles in two tests. This is typically performed by:

- **Calculating cumulative frequencies for both tests** in order to establish correspondence between each raw score and its percentile, i.e., to determine what percent of test-takers from the sample has lower scores then each raw score. Then,
- **Raw test scores are paired with their corresponding percentiles**, i.e., percentiles corresponding to the percent of test-takers that have raw scores below the raw score being paired.

For example, if we have tests A and B, we first calculate cumulative frequencies of the sample on test A. We then calculate cumulative frequencies for test B. Next, if we for example, establish that 10% of test-takers of test A have scores lower than 45, we look for the score on the test B that also has exactly 10% of test-takers scoring lower. We find out that, for example, exactly 10% of test-takers of test B have scores lower than 78. When we establish this, we conclude that score 45 on test A corresponds to the score 78 on test B, because both of these have the same percentage of test-takers scoring lower – in this example 10%. In other words, both of these scores correspond to the same percentile – 10th. The procedure is than repeated for all scores of both tests.

As it usually happens that there are many possible scores, equipercentile equating is often performed by selecting a certain number of scale points – percentiles that are then paired or sometimes only boundary values between different categories of results are paired, i.e., scores that define boundaries between categories that imply different interpretations of results. One possibility of such pairing is that a graph is made in which selected paired scores are marked from both tests, and a linear extrapolation is then made for score values between these selected points. A linear extrapolation is performed by drawing a straight line that connects points defined by paired scores from the two scales on the graph, the dimensions of which are scores on the two scales. The conversion of unpaired scores is then done by finding the point on that line that corresponds to the unpaired score that we have and the point on the other dimension corresponding to that point on the first, if found. Except for this graphic procedure, Kolen and Brennan (1995) describe an analytic procedure for equipercentile equating, i.e., a procedure that uses mathematical formulae to first identify percentiles corresponding to raw scores, and then to convert raw scores from one test into raw score of the other test in this way.

In their book about equating tests, Kolen and Brennan (1995) also present methods for **smoothing distributions** obtained by equipercentile equating, especially in those cases when pairing was done only for a small number of discrete values, while the majority of other values are converted using linear extrapolations. Smoothing of a distribution refers to procedures used to adapt the shape of the distribution so that it graphically has the shape of a smooth curve instead of a set of connected straight lines obtained by connecting discrete points. However, these authors state that it is not always clear if the equating procedure is better if a smoothed distribution is used or not, because there are cases when the non-smoothed distribution provided better results than the smoothed one.

A great advantage of equipercentile equating is that this procedure, aside from converting scores, also changes the shape of the distribution – after converting scores from test A to scores of test B, converted scores of the test A have the same distribution as test B scores. Of course, this happens in an ideal case, when scores of both tests may be considered as continuous variables. However, as scores from two tests are discrete variables in reality (because each test has only a limited number of possible different values), in practice there might be some differences between the two distributions – the distribution of original test scores and the distribution of scores of the second test that are converted to the original test scale using this procedure (Kolen & Brennan, 1995). The size of this difference will be even greater if equipercentile equating is done using a smaller number of selected points or if the number of different values on the two tests is smaller, so pairing scores with the same percentiles included some discrepancies (for example, if the 10th percentile from one test was paired with the13th percentile of the other tes, because there were no scores that corresponded to the 10th percentile exactly and similar).

However, in spite of these shortcomings, the distribution of scores converted using the equipercentile equating procedure would still be closer to the distribution of scores of the target scale than would be the case with scores converted using the procedure of linear equating (with linear equating, converted scores keep their original distribution completely). Another advantage of equipercentile conversion is that it cannot result in impossible values of converted scores, i.e., result in values outside the range of the target scale. Converted scales will be both within the theoretical and empirical range of the scale, i.e., it will not only be within the range of scores that can theoretically be obtained on that scale, but also inside the range of scores that real test-takers from the sample used for equating have on that scale.

When considering possible ways of presenting results of equipercentile equating, what is typically used are either tabular or graphic representations of pairs of corresponding scores from the two tests that can be used to convert scores of individual test-takers from the scale of one of the tests to the scale of the other. Another possibility is the existence of a set of instructions within the computer program for administering the test or converting scores that use a set of formulae on data from samples used for equating in order to convert individual results from the scale of one test to the scale of the other test.

Equating using alternate scoring schemes (Kolen & Brennan, 1995) is performed by changing the scoring method of one test in such a way that scores corresponding to the scale of the other test are obtained. It is possible to adjust the scoring method of both tests in order to obtain scores on the same scale. This can be done by adjusting the number of points given for individual items. For example, instead of the classic scoring system used in knowledge tests, where each correct answer carries one point, creating a score range from zero to the number of items, the number of points per item can be adjusted so that scores range from zero to a certain predefined number that can be the same for both tests. Or, with a theoretical justification, items can be assigned different numbers of points, but again fitted in such a way that it results in scores of the two tests being on the same scale, i.e., comparable with each other. This method of test equation is also applicable on tests that apply more complex scoring procedures, like those including corrections for guessing by subtracting a certain part of point from the total score for incorrect answers (better known as "negative points"), because such tests also allow the identification of discrete values that a test-taker may achieve and hence adjustment of the scoring method.

(External) criterion-based equating may be used when there is a clear and measurable criterion that is in a strong and known relationship with both tests. Equating is then performed by pairing scores from the two tests that correspond to the same value of the criterion. An advantage of this procedure is that it is clear that paired values of the test correspond to the same values of the criterion. If the criterion is a behavior or a variable these tests were created to predict, then the practical value of this method of equating the tests is great. However, an important shortcoming of this procedure is that the criterion variables needed for the successful application of this procedure are quite rare, and even when they exist, their values are often binary, making it possible to pair only the two boundary scores of the two tests instead of equating whole scales across their entire ranges. Of course, this binary pairing can sometimes be quite sufficient.

***

It should be noted that the listed methods for test equating do not represent a systematized overview of mutually exclusive categories of equating methods, but only an overview of some of the procedures and their names that can be found in the literature and encountered in practice. Some of the listed procedures may be treated as subcategories of another listed procedure – for example, mean-based equating is a special case of linear equating, equipercentile equating can be viewed as a special type of nonlinear equating, while true score equating, depending on the procedure used for establishing the relationship between the true and the total score, can be considered to be either a type of linear or nonlinear equating.

A common property of all these procedures except the procedure of trues score equating is that they can also be used for pairing scores on measures of different constructs, and not only with tests that measure the same construct. True score equating, on the other hand, due to the nature of the procedure that requires the same underlying latent trait to exist in both tests, can be used only in tests that measure the same construct and in which that construct is also a latent variable.

All of these listed procedures may also be used in situations when multiple tests need to be equated. In such cases, there is also an option to create a system of linking tests to each other and converting scores of each test to scales of each of the other tests or for converting all tests to the same, usually one of the standard scales (standard scales will be discussed in more details in the chapter about the interpretation of individual differences).

Another important aspect that should be taken into account when equating tests is **measurement error**. No matter how good the psychometric properties of equated tests are, measurement obtained by using them will always contain a certain error of measurement, and for this reason, correlations between two equated tests will not be 1, but always smaller than that. It is therefore very important when equating tests to be aware of the existence of this error and provide an assessment of the value of the measurement error, along with converted scores, either as a point statistic, or by defining a range of corresponding scores from the scale of the target test with a certain probability (a confidence interval). The data about assessed measurement error should be listed along with the values of converted scores. Aside from this, for the measurement error to be as small as possible, when equating tests, care should be taken that data be obtained on a sufficiently large sample – ideally a sample of over 500 test-takers, and the more the better, and also that this sample is created in such a way that it is as representative as possible for the intended populations of the tests.

The main principle on which test equating is based states that tests need to have something in common in order to be equated. This principle is called **the principle of overlapping sets**. The elements that are overlapping may be test-takers, such as in the case when the same group of test-takers completes both tests, thus providing results of both tests on the same test-takers to the researcher. Equating that is based on the same test-takers completing both tests is called **horizontal equating**. Procedures described previously all refer to situations when both tests have been administered to the same test-takers.

Overlap can also be secured by adding a certain number of the same items to each test, while each test is completed by a separate group of test-takers. Such a set of items that is added to both tests is called "an anchor" or "an internal anchor", and the equating procedure performed in this way is called **vertical equating** (Fajgelj, 2003). Fajgelj states that the optimal anchor size is 20 items, but that it should not be shorter than 10 items and that this should correspond to 5–15% of the total length of a test version. However, while this number of items could have been considered adequate in previous decades, when psychological practice was dominated by huge tests, with hundreds of items and when it was even acceptable to measure one single construct with a huge number of items, the current trend of creating short test versions (Armstrong, Allison, & Rounds, 2008; Ashton & Lee, 2009; Hedrih & Pedović, 2016; Rammstedt & John, 2007; Tracey, 2009; Vries, 2013) likely makes these numbers too large. An additional problem occurring in practice when tests to be equated are two language versions of the same tests is finding items that can be added to both versions. If the two versions of the test are to be administered to monolinguals from the two language populations for which the two test versions are intended, samples that, therefore, do not speak the same language, as is usually the case in a situation like this, verbal items cannot be used for making an anchor. Actually, what cannot be done is adding sets of the same verbal items, i.e., in the same language, to both tests, because the test-takers do not speak the same language, so the items would be intelligible to one sample, but unintelligible to the other. The possibility that then exists is to find a set of items in the two languages for which it is previously firmly known that there is full scalar equivalence between scores calculated from them. However, this is a condition that is very hard to meet in practice. And when this condition could be met, an obvious question arises – why would we want to create two new test versions when the measured constructs can be measured in a valid and equivalent way using only the anchor which is, by the way, also much shorter? The option that remains is to use nonverbal items to construct the anchor. The problem of language does not exist with nonverbal items. Nonverbal items can be added to both test versions with a reasonable expectation that test-takers will understand them, but aside from that, all the other problems listed in the previous part of this book remain, thus not allowing us to declare in advance that nonverbal items will function equally on test-takers speaking different languages and who belong to different cultures. Another possible option to be considered is to use anchor items in a third language that both groups know sufficiently, but for this to be an option at all, there needs to be such a language. Also, this third language would not be the first language of either group, bringing all the issues relating to answering a test in a foreign language. To summarize, there is no ideal solution. Every option that can be chosen has some shortcomings that will limit the quality of equating two language versions of a test. This is the reason why some authors even consider the expectation that full equating can be achieved unrealistic, i.e., that there can be full scalar equivalence of two language versions of a test (Cook & Schmitt-Cascallar, 2005).

On the other hand, for numerous practical purposes, full and precise equivalence and convertibility of scores of one language version into scores of another language version is not necessary. Sometimes, practical purposes are adequately fulfilled with rough comparability and sometimes even with the possibility that test-takers be sorted into several categories, albeit with a certain percentage of error. This is why a categorization of test linkage according to the "strength" of the link between tests and, with it, according to the level of comparability of scores and possibilities for interpretation of results that was proposed by Lin, and listed by Cook and Schmitt-Cascallar (2005), should also be mentioned. This categorization proposes the existence of the following methods of linking tests:

- Equating
- Calibrating
- Statistical Moderation
- Prediction

Equating represents the strongest level of linkage between tests, one in which scores of the linked tests are interchangeable. When two tests are linked in this way, it is completely the same whether the first or the second test will be used as the scores are completely comparable and equal. To establish the existence of this type of relation between tests it is not only necessary that the two tests have equal psychometric characteristics, but also that physical conditions of their administration be similar enough.

Calibrating represents a less demanding form of test linkage compared to equating. Tests for which the procedure of calibration is performed must measure the same construct, but it is possible that their reliability differs and that they also differ in the expression level of the measured construct on which they are the most useful. For example, it is possible that there are two tests linked in this way of which one is most discriminative at one part of the intensity range of the measured construct, while the other is most discriminative at another part of the intensity range. Due to this, it is also possible that distributions of scores of the two tests are also different.

Statistical moderation exists when external variables are used to link test scores, i.e., when equating is based on an external criterion. For this type of linkage, it is not necessary for the tests to measure the same construct, but it does require both tests to be in a strong relationship with the external criterion that is used for linking. One of the main shortcomings of this procedure is that it is highly dependent on the context, group and time. Due to this, it is possible that the established relationship between two tests varies depending on which group of test-takers is participating in the study or that it varies between research studies (Cook & Schmitt-Cascallar, 2005).

Prediction represents the weakest form of linking two tests. While there is any nonrandom relation between two tests it is possible to link their values, i.e., predict values of one test from the values of the other. Cook and Schmitt-Cascallar (2005) emphasize that prediction equations are always one-way, i.e., that separate equations must be created for predicting values of some test A from the values of test B, and for predicting values of test B based on values of test A.

Note

1 A nomological network is a network of relations a construct has with various variables different from that construct and usually not included in the test that measures the construct. Which variables the construct correlates with and in what way? An answer to this question is a description of the nomological network of the construct in question.

References

Armstrong, P. I., Allison, W., & Rounds, J. (2008). Development and initial validation of brief public domain RIASEC marker scales. *Journal of Vocational Behavior, 73*, 287–299. https://doi.org/10.1016/j.jvb.2008.06.003

Armstrong, P. I., Hubert, L., & Rounds, J. (2003). Circular unidimensional scaling: A new look at group differences in interest structure. *Journal of Counseling Psychology, 50*(3), 297–308. https://doi.org/10.1037/0022-0167.50.3.297

Ashton, M. C., & Lee, K. (2009). The HEXACO – 60: A short measure of the major dimensions of personality. *Journal of Personality Assessment, 91*(4), 340–345. https://doi.org/10.1080/00223890902935878

Browne, M. W. (1992). Circumplex models for correlation matrices. *Psychometrika, 57*(4), 469–497. https://doi.org/10.1007/BF02294416

Candell, G. L., & Drasgow, F. (1988). An iterative procedure for linking metrics and assessing item bias in item response theory. *Applied Psychological Measurement, 12*(3), 253–260.

Cattell, R. B. (1940). A culture-free intelligence test. *The Journal of Educational Psychology, 331*(3), 161–179. Retrieved from http://psycnet.apa.org.proxy.kobson.nb.rs:2048/fulltext/1940-04768-001.pdf

Chen, F. F. (2007). Sensitivity of goodness of fit indexes to lack of measurement invariance. *Structural Equation Modeling, 14*(3), 464–504. https://doi.org/10.1080/10705510701301834

Cheung, G., & Rensvold, R. (2002). Evaluating goodness-of-fit indexes for testing measurement invariance. *Structural Equation Modelling, 9*(2), 233–255.

Clauser, B. E., & Mazor, K. M. (1998). Using statistical procedures to identify differentially functioning test items. *Educational Measurement: Issues and Practice, 17*(1), 31–44. https://doi.org/10.1111/j.1745-3992.1998.tb00619.x

Cook, L., & Schmitt-Cascallar, A. (2005). Establishing score comparability for tests given in different languages. In *Adapting educational and psychological tests for cross-cultural assessment* (pp. 139–169). Mahwah, NJ: Lawrence Erlbaum Associates.

Costa, A., Foucart, A., Arnon, I., Aparici, M., & Apesteguia, J. (2014). "Piensa" twice: On the foreign language effect in decision making. *Cognition, 130*, 236–254. https://doi.org/10.1016/j.cognition.2013.11.010

Drasgow, F. (1984). Scrutinizing psychological tests: Measurement equivalence and equivalent relations with external variables are the central issues. *Psychological Bulletin, 95*(1), 134–135.

Ellis, B. B. (1989). Differential item functioning: Implications for test translations. *Journal of Applied Psychology, 74*(6), 912–921.

Fabrigar, L. R., Visser, P. S., & Browne, M. W. (1997). Conceptual and methodological issues in testing the circumplex structure of data in personality and social psychology. *Personality and Social Psychology Review, 1*(3), 184–203. https://doi.org/10.1207/s15327957pspr0103_1

Fajgelj, S. (2003). *Psihometrija.* Beograd: Centar za primenjenu psihologiju.

Hedrih, V. (2008). Structure of vocational interests in Serbia: Evaluation of the spherical model. *Journal of Vocational Behavior, 73*(1), 13–23. https://doi.org/10.1016/j.jvb.2007.12.004

Hedrih, V., & Pedović, I. (2016). Konstruktna validnost holističkih mera procene karakteristika radnog mesta po Holandovom modelu. In Đ. Čekrlija, D. Đurić, & A. Vasić (Eds.), *3. Otvoreni dani psihologije, Banja Luka, knjiga sažetaka* (p. 44). Banja Luka: Filozofski fakultet, Republika Srpska.

Hedrih, V., Stošić, M., Simić, I., & Ilieva, S. (2016). Evaluation of the hexagonal and spherical model of vocational interests in the young people in Serbia and Bulgaria. *Psihologija, 49*(2), 199–210. https://doi.org/10.2298/PSI1602199H

Hedrih, V., & Šverko, I. (2007). Evaluation of the Holand model of the professional intersts in Croatia and Serbia. *Psihologija, 40*(2). https://doi.org/10.2298/PSI0702227H

Hedrih, V., Šverko, I., & Pedović, I. (2018). Structure of vocational interests in Macedonia and Croatia – evaluation of the spherical model. *Facta Universitatis, Series: Philosophy, Sociology, Psychology and History, 17*(1), 19–36. https://doi.org/10.22190/FUPSPH1801019H

Hidalgo, D., & López-Pina, A. J. (2004). Differential item functioning detection and effect size: A comparison between logistic regression and mantel-haenszel procedures. *Educational and Psychological Measurement, 64*(6), 903–915. https://doi.org/10.1177/0013164403261769

Hofstede, G. (2011). Dimensionalizing cultures: The Hofstede model in context. *Online Readings in Psychology and Culture, 2*(1). https://doi.org/10.9707/2307-0919.1014

Hofstede, G., Neuijen, B., Ohayv, D. D., & Sanders, G. (1990). Measuring organizational cultures: A qualitative and quantitative study across twenty cases. *Administrative Science Quarterly, 35*(2), 286–316.

Hogan, R., & Blake, R. (1999). John Holland's vocational typology and personality theory. *Journal of Vocational Behavior, 55*(1), 41–56. https://doi.org/10.1006/jvbe.1999.1696

Holland, J. L. (1959). A theory of vocational choice. *Journal of Counseling Psychology, 6*(1).

Holland, J. L. (1994). *Self-directed search: Assessment booklet, a guide to educational and career planning.* Odessa: Psychological Assessment Resources, Inc.

International Test Comission. (2017). *ITC guidelines for translating and adapting tests* (2nd ed.). https://doi.org/10.1027/1901-2276.61.2.29

Keysar, B., Hayakawa, S. L., & An, S. G. (2012). The foreign-language effect: Thinking in a foreign tongue reduces decision biases. *Psychological Science, 23*(6), 661–668. https://doi.org/10.1177/0956797611432178

Kolen, M. (2004). Linking assessments: Concept and history. *Applied Psychological Measurement, 28*(4), 219–226. https://doi.org/10.1177/0146621604265030

Kolen, M., & Brennan, R. (1995). *Test equating: Methods and practices.* New York: Springer-Verlag.

Kristjansson, E., Aylesworth, R., Mcdowell, I., & Zumbo, B. D. (2005). A comparison of four methods for detecting differential item functioning in ordered response items. *Educational and Psychological Measurement, 65*(6), 935–953. https://doi.org/10.1177/0013164405275668

Lorenzo-Seva, U., & ten Berge, J. M. F. (2006). Tucker's congruence coefficient as a meaningful index of factor similarity. *Methodology, 2*(2), 57–64. https://doi.org/10.1027/1614-1881.2.2.57

Nagy, G., Trautwein, U., & Lüdtke, O. (2010). The structure of vocational interests in Germany: Different methodologies, different conclusions. *Journal of Vocational Behavior, 76*, 153–169. https://doi.org/10.1016/j.jvb.2007.07.002

Prediger, D. J. (1982). Dimensions underlying Holland's Hexagon: Missing link between interests and occupations? *Journal of Vocational Behavior, 21*, 259–287.

Rammstedt, B., & John, O. P. (2007). Measuring personality in one minute or less: A 10-item short version of the big five inventory in English and German. *Journal of Research in Personality*, *41*(41), 203–212. https://doi.org/10.1016/j.jrp.2006.02.001

Rounds, J., & Tracey, T. J. (1993). Prediger's dimensional representation of Holland's RIASEC circumplex. *Journal of Applied Psychology*, *78*(6), 875–890.

Serpell, R. (1979). How specific are perceptual skills? A cross-cultural study of pattern reproduction*. *British Journal of Psychology*, *70*(3), 365–380. https://doi.org/10.1111/j.2044-8295.1979.tb01706.x

Stark, S., Chernyshenko, O. S., & Drasgow, F. (2006). Detecting differential item functioning with confirmatory factor analysis and item response theory: Toward a unified strategy. *Journal of Applied Psychology*, *91*(6), 1292–1306. https://doi.org/10.1037/0021-9010.91.6.1292

Šverko, I., & Hedrih, V. (2010). Evaluacija sfernog i heksagonalnog modela strukture interesa u hrvatskim i srpskim uzorcima. *Suvremena Psihologija*, *13*(1), 47–62.

Tracey, T. J. G. (1997). Randall: A Microsoft FORTRAN program for a randomization test of hypothesized order relations. *Educational and Psychological Measurement*, *57*(1), 164–168.

Tracey, T. J. G. (2009). Development of an abbreviated personal globe inventory using item response theory: The PGI-short. *Journal of Vocational Behavior*, *76*, 1–15. https://doi.org/10.1016/j.jvb.2009.06.007

Van De Vijver, F., & Poortinga, Y. H. (2005). Conceptual and methodological issues in adapting tests. In R. Hambleton, P. Merenda, & C. Spielberger (Eds.), *Adapting educational and psychological tests for cross-cultural assessment* (pp. 39–64). Mahwah, NJ and London: Lawrence Erlbaum Associates.

Vries, R. (2013). The 24-item brief HEXACO inventory (BHI). *Journal of Research in Personality*, *47*, 871–880.

Wu, A. D., Li, Z., & Zumbo, B. D. (2007). Decoding the meaning of factorial invariance and updating the practice of multi-group confirmatory factor analysis: A demonstration with TIMSS data. *Practical Assessment, Research & Evaluation*, *12*(3), 1–26.

5

INTERPRETATION OF INDIVIDUAL RESULTS

Introduction

After creating or adapting a test and examining its validity or measurement equivalence with the original test version, the question of how to interpret individual results obtained by using the test arises next. No matter how good the psychometric properties of a test are, scores by themselves do not mean anything, nor can numerical values from the test by themselves be treated as data about the test-taker. The fact that the test-taker achieved, for example, score 56 on the test does not mean anything by itself and without a reference frame for interpreting the meaning of different scores. Therefore, to interpret results obtained by testing a reference frame is needed, one that would provide meaning to the numbers. But what can such a frame be like?

When considering options for this, we should first ask ourselves about all the different purposes for which psychological tests are used, i.e., about all the different tasks a psychological test needs to fulfill. Maybe the most well-known use of psychological tests is their use in diagnostics – a test is applied with an intent to establish if a person has certain psychopathological manifestations important for obtaining a diagnosis. Tests can also be used to determine if a person has certain skills or abilities required for performing a job or an activity. But tests can also be used to establish the extent to which test-takers possess a certain psychological trait or how pronounced a certain psychological state is with them. Tests are sometimes used to rank test-takers on some measured property, like for example, in some selection situation. If we extend the definition of tests to include tests of knowledge or content-oriented tests, then the tests can be also used to establish the extent to which a person has mastered certain content or attained knowledge contained in some precisely defined program, like, for example, school programs for a certain grade. Tests are also used to establish which of the compared traits is the most pronounced and it is sometimes important to know where the results of a person are in comparison to some population that is important for the purpose of testing with regard to a measured trait or a set of measured traits. Sometimes there is a need to establish the relation between an individual and a population with regard to a set of examined traits. Tests are also sometimes used to follow the progress of a test-taker (for example, during a training program) in relation to a group of reference or to the test-taker him/herself. Sometimes the goal of test application is to obtain data needed for a complex assessment of the cognitive and conative properties of an individual. Many, many more examples of test application could be found, but it is obvious that these diverse examples of test application can certainly not all be covered by a single method for interpreting individual results, nor with a single strategy for interpreting tests.

Approaches to interpretation of individual results

Two basic approaches to interpreting individual results of psychological tests found in literature are norm-referenced assessment and criterion-referenced assessment. In line with these two basic approaches, tests can also be categorized into criterion-based tests and norm-based tests (Berk, 1986; Fajgelj, 2003; Geisinger, 1994).

The defining characteristic of **criterion-referenced assessment** is that conclusions about results of individual test-takers and their interpretation are based on comparing the achievement of the test-taker with some external criterion. Test performance is strongly linked to that external criterion so that it can be established what kind of performance test-takers with a certain value of the criterion variable have. In the other variant, the criterion itself is contained in the test, i.e., the test requires that the test-taker manifests the criterion behavior and then, in the process of evaluation, a conclusion is made whether the participant was successful in it or not.

In the scope of **norm-referenced assessment**, i.e., norm-based tests, the interpretation of which is based on norms, inferences about results of an individual test-taker are made by comparing the performance of the test-taker whose results are being interpreted to performances of members of a certain population, usually the population this test-taker belongs to. As data about the population as a whole are usually not available and they cannot be practically acquired, the population with which the performance of the test-taker is to be compared is typically represented by a sample assembled in such a way that it is as representative for that population as possible. Interpretations of results of a test-taker are performed by determining the position of scores of that test-taker on the distribution of the sample and then generalizing the conclusion about the position of the test-taker on the sample to his/her position in relation to the whole population.

Aside from these two basic approaches, different authors describe other types of approaches. One such approach is the **cohort-referenced assessment** (Wiliam, 1998), a name for an approach to test assessment where results of an individual test-taker are compared with results of the group of test-takers participating in the same testing event, usually with the goal of forming a unified ranking list and later selection of candidates that will be considered to have passed the selection procedure, for example, those that will be accepted into a certain educational program. In statistics, a **cohort** is a name used to describe a group of examinees with some common characteristic like, for example, a group of people born on the same year or group of people who all performed a certain action (like, for example, applying to a public call at a similar time). Due to this, they all participate in the same testing procedure. The idea behind this approach is that it is enough that results be comparable within the testing situation, so that ranking can be done. Results are not generalizable to the wider population, i.e., the performance of test-takers on the test does not provide any information about the level of expression of the measured construct nor does it provide any information about what would the achievement of the test-taker be like in an another similar testing situation, because it is assumed that the group of test-takers – cohort – would be completely different in another testing situation.

Another approach is the **construct-referenced assessment** (Wiliam, 1998) approach in which assessors assess the performance of the test-taker on a test. Dylan William proposed this approach, having first in mind tests of educational achievement and proposes the use of this approach in situations when learning outcomes cannot be clearly defined. Although they do not have a clear definition of learning outcomes that should be evaluated in the test and how precisely it should be evaluated, assessors share a common idea of what is measured, what is the construct the presence of which should be evaluated in the text and what, in general, favorable outcomes look like. Test authors then assess tests and harmonize these assessments, and assessments obtained in this way are then used as benchmark assessments for other assessors. New assessors are then trained by being tasked with assessing these same tests, and their assessments are then compared to benchmark assessments provided by authors of the test or of the group that organizes the training. The goal of the training is to achieve intersubjective agreement. For the trainees to be considered competent to apply and evaluate the test, it is necessary that they learn to assess the test in a way that results in assessments that are sufficiently close to benchmark assessments. In situations where there are no benchmark assessments (for example, in situations of assessing unstandardized school tests), the focus is placed on achieving congruence between assessors (in the example with school tests, these assessors would be teachers who are doing the assessment). Approaches similar to this one can also be found in the area of assessing psychological constructs and not only in the area of educational assessment. For example, the assessment system for the Mirror interview (Buhl-Nielsen, 2006; Kernberg, Buhl-Nielsen, & Normandin, 2006; McBirney-Goc, 2016) utilizes an approach that is very similar to this approach, and such is also the case with the Adult Attachment Projective Picture System – AAP (George & West, 2001). It should be noted that a construct-referenced assessment approach in this form is applied with open-ended tests and in a system for qualitative assessment of psychological and educational constructs.

One more approach that can be found in the literature, again primarily in the area of educational assessment, is the **curriculum-based assessment** (Burns, 2002; Deno, 1985). With this approach, interpretation is based on the level of adoption of knowledge contained in a curriculum of the educational process the test-taker is attending. Results are typically presented as a percentage of knowledge of the curriculum content. This approach is linked to interventions in the educational process and assessments can also be made during the educational process allowing the results to be using for adjusting the educational process to the test-taker.

Although authors involved in these other approaches insist on their distinctiveness from the "classic" approaches to test assessment – the norm-referenced and criterion-referenced approaches – even a superficial analysis shows that these other approaches may more or less be considered to be special subtypes of norm-referenced and criterion-referenced approaches, albeit with some special properties. For this reason, the following text will focus in detail on the properties of norm-referenced and criterion-referenced approaches to interpreting individual results of test-takers on psychological tests, with some attention devoted to specifics of some of the other approaches listed in this context.

Criterion-referenced and norm-referenced approaches to interpreting individual results

Criterion-referenced assessment approach

A key property of criterion-referenced assessment is the existence of an external criterion used to make the assessment – an external criterion with which performance of test-takers is compared. Criterion used for assessment in this approach must be clear, easily measurable, relevant for the purpose of testing and must not be dependent on the results of other test-takers. In the criterion-referenced assessment approach, conclusions about the performance of any individual test-taker are in no way dependent on the performances of other test-takers.

In an ideal situation, there is a natural criterion, i.e., a criterion behavior which separates test-takers into natural categories according to the value they have on the criterion variable. For example, the skill of swimming in a pool filled with water could be one such natural criterion – a person who knows how to swim in a pool is the one who can maintain him/herself on the surface of water without holding to the edge of the pool, touching the bottom or using any aid for keeping oneself afloat. A person who does not fulfill this criterion is the one who would drown in such a situation. In a similar fashion, a person who can drive a car is the one who can drive a car from one place to another under conditions of normal traffic, without causing an accident and while acting in accordance with traffic regulations. For a person who would cause a crash or could not perform the task without braking traffic regulations, we would conclude that he/she cannot drive a car. Or, for an example from clinical practice, a criterion variable could be whether a person has hallucinations or not. A person that reports having sensory stimuli that do not exist in reality is a person having hallucinations. A person that does not perceive sensory stimuli that do not exist does not have hallucinations.

These three examples – if a person can swim or not, drive a car or not or if a person has hallucinations or not – are examples of natural criteria. In all three examples, criteria are binary variables – can swim/cannot swim, can drive a car/cannot drive a car, has hallucinations/does not have hallucinations. This is one of the typical properties of criterion-referenced tests – criteria usually employ a binary format for expressing results – a person either possesses or does not possess certain skill or ability, can or cannot perform this or that action, manifests or does not manifest this or that set of psychopathological symptoms etc. Criterion variables that have more categories, i.e., those that would be ordinal instead of binary, could possibly be created, but the tradeoff would usually be giving up on having clear, natural categories and their replacement with categories of debatable distinctiveness. In the example with swimming skills, an ordinal criterion could be created by dividing the category of swimmers into multiple categories according to, for example, swimming speed or the number of swimming styles a person knows. However, it is obvious that there are multiple ways in which such categories could be created and that there are multiple decisions to be made when creating them. Also, some of these decisions are such that they potentially compromise the unidimensionality of the measured trait or skill. For example, should the number of swimming styles a person knows be used for distinguishing categories of swimmers, or should it be swimming speed? Or both? Is the number of swimming styles a person knows the same skill as the ability to maintain oneself afloat, or is it something else? These questions illustrate a problem typically appearing in situations when an attempt is made to formulate an ordinal criterion variable instead of a binary one.

A common property of all these criteria is that that the criterion clearly shows what type of behavior can be expected from a person having a particular value of the criterion variable. Because the criterion behaviors are clearly defined, it is also clear what people fulfilling or not fulfilling that criterion can or cannot do.

However, it is not possible to create equally valid criteria for all constructs and all tests. For many psychological constructs, such as basic personality traits, cognitive traits and other similar wide-scope psychological traits, it is typically not possible to formulate valid criteria. While it is relatively easy to define how exactly swimming skill is manifested, the same cannot be said for a person that is an extravert, that is open to experience or for an intelligent person. While psychologists have a clear idea of the characteristics of people like this, converting these general behavior tendencies into precise, clear-cut and easily measurable criteria is something else entirely, and a task that cannot typically be done in a universally valid way. Even if we tried to define criteria for such tests, such criteria would turn out to be very arbitrary. This is the reason why criterion-referenced assessment is not in general use with all psychological tests. Things become additionally complicated when the component of cross-cultural variability is included in the assessment of manifestations of basic personality traits. In such a situation, it comes to attention that the same traits may have different manifestation in different cultures and that the same observable behaviors can be incited by different traits or latent variables in different cultures. Due to this, criterion-referenced assessment is most commonly used in (Fajgelj, 2003):

- **Content oriented tests** – tests intended to asses if a person has adopted necessary knowledge from the domain covered by test contents;
- **Mastery tests** – tests intended to assess if a person has mastered a skill or attained specific knowledge; and
- **Tests aiming to assess the possession of a certain trait** – tests intended to assess if a person possesses certain traits relevant for the purpose of testing in a sufficient amount or not. An example could be tests that assess if a person has certain psychopathological symptoms or if he/she achieves certain predefined results at work or if he/she possesses properties necessary to achieve such results.

Aside from these types of tests, attempts to assess some wider psychological constructs, like for example attachment styles or dimensions, in a way resembling the criterion-referenced approach are notable in the last few decades (George & West, 2001; Kernberg et al., 2006; McBirney-Goc, 2016). However, lacking natural criteria that could be used in tests measuring these psychological constructs, these attempts are usually more in line with the construct-referenced assessment approach to the interpretation of results, although authors may provide more or less detailed instructions and guidelines for interpreting test results, like lists of possible answers of test-takers and how to interpret them, systems for analyzing answers to various components and systems for allocating points to each component in accordance to the value of the component and the like.

When construction of criterion-referenced tests is in considered, due to the need that the test be in a strong relationship with the criterion, practically the only property of test items that needs to be taken care of during construction and item selection is item discrimination in regard to the criterion. As long as items discriminate between different values of the criterion, i.e., as long as test-takers with different values on the criterion variable achieve different scores on items and these items cover all the important aspects of the criterion, other item properties are mostly unimportant.

The situation is similar with psychometric properties of a test as a whole. Literally the only important psychometric property of a criterion-referenced test is its criterion validity, i.e., correlation with the criterion. If the other psychometric properties are also good, that is a sure plus, but if they are not, it is of no particular importance as long as it is certain that the criterion validity of the test is good. Aside from this, due to the binary assessment format that is typical in criterion-referenced tests, coefficients of internal consistency will tend to underestimate the reliability of these tests. There are also many situations where internal consistency of a criterion-referenced test cannot be meaningfully calculated because the measured construct is not a latent variable, hence the primary condition for estimating reliability using internal consistency coefficients is not fulfilled.

Norm-referenced tests

The idea underlying the norm-referenced tests is that performance of an individual test-taker can be assessed by comparing it to a certain population, which is usually the population the individual test-taker belongs to or a population to which the performance of this test-taker can be meaningfully compared. If the performance of this test-taker is better than performance of an average member of the reference population, this means that that the level of expression of the measured construct in this test-taker is above-average or high. If the performance of this test-taker is lower than the typical performance of members of the reference population, this mean that the level of expression of the measured construct in this test-taker is low or below average. The conclusion about the level of expression of the measured construct in every individual test-taker depends on the performance of that test-taker in comparison to the reference population.

The population with which the individual test-taker is compared in the scope of norm-referenced approach is called **the normative population or the reference population**. However, in practice, data about the normative population are usually not available, so the group that is really used as a reference for comparing scores of individual test-takers is a sample taken from the normative population. The sample that provides results with which results of individual test-takers are compared is called **the normative sample**. In an ideal case, a normative sample is representative of the normative population, i.e., it is equal in all properties to the population, except in size. However, as representativity of a sample for a population cannot be established for certain, and as financial resources available to researchers for conducting a normative study are, usually, far from endless, the requirement that the sample be representative is in practice often replaced by the requirement that the sample be large enough and obtained using the best sampling procedure that researchers are able to conduct with the resources they have available. A sufficiently large sample, in a situation when population size is very large or effectively unlimited (for example, population of the UK or the US) means at least 500 test-takers, ideally as many more as possible. On the other hand, when a normative sample is created for some limited and relatively small population in mind (for example, professional sports judges in a mid-sized city), it is then sufficient that the sample is a substantial part of the population and if the population is sufficiently small, it is sometimes possible to include the whole or almost the whole population into the sample. Although, for practical reasons, when sampling from large populations, there is little point in insisting that the normative sample be collected using this or that specific sampling procedure. Researchers conducting a normative study need to take care that they, whenever possible, avoid having a sample that is selected in regard to the level of the construct that is measured by the test. A normative sample should encompass the full range of the measured construct in the reference population.

After administering the test to the normative sample, results of test-takers from the sample are systematized and presented in the form of **norms**. Norms are a document that contains data about what part of the normative sample has what scores on the test to which the norms refer, i.e., contains a clear overview of the distribution of the normative sample. Psychologists using the test in practice then use these norms to interpret results of individual test takers (instead of working with the entire sample, to which they usually do not have access).

In the scope of the normative approach, the results of individual test-takers can be expressed as a percentile rank in relation to the normative sample or in the form of a standard score. When the performance of a test-taker is expressed as a percentile rank, it represents the percentage of test-takers from the normative sample that have lower scores than the test-taker in question. Performance of the test-taker need not, of course, be expressed exclusively in the form of percentiles – other fractiles are also acceptable – deciles, quintiles, quartiles, etc. Norms expressed in the form of fractiles are jointly called **fractile norms**, or according to the specific type of fractile used to express test performance – percentile norms, decile norms, quartile norms, etc. Expressing performance on a test as a standard score is essentially the same, with the main difference being that standard scores can be treated as interval measures while percentile ranks are ordinal. Aside from this, when multiple tests that measure related constructs are all converted to the same standard scale, psychologists working in practice with that sort of construct can easily learn the rules for interpreting scores on that standard scale, allowing them to easily interpret results on that scale regardless of the test from which they originate. However, it is important to have in mind that in whatever way performance is expressed – as a fractile rank of the test-taker or as a standard score – it never represents anything other than the size of that test-takers score in relation to scores of test-takers from the normative sample. The result expressed in this way shows nothing about the level of expression of the measured trait in any absolute or criterion-like way. However, this also does not imply that interpretations will change much if the normative sample changes. Although changes between normative samples are possible and they do happen, when normative samples are collected in a valid way, so that they are as representative for the population as possible, differences between normative samples tend to be limited and there are studies showing substantial longitudinal stability of certain measures obtained using the norm-referenced approach (Fagan, Holland, & Wheeler, 2007; Hopkins & Bracht, 1975; Rose, Feldman, Jankowski, & Rossem, 2012).

When considering psychometric characteristics of norm-referenced tests, lacking a criterion that could be used to describe behaviors corresponding to certain test scores, construct validity becomes prominent. If it is established that a test measures the construct for which it is intended or, in other words, if it is established that it is construct valid, it becomes justified to use the existing research data about behavioral tendencies of people with a certain level of construct to attribute these tendencies to test-takers whose test scores correspond to those levels of the construct. For this reason, it is important to first examine the reliability of the test, and, after that, all other aspects of construct validity that can be examined for the given test on samples from populations to which it will be applied.

Standard scales

A very well-known standard scale and a scale with wide application in statistics is the **z scale**. The definition of the z scale is that it is a scale with a mean of 0 and a standard deviation of 1. Although widely used in statistics, the z scale is not too popular as a standard scale to which raw test scores will be converted for interpretation purposes. Results converted to the z scale are typically non-whole numbers (numbers with a decimal), performance of the average test-taker is 0, and all test-takers with performance below the 50th percentile have negative values. Both zero and negative values as measures of a person's performance tend to have a negative connotation in everyday life, while people generally find it harder to work with non-whole numbers than with natural numbers. Due to this, except with a certain number of psychometrically oriented researchers and test authors, z scale is generally not popular as a scale for expressing performance of test-takers on psychological tests.

A widely popular scale is the **T scale**, and it is typically encountered as a standard scale of different clinical and conative tests. The arithmetic mean of the T scale is 50 and standard deviation is 10. Raw scores converted to the T scale are generally easy to express as whole numbers, because non-whole numbers can easily be rounded without any particular loss in precision. One of the most popular tests using the T scale is the clinical test Minnesota Multiphasic Personality Inventory, the well-known MMPI (Greene, 2000; Ward, 1991), a test that had several revisions, versions and editions, and which is currently in clinical use by psychologists in many countries throughout the world. Thanks to the T scale to which raw scores of this test are converted, practically every clinical psychologist knows that when interpreting MMPI results, one should primarily pay attention to scales that exceed the T score of 70 (or 65 in the MMPI-2 version [Greene, 2000]). MMPI is used here as an example, but there are other conative tests, first of all personality inventories, results of which are interpreted in a norm-referenced way, that include T scores as the main or as one of the options in interpreting results.

Maybe the most popular standard scale is **the intelligence quotient scale, or IQ scale**. The arithmetic mean of the IQ scale is 100, while the standard deviation is 15. The name "intelligence quotient" is at this point more than 100 years old and it is attributed to the German psychologist William Stern (Lamiell, 2012; Stern, 1912), who so named a method of calculating scores on an intelligence test he presented in his book. However, the term became popular only when his book, published in 1912 in the German language, was translated into English and distributed in the US. In the beginning, IQ was calculated as a ratio between mental and chronological age, that was then multiplied by 100 to obtain a result on a scale centered on 100. Mental age is an archaic measure of performance of children on intelligence tests first proposed by Alfred Binet with the help of Theodor Simone, and it was first used in the famous Binet-Simone scale (Boake, 2002). Thanks to the fact that performance of children on intelligence tests rises with age, it is possible to create expectations about the average performance that is to be expected from children of a certain age. The range of possible scores on that test is then divided into mental ages, and the test-taker is then attributed a mental age corresponding to his/her performance. This is then divided by their chronological age (how old the test-taker really is) and then multiplied by 100 to obtain the IQ. The concept of mental age could not be meaningfully applied to adult intelligence and it also suffered numerous criticisms as a measure of children's intelligence, so it is mostly abandoned today. However, the IQ scale, as a standard scale with fixed characteristics, i.e., predefined mean and standard deviation remains popular and widely used even today.

Many tests of cognitive abilities that are used today use the IQ scale for presenting results. Probably the most popular test of this sort is the Wechsler Adult Intelligence Scale – WAIS, the current version of which is the WAIS-IV (Benson, Hulac, & Kranzler, 2010; Wechsler, 2008), but the IQ scale is also used by many other tests of intelligence or cognitive abilities. Aside from its application for presenting results of tests of cognitive abilities, attempts to use the standard IQ scale in tests measuring constructs for which it is not clear whether they are cognitive or conative traits is notable in the last few decades. Of such applications, probably the most notable is application in tests intended to measure the construct of emotional intelligence when expressed as a quotient of emotional intelligence or EQ (Bar-On, 2004; Dawda & Hart, 2000).

Another standard scale that can be encountered in the literature is the **C scale**. The arithmetic mean of the C scale is 10 and its standard deviation is 5 (Fajgelj, 2003).

Types of norms

It was mentioned earlier that a document called "norms" is created based on the application of the test on a normative sample and that psychologists use these norms for interpreting results of individual test-takers by comparing their scores with these norms instead of directly comparing them with the normative sample. For this reason, norms are an obligatory part of a test manual. The procedure of creating norms is called **test calibration or norming**.

What norms should be used in a test, i.e., which population should results of test-takers be compared to in order to be most adequately interpreted? The first answer and the one that seems the most obvious is that test-takers should be compared with the general population, i.e., with the intended population of the test. Such norms are called **universal norms**. For norms to really be universal it is necessary that the normative sample be representative of the general population and that this population is homogenous, i.e., that there are no groups on which tests shows differential functioning.

How big could the population for which universal norms are created be? Guidelines for adapting tests of the International Test Commission (International Test Comission, 2017) explicitly denounce the practice of using norms created for a population that uses one language version of the test on a population using another language version without proof that such use is adequate. For norms to be applicable to test-takers doing another language version, it is first necessary to obtain empirical evidence that there is full scalar equivalence between the two versions. The spirit of norm-referenced approach would also require the normative sample to then consist of members of both linguistic populations and to be representative for the joint population consisting of both groups. Of course, such a requirement is not easy to fulfill in practice. The rate at which researchers encounter different language versions between which there is absolutely no differential functioning, not even DIF that manifests as different difficulties of some items, is far from regular. As linguistic borders often follow state borders, another factor to be taken into account when making norms are the legal regulations about psychological testing in the country in which a test is used. Regulations usually require tests that enter commercial use and that are used in psychological practice to pass some certification or quality control procedure with the national institutions competent for psychological testing and one of the main indicators of quality used in such processes is the existence of norms for the population of the country that is to issue the certificate for the test. For this reason, the most encompassing universal norms are usually national norms – norms intended for the population of a country; or language norms, used when there are groups speaking different first languages within the population of a country.

However, universal national or language norms are, sometimes neither are sufficient nor adequate for practical use. One notable example of inadequacy of universal norms are situations of cognitive testing of children. If we applied universal norms to the performance of children on cognitive tests, we would obtain results showing that cognitive abilities of children rise with age. In the spirit of universal norms, we could conclude that children are born mentally handicapped and that they approach the cognitive performance of adults more and more as they age. However, we know that such performance of young children is normal and not a result of their weak cognitive capacities. We also know that this is a transient state that quickly changes with age, while the idea of assessing cognitive abilities is to obtain assessments that are relatively permanent. Also, psychologists and other parties involved in assessing cognitive abilities of children are essentially not interested in comparing the current performance of children to that of adults, i.e., the general population, because it is clear that it will be weak at this early age. Instead, they are interested in predicting what the cognitive abilities of children will be when they grow up and become adults. Due to this, it makes much more sense to compare the performance of a child with other children of the same age, then with the general population (of adults). To achieve this, test publishers and psychologists created the so-called **age norms**. Age norms are norms based on a normative sample consisting of test-takers of a precisely defined age. Age norms include separate norms for every age or age interval. Age norms are created for children and adolescents, but there are also situations in which norms are created for adults of different ages. Such norms for adults are usually made with wider age intervals than norms for children. While with children, separate norms may be created for intervals of only one year or even months, norms for adults can be made in intervals of 5–6 or maybe 10 years, and sometimes the whole age span between, for example, 25 till the oldest age can be divided in only a couple of categories for which separate norms are made.

In his book, Fajgelj (Fajgelj, 2003) lists local, class, school and occupational norms. **Class norms** are similar to age norms, with the only difference being that separate norms are made for different grades in school instead of ages. **School norms** are norms that are created for a specific school or a group of schools.

Another type of norms are **occupational norms**. A defining property of universal norms is that they cover the whole range of intensities of the measured construct in the general population, while tests are typically created to be the most discriminant at the middle level intensity of the measured construct. However, there are occupations that require people working in them to have a very high (or low) level of a certain trait or a set of traits that are important for performing activities required by that occupation. If universal norms were applied to these people, it would quickly become obvious that they do not allow for a sufficiently precise differentiation of people in that occupation in regard to these traits. Universal norms would show that all persons in that occupation are more or less on the same scale point or that their trait levels fall within a very narrow range, thus not allowing the needed differentiation between them to be made. Aside from this, for concluding if the level of the measured trait of test-takers in an occupation is high, low or just barely sufficient for performing activities included in that occupation, it is typically useless to know where performance of these test-takers is in comparison to the general population. What is needed is comparison between the test-takers and other members of that occupation.

Local norms are norms that use inhabitants of a certain area as the reference populations – inhabitants of a geographical area, a settlement or a group of settlements. Local norms can be particularly useful in areas that have certain specificities – cultural, linguistic or other specific traits compared to the general population. If national norms were used on residents of that locale, it could be expected that the test would show differential functioning. They are also useful when there is no differential functioning, but the local population differs sufficiently from the general population that the position of the test-taker in relation to the national norms cannot be used as an indicator of his/her position in relation to the local population.

Although a topic of much controversy, psychological tests also use gender or sex norms. **Gender norms** are norms in which the reference population are just members of a single gender and separate norms are then created for males and females. Gender norms are encountered in various systems for assessing physical abilities, but also in measures of various psychological constructs. With psychological constructs, gender norms have their place in numerous situations where tests show differential functioning (but not construct inequivalence) for members of different genders, making direct comparison between males and females unjustified and then also the use of universal norms for score comparison.

Gender norms become controversial when they are applied in the domain of work and particularly in the area of selection. Excluding persons of one gender from some occupations was often, in the past, justified by listing real or made-up differences in average performance between males and females in job-related traits. However, differences in mean performance of groups of different genders do not mean that distribution of groups by gender have no overlap, i.e., that no two members of different genders can have the same performance. In the area of work, there is a famous discussion in the US about the use of tests of physical abilities in the selection of people for positions of firefighters. While some US cities seem to avoid joint rankings of males and females or, in other words, use separate norms for each gender (gender norms) (www.nytimes.com/1987/10/06/us/court-refuses-suit-by-women-over-fire-test.html), application of the same test for both genders in New York was a topic of several court processes. Probably most famous of them was the court process from the 1970s when the New York lawyer Brenda Berkman (https://en.wikipedia.org/wiki/Brenda_Berkman), who unsuccessfully applied for a position of a firefighter, sued the firefighting department for discrimination, stating that the test of physical abilities used in the admission procedure – the test that no female candidate managed to pass – was not valid in the sense that the test tasks were not relevant for the job. She won the process and the procedure was repeated by having female candidates complete another test, created just for that purpose and which, according to the available data, contained tasks more relevant for the job of a firefighter. However, the controversy about how to correctly assess physical abilities of firefighters continued.

Temporal stability of norms

When norms are first created, how long do they remain valid? Could it be considered that norms, once made correctly, will be valid forever or should they be reevaluated from time to time? What happens if results show that norms need to be changed? If norms are changed, standard scores obtained using those norms and those using new norms become incomparable. On the other hand, if norms do not change and the distribution of performance of the reference population changes, standard scores no longer adequately reflect the position of the test-taker in relation to the reference population.

There are two approaches to this problem – **norm freezing** (Fajgelj, 2003) and **periodic re-creation of norms**. Norm "freezing" or a system of scoring based on a fixed reference group (Fajgelj, 2003) is done by having norms once obtained on a normative sample at one time point used in future interpretations of individual results, regardless of whether the performance distribution of the general population changed in the meantime or not. The main advantage of the "freezing" strategy is that standard scores and percentile ranks of different test-takers can always be compared with each other regardless of when the testing was conducted. This is possible because results of all test-takers are interpreted by comparing them with the same normative sample – the one on which the "frozen" norms are based. A shortcoming is that, in time, changes to population values may happen that can make these norms no longer relevant, i.e., a discrepancy between the position of a test-taker when compared to norms and his/her position if he/she would be compared to the current population values can at a point became unacceptably high.

The idea of the second approach is that normative studies should be repeated periodically. After a certain period, a normative study is done again and new norms are created that are used onward instead of the old norms. The period between normative studies may follow some rule defined by the publisher or the test authors, but may also follow some natural cycles related to test use. For example, new norms can be created every year, every two years, every five or 10, but the period can also be nonsystematic, like in the case when new norms are created for a new test edition. In this last case, the content of the test is usually upgraded or changed, so new norms need to be created anyway because the test has been changed as methodological standards require (International Test Comission, 2017). An advantage of the strategy of periodic re-creation of norms is that it secures that the test always has norms that more or less reflect the current population values, so their users have valid data on the performance of test-takers in relation to the current reference population in regard to the measured trait. However, the strategy of periodic re-creation of norms means that results of persons who took the test at different times are compared to different normative samples and, because of that, standard scores and fractile/percentile ranks of different test-takers are not comparable if they were obtained using different norms. A psychologist working with such a test, if he/she intends to compare the performance of different test-takers, or follow the performance of a test-taker over a longer time period, needs to strictly pay attention to which norms were used to calculate standard scores and at what time points. This then makes the comparison impossible or much harder. An additional property of the strategy of periodic re-creation of norms is that it requires additional resources to be allocated to covering the expenses of the norming study every time new norms need to be created. In this way, the publisher or the author incurs additional expenses, expenses he/she does not have with "frozen" norms. On the other hand, with commercial tests, the author or the publisher may transfer these costs to users and earn on top of that if he/she uses the opportunity when new norms are created to also upgrade the test if necessary and sell the whole package – the upgraded test + new norms to users again as a new edition of the test. Even when the author/publisher does not sell the whole test version to the end-users, but only usage rights (by for example charging for the number of test application, instead of the whole test with the manual, a strategy often used with tests applied and evaluated online), periodic upgrading of norms and the test leaves an impression with the users that the author/publisher is still working on the test and maintaining it.

There is also the possibility that test users or publishers/authors combine these two approaches and offer one or a few packages of "frozen" norms along with the test, but also do periodic re-creation of norms. The test user may then choose in every particular situation whether he/she will base his/her interpretation on the current or on "frozen" norms. Such a combined approach does not create additional expenses to the author/publisher in comparison to periodic recreation of norms, because "old" norms are certainly already available and the test manual just needs to be supplemented with new norms.

An additional consideration that needs to be made when discussing temporal stability of norms is how the change in norms can happen. A logical answer would be that, in time, population values on the measured trait may change, which is then reflected in test performance. But it is also possible that the way the measured construct is manifested in behavior changes. In time, changes in cultural norms or cultural properties may occur along one of the dimensions of cultural differences and this is then reflected in the way test-takers respond to tests, especially with conative tests. For example, although I found no longitudinal studies on the topic, it can be pretty well argued that culture in many countries of Eastern Europe changed in the direction of individualism on the dimension of individualism-collectivism, and possibly on some other dimensions as well during the last decades of the 20th century (Hofstede, 2011).

Some tests, especially cognitive tests, can be learned and members of the population can become proficient in solving tasks of a certain type. For example, in the second part of the 20th century, there was a notable leap in the performance of people in the developed world on cognitive tests. This effect was named **the Flynn effect**, after the psychologist from New Zealand, James Flynn, who first described this effect. The nature of this effect was a topic of much discussion in science, with different authors offering different explanations. These explanations ranged from stating that the effect is caused by improved food quality or better healthcare to attributing the effect to improved quality and wider availability of education (Teasdale & Owen, 2005). However, this trend of increased performance that was particularly noticeable in the second part of the 20th century seems to have stopped somewhere in the 1990s or even reversed at the beginning of the 21st century (Sundet, Barlaug, & Torjussen, 2004; Teasdale & Owen, 2005) in countries in which physical quality of life and education conditions did not worsen, at least not visibly. In this light, maybe the best explanation of this effect was provided by Flynn himself in his 2007 book (Flynn, 2007) in which he argued that the observed increase in performance on cognitive tests cannot be a consequence of an increase of cognitive abilities. Namely, if we used modern norms to evaluate performance of people from the beginning of the 20th century we would find that people who were classified as having normal intelligence according to norms of the time would be classified as mentally handicapped to a lesser or greater degree according to modern norms. Given such classification in accordance with modern norms, it should than be expected that such people would not be able to perform numerous everyday activities such as reading, writing, and performing various job-related activities, as is the case with modern persons with the same test performance. However, we know that this is not the case – people from the beginning of the 20th century whose test performance was equal to test performance of modern mentally handicapped persons were well able to master reading, writing and other everyday skills – skills which modern people with the same test performance are unable to master. This clearly shows that explanation for the change in performance on cognitive tests cannot be that modern generations are smarter, but only that there is some reason why tests are easier for them, i.e., they are more skillful in solving tasks of cognitive tests. Given that intelligence tests and cognitive tests in general were a new thing at the beginning of the 20th century, and that the tasks they contained were unknown to most people, while modern people are much more familiar with them, with similar tasks now encountered in various educational and entertainment programs and publications, an obvious conclusion is that, in time, people simply became more skillful in solving such tasks. This also explains the plateau registered in the 1990s (Sundet et al., 2004) and also a possible decrease in scores on some samples (Teasdale & Owen, 2005), which will probably turn out to be just an oscillation in group level performance due to small changes in the population or properties of the studied sample. In this way, the Flynn effect shows that performance of a population may also change when members of the population become more skillful in solving tasks included in the test, with no real increase

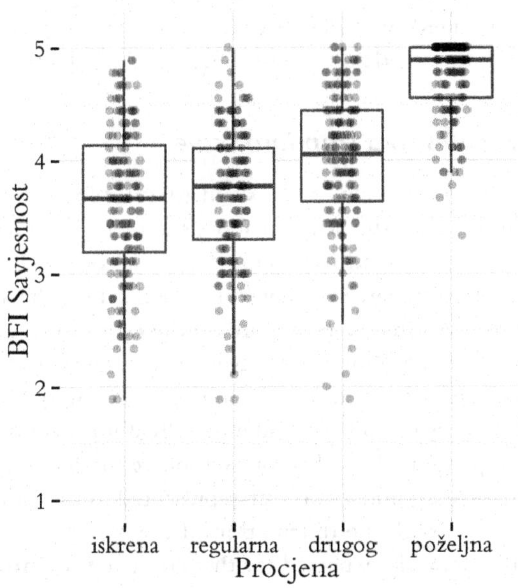

FIGURE 5.1 Distributions of responses to the Conscientiousness scale under different instructions. From left to right, test-takers were instructed to respond honestly (iskrena) received standard scale instruction (standardna), and they were evaluated by their friend (drugog). In the far right is the distribution obtained when test-takers were instructed to present themselves in the best possible way (poželjna). These results show that different instructions can produce different test results – when instructed to present themselves in the best possible way, participants gave responses indicating a much-elevated level of conscientiousness compared to both the situation when they were asked to be honest, and the situation when they received the standard test instruction.

in the level of the measured construct. Special care should be taken about this effect in situations when a test that can be learned is used on a population for a long time. There are authors who claim that a similar effect can also be observed on conative tests in situations when such tests are used to make decisions that are important to test-takers – the so-called high-stakes testing, such as, for example, testing in the scope of selecting candidates for a job or selection of people inside an organization to be promoted. With such tests, it is possible that test-takers learn what answers result in favorable outcomes and then give such answers – so-called socially desirable answers in the testing situation. For example, a study performed by Dr. Siniša Lakić from the University of Banja Luka in the scope of his doctoral research showed that, when given instructions to present themselves in the best possible light on a personality test, test-takers (students in his case), have no problem in giving answers that increase their scores on the Conscientiousness personality dimension compared to a situation when they were not given such instruction (Figure 5.1). Conscientiousness is a personality trait often used in job selection procedures. The same test-takers, when asked to be as honest as possible, gave responses on Conscientiousness that resulted in scores that were somewhat lower compared to the results obtained with the standard test instruction (Lakić, 2014)

Converting raw scores to a standard scale

When creating norms and after choosing a standard scale to which the raw scores will be converted, the next step is the decision about the method with which raw scores will be converted to that standard scale. This issue more or less does not exist if raw scores are only converted to percentiles or some other type of fractiles, i.e., if fractile norms are created, because fractile norms are on the ordinal measurement level, but the issue does exist if the intention is to convert raw scores to a standard scale that is at an interval level of measurement. A problem might arise in this situation if it turns out that the distribution is not normal and especially if it turns out that it is not due to a problematic sampling method, that for example resulted in test-takers of certain levels of performance being under- or over-represented in the sample.

If everything is okay with the distribution of raw scores, i.e., if it is normal or of a shape that is theoretically expected for that construct, a **simple linear transformation** of raw scores to the standard scale is completely adequate. If the shape of the distribution is not good, then one of the procedures for normalizing raw scores can be performed first with the goal of "repairing" the distribution, after which a linear transformation can be used to convert scores to a standard scale. Alternatively, it is possibly to conduct an equipercentile conversion of raw scores to a standard scale by first selecting points on the standard scale that will be paired with raw scores and used to create norms, then using a mathematical function in statistics software to find percentiles corresponding to these standard scores and finally inspect the distribution of raw score cumulative frequencies to identify raw scores corresponding to selected points of the standard scale by pairing scores with equal percentile values.

It is also possible to apply other methods for converting raw scores into standard scores, especially if theoretical reasons require that a specific transformation procedure be used.

These conversion procedures are conducted in a way that was described in the subchapter about test equating, with the difference that raw scores are here converted to scores on standard scales with fixed properties instead of the scales of another test. This also means that the true score equating procedure, described in the previous chapter, cannot be applied here, while the other procedures can.

Dimensional interpretation of individual results vs. profile analysis

After raw scores are converted to corresponding standard scores (or percentiles or other fractiles), it is time to consider what kind of behavior can be expected from a person whose test performance corresponds to a certain standard score. A standard score, as well as a percentile, provides information about where is the performance of that person compared to the normative sample, but this in itself still does not tell us what kind of behavior can we expect from such a person. With criterion-referenced tests this problem does not exist. When we know the performance of a person on the test, we also know his/her value of the criterion, whether he/she fulfills it or not and, with this, we also know what behavior to expect, because this stems from the nature of the criterion. This is not the case with normative tests. Position on a distribution by itself tells nothing about the behavior that can be expected and additional knowledge of the measured construct and properties of people with different levels of expression of that construct is needed.

It becomes more complicated when the test measures more than one construct, like is the case with tests measuring different forms of intelligence or personality inventories measuring multiple personality traits. Theory underlying the test operationalizes personality as an entity comprised of multiple dimensions that are measured separately, but which influence various and wide aspects of behavior. However, it is well-known that behavior is influenced by the integral personality and that elements of behavior influenced by only a single personality trait are very rare. So, how do we create the description of behavior of an individual based on knowing the position of that individual on the normative sample and through it on the normative population. There are two approaches:

- Dimensional approach
- Profile analysis approach

With the **dimensional approach** to interpretation of individual results, every construct or dimension the test measures is treated as a separate trait and is interpreted separately. The intensity range of each trait is, for ease of interpretation, divided into several categories and descriptions of behavior of people in each category are created based on theory and previous research studies on that trait. Descriptions of each category of each of the measured constructs is then included in the test manual or software for interpreting tests, and test users then form descriptions of the test-taker by combining descriptions of each category that test-taker belongs to. One way to do that is to concatenate descriptions of categories a test-taker belongs to on each of the traits so that the final description of the test-taker is a mechanical sum of descriptions of categories he/she belongs to on the measured trait. Another method, used by psychologists who are more experienced in assessment, is to start from descriptions of categories provided in the manual, but to then take from those descriptions those characteristics that are relevant for the purpose of testing, integrate them in his/her description and to then additionally harmonize parts of descriptions based on various measured traits, especially if it so happens that contradictory behavior descriptions stem from descriptions of categories the test-taker belongs to on different variables.

A great advantage of the dimensional approach to interpretation of individual results is that a system for interpreting individual results that follows this approach is quite easy to create. If measured constructs are somewhat known or established in the psychological science, a search of the literature can surely provide studies exploring the relation of measured construct with various observable behaviors (e.g., Barrick & Mount, 1991; Le Vigouroux, Scola, Raes, Mikolajczak, & Roskam, 2017; Van Dijk et al., 2016). Also, during the "life" of the test, it can be expected that the quantity of available data will increase, either due to studies conducted by test authors themselves, by other authors using the test or due to studies using other tests measuring the same or similar constructs, but results of which can be generalized to constructs measured by the test. These studies are the basis for creating descriptions of categories and also for changing or supplementing those descriptions in later editions of the test. The main shortcoming of the dimensional approach comes from the fact that observable behaviors are rarely influenced by only one psychological construct. Due to this, the validity of descriptions of observable behaviors that could be expected from persons with a certain trait level is often limited. It may also happen that descriptions of behaviors or personal characteristics for different constructs are contradictory. It is also possible that a concrete test-taker has such a configuration of the measured construct with other personal and environmental factors that his/her observable behavior significantly deviates from the description provided by the dimensional approach. This is the reason why psychologists interpreting test results should not take test results to be the final verdict about the test-taker, but should always compare the results of the test with their own assessment of the test-taker. To support this stance, authors of the test should themselves refrain from using definite or firm predictions in their descriptions, but should instead speak of tendencies and regularities in behavior. However, this approach also increases the risk of appearance of the **Barnum effect**, i.e., the risk of writing descriptions of categories in such a way that they include all possibilities and thus making them fit all people regardless of their personal properties (e.g., Snyder, Shenkel, & Lowery, 1977). Because the safest way not to make any errors in prediction is to not predict anything, personality descriptions that would consist of statements that are valid for all people would never be wrong, but would also be cognitively worthless as we would not learn of any specific properties of the test-taker from them.

The **profile analysis approach** is based on the recognition of the fact that there are practically no behaviors that are influenced by only one psychological trait. Observable behavior is a result of interaction between environmental factors and personality as a whole, and not of individual traits. Due to this, multiple or all personality traits should be considered together and conclusions about properties of a person should be based on considering the configuration, the pattern of measured traits and not on consideration of individual traits. In psychology, this approach takes two forms:

- The typological approach
- The profile analysis approach proper

The typological approach is based on dividing the studied domain of behavior into a certain number of categories – types and the interpretation of individual results is done by determining the type or category the person belongs to. The person is placed in a category and assigned the description corresponding to that category. The typological approach is applied by creating tests that assess category membership instead of assessing latent dimensions, but these tests can also be made to assess latent dimensions that are then combined to determine category membership. Tests intended to categorize test-takers into types based on sufficiently developed theoretical models typically provide both measures of latent dimensions and data needed to categorize test-takers into types. Other tests that work with types can often be rescored so that they provide assessment of latent dimensions, even if they were not intended to provide such data initially. For example, the Personal Globe Inventory, an inventory of vocational interests, is based on the spherical model of vocational interests and it provides data on 18 types of vocational interests included in the spherical model, but it also provides scores of test-takers on three latent dimensions of vocational interests (Hedrih, 2008; Tracey, 2002). A test intended to asses types/categories within a typology such as the Meyers-Briggs Type Indicator, can be rescored to provide measures of the Big Five personality traits (Harvey, Murry, Markham, & Pamplin, 1995), even though test authors did not have such a rescoring in mind.

When considering types themselves, it is likely that there are no types in nature. Types are a convenient "invention" of psychologists and researchers that help them view and describe individual differences in behavioral tendencies in a way that is simpler than describing and interpreting scores on multiple dimensions and deciphering the ways in which these dimensions combine to create unique behavior of the person. It is much easier to say that a person is an "introverted type"(McCrae & Costa, 1989) or an "artistic type" (Holland, 1959) or that he/she belongs to the "secure attachment style" (e.g., Bartholomew & Horowitz, 1991; Mihić, Zotović, & Petrović, 2007), than operate with multiple independent dimensions, describe properties of the test-taker on each of them, and then think of ways to combine them. But things are not like that in nature. If they were, if psychological types existed, what we would see when observing multivariate distributions of test-takers by intensities of measured latent traits would be test-takers grouping around multiple different and relatively distant points in the statistical space of measured latent dimensions. In other words, distributions of individual differences would be bimodal, three-modal, polymodal, etc. But this is not what happens. What is typically obtained are normal distributions of values of test-takers on measured latent traits, i.e., groupings around a single central point, with frequencies of test-takers decreasing with distance from that central point (e.g., Tracey & Rounds, 1995). And not only is the normal distribution what is typically obtained, normal distribution is also the distribution shape researchers theoretically expect when studying individual differences and that is why they gladly use procedures to normalize the distribution when the empirical distribution deviates from normal. When deviations from normal distribution happen, researchers usually attribute them to shortcomings of the instrument used and only rarely to real properties of the population. Of course, selected, artificially created groups of people can be exceptions to these rules, and this is also the case with artificially created groups with certain characteristics in which we can also obtain real types, but the previous discussion of types refers to natural, homogenous human populations.

When considering theoretical psychological models that were initially conceived as exclusively typological, later studies have typically shown that there are latent dimensions underlying the types (e.g., Furnham, 1996; McCrae & Costa, 1989; Prediger, 1982) and that the division of the latent space defined by these dimensions is arbitrary (Tracey & Rounds, 1995), so that it can easily be replaced by a different typology covering the same latent space (e.g., Tracey, 2002). References included here refer to examples of the Holland's model of vocational interest and the MBTI typology, but conclusions and approaches used in the referenced papers can likely be generalized to other typologies as well.

Although types do not really exist, but represent more or less arbitrary groupings of people (Tracey & Rounds, 1995), they represent very useful tools for psychologists, both practitioners and researchers. Dividing a certain domain into types allows researchers to focus their further studies on people with specific configurations of values on latent dimensions and in that way improve the body of knowledge about people with such configurations of latent traits. The typological approach described here has the advantage of typically involving only a small number of categories that can be studied in detail, so in time, through sequences of studies, data about common tendencies in the behavior of people of each type may accumulate. This surely represents a valuable contribution to theoretical knowledge.

How are types created? Older typological theories started from an assumption that the types they propose exist as natural groups without considering the underlying latent dimensions. This is usually not the case with modern theories, where authors are often aware that they are "inventing" types as useful tools for describing individual differences. They often even define types through their relations with latent dimensions. This may be done by defining positions of types in the statistical space defined by latent dimensions, as is the case with the spherical model of vocational interests (Tracey, 2002), but can also be done by dividing the whole latent space into sections corresponding to types, as is the case with attachment styles/types (Bartholomew & Horowitz, 1991; Mihić et al., 2007). In the area of attachment, belonging to a certain attachment type is defined by a configuration of scores on two attachment dimensions – model of self and model of others the person has and, in this way, positive scores on both classify a person as belonging to the secure attachment type, negative on both classify a person as disorganized attachment type and so on (Mihić et al., 2007). In this way, the whole two-dimensional space is defined by these two attachment dimensions and divided into four sections each of which corresponds to one attachment type. The decision on how to define types in space of latent dimensions and how they will be distributed is primarily driven by theoretical reasons and the ways in which the typology will be used.

The profile analysis approach proper starts from observing the configuration of test-takers scores on measured constructs and compares them to configurations listed in the test manual or a separate publication containing profiles. These configurations are called **profiles**. Results of these tests usually contain a graphical overview of profiles in order to make it easier to observe relations between scores, i.e., to visualize the profile. Such tests are usually accompanied by special forms in which results are to be drawn to create a graphic profile if the test is administered in paper form. If the test is administered in electronic form, the presentation of results usually includes a graphic presentation of the profile. For example, the Emotion Profile Index (Plutchik, 1989; Plutchik & Kellerman, 1974) contains a form with a circular graph in which percentile ranks of the test-takers should be marked in order to obtain a profile. The test is then interpreted either dimensionally (Kurbalija & Šakotić Kurbalija, 2014) or by comparing the profile with reference profiles from the manual.

The clinical test MMPI (Greene, 2000) contains a graph in which T scores of the test-taker are to be marked, and then the profile is drawn by connecting the marks. Depending on the MMPI version, T score 65 or 70 is bolded on the graph, because interpretation rules state that T scores above that level point to clinically relevant score levels and the profile interpretation is based, to a great extent, on determining if scores are above or below that threshold. When a profile is drawn, it is compared to reference profiles from the test manual or profiles from a type of publication called **profile atlas**. This is done by hand by the psychologists or by a computer program when the test version is administered or interpreted via computer.

During the second half of the 20th century, profile atlases were popular. These were voluminous publications containing sometimes hundreds of different profiles with descriptions of each. These descriptions were based on properties of individual test-takers with profiles of their test scores. Descriptions were often based on data about the test-taker that were obtained from other sources, their medical histories firstly. For example, the profile atlas of Hathaway and Meehl (1951) contains descriptions of 968 patients, tested with the version of MMPI that was current at the moment, with clinical and other available data for each patient. The idea underlying the use of these atlases is that a psychologist using the test interprets the results of the test-taker he/she is testing by finding a profile in the atlas that is the most similar to the profile of the test-taker whose results he/she is interpreting. The psychologist should than attribute to the current test/taker properties of the patient with that profile listed in the atlas.

Operationalized like this, this version of profile analysis approach could be treated as a form of typological approach as these profiles are essentially types. The only difference is that profiles obtained in this way (profiles from the atlas) are not theory-based categories, but results of individual empirical observations; while the number of categories is huge – in the case of the atlas of Hathaway and Meehl the effective number of categories on hand is 968! In fact, as this atlas was not the only atlas available and individual atlases do not pretend to be complete and exclusive categorizations, the effective number of categories, combined from different atlases, is even higher.

The essential problem with this approach, at least for practicing psychologists working with hardcopy atlases who need to compare the profile of the current test-taker with the atlas, is that these voluminous atlases are practically unsearchable. A psychologist holding the test-taker's profile in one hand and going through the atlas with the other is not really in a situation to spend hours and hours sifting through the atlas and comparing profiles for each individual test-taker. Also, he/she is not really able to compare the profile of every test-taker with hundreds of profiles from the atlas, so, in reality, psychologists compared test-takers' profiles with only a select few profiles from the atlas, or only with profiles listed on a select few pages. And, even if there were an automated system for doing comparisons, like a computer program that would calculate profile similarity between the test-taker and profiles from the atlas, the problem remains that profiles listed in the atlas are not theoretical types, but only descriptions of concrete people that had a certain profile on the test. This typically means that when reading the profile description, one cannot determine which of the listed characteristics are common characteristics of all people with such a profile, and which are specific properties of concrete test-takers whose data were entered into the atlas that have nothing to do with psychological characteristics represented by the profile.

An additional problem is also that when profile similarity of a test-taker with each profile from the atlas is calculated, the test-takers profile will typically be similar to a number of reference profiles, but with discrepancies, even when the degree of similarity is calculated quite precisely. Also, it is possible that the profile of the test-taker be very similar to a reference profile the description of which is obviously and plainly wrong for the test-taker. It is then up to the psychologist to decide which of the multiple profiles with almost equal levels of similarity to the profile of the test-takers should be chosen to be corresponding to the test-taker. The psychologist may do that by reading the descriptions with each of the corresponding reference profiles and then attribute to the test-taker the description or parts of the description that is most in accordance with the psychologist's personal assessment of the test-taker. However, such approach compromises the objectivity of test evaluation, thus nullifying one of the defining properties of a psychological test.

Due to these problems, interpretation of results using profile atlases has been largely abandoned in modern psychological practice. What did remain is a combination of the profile analysis approach with the dimensional approach. Instead of interpreting every test result by comparing it with a large number of poorly researched profiles, test manuals started to include descriptions of a few or a small number of profile properties of which have been verified and studied in detail. If it happens that the score configuration of a test-taker corresponds to one of the profiles, properties of that profile are then attributed to the test-taker. If the score configuration does not correspond to one of the listed profiles, results are interpreted in line with the dimensional approach. Test manuals often also include lists of characteristics that are crucial, i.e., that should primarily be considered in deciding if a score configuration corresponds to a profile or not. The representation of the reference profile need not be in graphic form, but can also be given as a description or as a list of boundary conditions. For example, the description of a profile might state that test-takers with standards scores above 70 on constructs A and B and also scores between 30 and 40 on C and below 30 on D correspond to that profile. Profile description need not include all constructs measured by the test, only those that are relevant for the decision if a person's score configuration corresponds to that profile or not.

When looking at score configurations or profiles as a whole, they can be described using the following properties:

- **Profile level** – refers to the average level of expression of the measured traits, i.e., how high the scores are on average. There are profiles consisting of scores that tend to be high, close to the upper end of the reference distribution, low profiles, medium profiles, etc.
- **Profile dispersion** – represents the extent to which test-takers standard scores differ between the measured constructs. As all scores are converted to the same standard scale before creating a profile, these scores can be compared to each other in regard to the position on the normative distribution they represent for each of the measured constructs. Based on this, we can have highly dispersed profiles – profiles in which test-taker's scores are high on some of the measured constructs, and low on all the other and where there is a general tendency for test-taker's score on different constructs measured by the test to be very different. On the other pole are profiles with low dispersion where the test-taker tends to have similar standard scores on all measured constructs.
- **Profile shape** – refers to which standard scores are high (on which of the measured construct), which are low, which standard score (the standard score on which of the measured construct) is higher than which standard score, and what the profile curve looks like.

These profile properties are more or less independent of each other, and sometimes one of these properties is necessary to identify a profile, and sometimes another. Sometimes, score configurations that visually look very different might belong to the same profile type, because only one or two of these three properties are relevant for identification. For example, a profile might require that a score configuration have a certain shape, regardless of its dispersion or level. Some profiles may be primarily defined by their level (for example, an extremely high profile, where all scores are very high), regardless of shape or dispersion. Or it may be shape and dispersion that are important, but not the level and so on.

Methods for assessing the similarity of two profiles include:

Visual expert assessment by the psychologist – the psychologist administering the test visually compares the graphical representation of a test-taker's profile with graphical representations of reference profiles and decides which profile corresponds the most to the test-taker's profile. The psychologist need not base his/her decision on the visual assessment of profile similarity alone, but may also use his/her theoretical knowledge of profile properties (i.e., knowing which profile properties are important and which are not) and additional data available about the test-taker to make the decision.

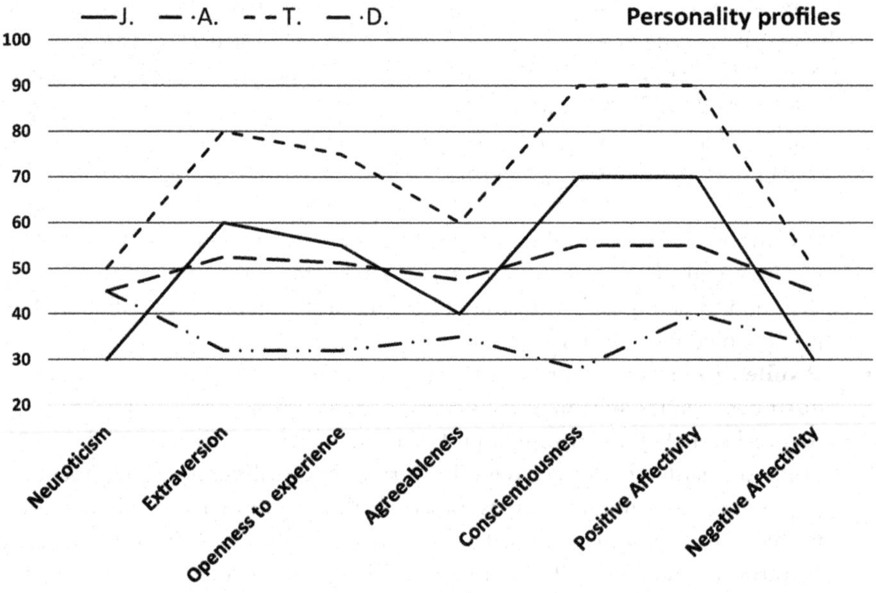

FIGURE 5.2 Graphical presentation of profiles. In this example, profiles T (shorter interrupted line) and J (solid line) have the same shape but different elevation. Profiles J and A (longer interrupted lines) have the same elevation and shape, but different dispersions. Profiles T and A have different dispersions and elevations, but the same shape. Profile D (interrupted line with double dots) is a profile of low elevation, of different shape than the other profiles. Profiles in the picture are based on fictitious data.

Descriptive criteria/criteria defining boundary conditions – the reference profile is described by words; words are used to define boundary properties of the profile. The psychologist then checks if the test-taker's score configuration fulfills these conditions. For example, a description of a reference profile might require that scores on certain measures be in a certain range, on some other measures within another range and that profile as a whole has a certain property (e.g., to be high or low or highly dispersed, etc.). Results are then inspected to determine if they fulfill these conditions.

Correlation between profiles – test-taker's profile is represented as a series of numbers (the standard score on each measured construct being one number), reference profiles are represented in the same way and a correlation is calculated between them. It should be taken into account here that correlation is only sensitive to the profile shape, but not the level or dispersion. Due to this, calculating correlation is a method of choice only when neither dispersion nor profile level are important for deciding about the correspondence of the two profiles and when it is adequate that the decision be based only on shape similarity. Calculating correlations as similarity measures requires the reference profile to be presented as a specific score configuration and not defined as boundary conditions.

Distance – test-taker's profile and reference profiles are points in a multidimensional statistical space and their distances in that space are calculated using one of the methods for calculating distances. The type of distance that is calculated determines the properties of this approach to calculating profile similarity. For example, Euclidian distance will be dependent on all three profile properties – shape, dispersion and level; but Chebyshev's distance will depend only on one – the biggest difference between the standard score of the test-taker and the reference profile, etc.

Cattell's profile similarity coefficient, known as Rp (Cattell, 1969), and other statistical methods.

Which of these methods will be applied with the test depends on the characteristics of that test, and ways in which profiles are defined and described. Statistical procedures for calculating profile similarities are suitable when a comparison is made by a computer and much less when the comparison is done by hand by a psychologist. Of course, visual assessment of profile similarity can only be performed when the psychologist him/herself makes the comparisons between profiles.

When profile comparison is done using a computer, this typically does not exclude the psychologist from the assessment. The results might show multiple reference profiles, which are the most similar to the test-taker's profile, and it will then be up to the psychologist to decide whether it is correct to attribute the description of the most similar reference profile to the test taker, or would it be better to choose some of the other profiles – maybe none of them.

References

Bar-On, R. (2004). The bar-on emotional quotient inventory (EQ-i): Rationale, description and summary of psychometric properties. In G. Geher (Ed.), *Measuring emotional intelligence: Common ground and controversy* (pp. 115–145). Hauppauge, NY: Nova Science Publishers. Retrieved from http://psycnet.apa.org.proxy.kobson.nb.rs:2048/record/2004-19636-006

Barrick, M., & Mount, M. (1991). The big five personality dimensions and job performance: A meta-analysis. *Personnel Psychology*, *44*, 1–26. Retrieved from http://jwalkonline.org/docs/Grad Classes/Fall 07/Org Psy/big 5 and job perf.pdf

Bartholomew, K., & Horowitz, L. M. (1991). Attachment styles among young adults: A test of a four-category model childhood attachment and internal models. *Journal of Personality and Social Psychology*, *61*(2), 226–244.

Benson, N., Hulac, D. M., & Kranzler, J. H. (2010). Independent examination of the Wechsler adult intelligence scale – fourth edition (WAIS – IV): What does the WAIS – IV measure? *Psychological Assessment*, *22*(1), 121–130. https://doi.org/10.1037/a0017767

Berk, R. A. (1986). A consumer's guide to setting performance standards on criterion-referenced tests. *Review of Educational Research Spring Hambleton & Eignor*, *56*(1), 137–172.

Boake, C. (2002). From the Binet±Simon to the Wechsler±Bellevue: Tracing the history of intelligence testing. *Journal of Clinical and Experimental Neuropsychology*, *24*(3), 383–405.

Buhl-Nielsen, B. (2006). Mirrors, body image and self. *International Congress Series*, *1286*, 87–94. https://doi.org/10.1016/j.ics.2005.09.149

Burns, M. K. (2002). Comprehensive system of assessment to intervention using curriculum-based assessments. *Intervention in School and Clinic*, *38*(8), 8–13.

Cattell, R. B. (1969). The profile similarity coefficient, rp, in vocational guidance and diagnostic classification. *British Journal of Educational Psychology*, *39*(2), 131–142. https://doi.org/10.1111/j.2044-8279.1969.tb02056.x

Dawda, D., & Hart, S. D. (2000). Assessing emotional intelligence: Reliability and validity of the bar-on emotional quotient inventory (EQ-i) in university students. *Personality and Individual Differences*, *28*, 797–812.

Deno, S. L. (1985). Curriculum-based measurement: The emerging alternative. *Exceptional Children*, *52*(3), 219–232. https://doi.org/10.1177/001440298505200303

Fagan, J. F., Holland, C. R., & Wheeler, K. (2007). The prediction, from infancy, of adult IQ and achievement. *Intelligence*, *35*, 225–231. https://doi.org/10.1016/j.intell.2006.07.007

Fajgelj, S. (2003). *Psihometrija*. Beograd: Centar za primenjenu psihologiju.

Flynn, J. (2007). *What is intelligence? Beyond the Flynn effect*. Cambridge: Cambridge University Press.

Furnham, A. (1996). The big five versus the big four: The relationship between the Myers-Briggs type indicator (MBTI) and NEO-PI five factor model of personality. *Personality and Individual Differences*, *21*(2), 303–307.

Geisinger, K. F. (1994). Cross-cultural normative assessment: Translation and adaptation issues influencing the normative interpretation of assessment instruments. *Psychological Assessment*, *6*(4), 304–312.

George, C., & West, M. (2001). The development and preliminary validation of a new measure of adult attachment: The adult attachment projective. *Attachment & Human Development*, *3*(1), 30–61. https://doi.org/10.1080/14616730010024771

Greene, R. (2000). *The MMPI-2: An interpretive manual* (2nd ed.). Needham Heights, MA: Allyn & Bacon.

Harvey, R. J., Murry, W. D., Markham, S. E., & Pamplin, R. B. (1995). *A big five scoring system for the Myers-Briggs type indicator*. Annual Conference of the Society for Industrial and Organizational Psychology.

Hathaway, S., & Meehl, P. (1951). *An atlas for the clinical use of the MMPI*. Oxford: University of Minnesota Press.

Hedrih, V. (2008). Structure of vocational interests in Serbia: Evaluation of the spherical model. *Journal of Vocational Behavior, 73*(1), 13–23. https://doi.org/10.1016/j.jvb.2007.12.004

Hofstede, G. (2011). Dimensionalizing cultures: The Hofstede model in context. *Online Readings in Psychology and Culture, 2*(1). https://doi.org/10.9707/2307-0919.1014

Holland, J. L. (1959). A theory of vocational choice. *Journal of Counseling Psychology, 6*(1).

Hopkins, K. D., & Bracht, G. H. (1975). Ten-year stability of verbal and nonverbal IQ scores. *American Educational Research Journal, 12*(4), 469–477.

International Test Comission. (2017). *ITC guidelines for translating and adapting tests* (2nd ed.). https://doi.org/10.1027/1901-2276.61.2.29

Kernberg, P., Buhl-Nielsen, B., & Normandin, L. (2006). *Beyond the reflection: The role of the mirror paradigm in clinical practice*. New York, NY, US: Other Press.

Kurbalija, D., & Šakotić Kurbalija, J. (2014). Crte ličnosti merene testom Profil indeks emocija (PIE): Preliminarne norme za srednjoškolce. *Psihološka Istraživanja, 17*(2), 159–178.

Lakić, S. (2014). *Multimetodna validacija psihometrijski definisanog konstrukta savjesnosti*. Univerzitet u Banjoj Luci, Republika Srpska, Bosnia & Herzegovina.

Lamiell, J. T. (2012). Introducing William Stern (1871–1938). *History of Psychology, 15*(4), 379–384. https://doi.org/10.1037/a0027439

Le Vigouroux, S., Scola, C., Raes, M.-E., Mikolajczak, M., & Roskam, I. (2017). The big five personality traits and parental burnout: Protective and risk factors. *Personality and Individual Differences, 119*, 216–219. https://doi.org/10.1016/j.paid.2017.07.023

McBirney-Goc, E. (2016). Utilization of the mirror interview to explore the influences of parents and objectification on the body and disordered eating behaviors. *The New School Psychology Bulletin, 13*(2).

McCrae, R., & Costa, P. J. (1989). Reinterpreting the Myers-Briggs type indicator from the perspective of the five-factor model of personality. *Journal of Personality, 57*(1), 17–40.

Mihić, I., Zotović, M., & Petrović, J. (2007). Stresna iskustva u odrastanju i afektivna vezanost adolescenata. *Psihologija, 40*(4), 527–542. https://doi.org/10.2298/PSI0704527M

Plutchik, R. (1989). Measuring emotions and their derivatives. In *The measurement of emotions* (pp. 1–35). Academic Press. https://doi.org/10.1016/B978-0-12-558704-4.50004-9

Plutchik, R., & Kellerman, H. (1974). *Emotion profile index*. Western Psychological Services. Los Angeles, USA.

Prediger, D. J. (1982). Dimensions underlying Holland's Hexagon: Missing link between interests and occupations? *Journal of Vocational Behavior, 21*, 259–287.

Rose, S. A., Feldman, J. F., Jankowski, J. J., & Van Rossem, R. (2012). Information processing from infancy to 11 years: Continuities and prediction of IQ ☆. *Intelligence, 40*, 445–457. https://doi.org/10.1016/j.intell.2012.05.007

Snyder, C. R., Shenkel, R. L., & Lowery, C. (1977). Acceptance of personality interpretations: The "Barnum effect" and beyond. *Journal of Consulting and Clinical Psychology, 45*(1), 104–114.

Stern, W. (1912). *Die psychologischen Methoden der Intelligenzprüfung und deren Anwendung an Schulkindern* (No. 5). J.A. Barth.

Sundet, J. M., Barlaug, D. G., & Torjussen, T. M. (2004). The end of the Flynn effect? A study of secular trends in mean intelligence test scores of Norwegian conscripts during half a century. *Intelligence, 32*, 349–362. https://doi.org/10.1016/j.intell.2004.06.004

Teasdale, T. W., & Owen, D. R. (2005). A long-term rise and recent decline in intelligence test performance: The Flynn effect in reverse. *Personality and Individual Differences, 39*, 837–843. https://doi.org/10.1016/j.paid.2005.01.029

Tracey, T. J. G. (2002). Personal globe inventory: Measurement of the spherical model of interests and competence beliefs. *Journal of Vocational Behavior, 60*(1), 113–172. https://doi.org/10.1006/jvbe.2001.1817

Tracey, T. J. G., & Rounds, J. (1995). The arbitrary nature of Holland's RIASEC types: A concentric-circles structure. *Journal of Counseling Psychology Rounds & Tracey Rounds & Zevon*, *42*(4), 431–439.

Van Dijk, S. D. M., Hanssen, D., Naarding, P., Lucassen, P., Comijs, H., & Oude Voshaar, R. (2016). Big five personality traits and medically unexplained symptoms in later life. *European Psychiatry*, *38*, 23–30. https://doi.org/10.1016/j.eurpsy.2016.05.002

Ward, L. C. (1991). A comparison of T scores from the MMPI and the MMPI-2. *Psychological Assessment*, *3*(4), 688–690.

Wechsler, D. (2008). Wechsler adult intelligence scale – fourth edition (WAIS – IV). San Antonio, TX: NCS Pearson, 22, 498.

Wiliam, D. (1998, September 18). *Construct-referenced assessment of authentic tasks: Alternatives to norms and criteria*. Retrieved April 7, 2018, from www.leeds.ac.uk/educol/documents/000000793.htm

6

RIGHTS OF TEST-TAKERS, LEGAL AND ETHICAL ISSUES OF PSYCHOLOGICAL TESTING

Introduction

In the scope of psychological testing and in psychological practice in general, psychologists come in contact with a wealth of information about their clients/ patients/test-takers, i.e., people they work with. Many pieces of this information contain intimate details about the test-taker, his/her health status or about the social network he/she lives within. Also, this information serves as a basis for making decisions that impact the life of the test-taker. For example, it may depend on the testing results whether a person will get a job or not; whether a person will obtain guardianship over a child; a scholarship or funds in the scope of some public call; whether ailments the person has will be treated in one way or another; whether the person will be sent to hospital for treatment or to prison; whether the person will obtain and maintain the right to drive a car, truck, airplane or another vehicle; and many other things. If testing results made by psychologists turned out to be incorrect, misinterpreted or if intimate data that the test-taker gave to the psychologist during testing in good faith were to leak to public or to people they were not intended for, significant damage could occur of the test-taker. Additionally, if such things happened, the public would quickly loose trust in the profession of psychologists and people would become less willing to come to a psychologist for help or to entrust them with sensitive information about themselves. Trust between a psychologist and his/her client is necessary for psychologists to be able to provide their services. It is very probable that society would quickly eliminate positions and situations that rely on psychological tests and psychological assessment if psychologists could not be trusted. For psychologists working in cross-cultural contexts, like is the case of psychologists who work outside their country of origin or with members of different cultures and ethnic groups, in multicultural areas, those who work with mobile populations like migrants, refugees and employees of multinational companies, challenges are even higher.

These are the reasons why psychological practice is regulated by a number of defining principles and rules of conduct in psychological practice and in particular when doing psychological testing/assessment. Some of these norms, those dealing with copyright and rights of authors, were presented in a separate chapter. This chapter will focus on legal and ethical norms that deal with rights of test-takers in relation to psychological assessment/testing and also about the duties of psychologists in this procedure and also rules dealing with the treatment of the test-taker and data resulting from psychological testing.

Two main groups of legal norms that regulate psychological testing practice are those dealing with the **protection of personal data** and **ethical regulation of the profession of psychologists**, primarily encoded in ethical codes of national psychological associations.

Personal data protection

Personal data is any information relating to an identified or identifiable individual ("data subject"). This is a definition given by the Convention for the Protection of Individuals with regard to Automatic Processing of Personal Data (1981), a convention that provides a common legal frame for laws and regulations dealing with the protection of personal data in all member countries of the Council of Europe, including the United Kingdom. This convention defines "automatic processing" as including the following operations if carried at least in part by automated means: storage of data, carrying out of logical and/or arithmetical operations on those data, their alteration, erasure, retrieval and dissemination. Recognizing that collection of personal data occurs in many social activities, and also taking into account that computer technology enables easy storage and use of personal data (automatic processing), this convention provides guidelines for avoiding misuse of personal data and protecting from it, but also provides a legal frame for free transfer of legally obtained data between Council of Europe member countries. This convention is the reason why the laws of all Council of Europe member countries that regulate data protection are very similar in their main provisions, but has also strongly influenced legal solutions concerning data protection throughout the world.

The Convention for the Protection of Individuals with regard to Automatic Processing of Personal Data (1981) was so far ratified and entered into force in all countries members of the Council of Europe. The convention entered into force in the United Kingdom in 1987. In line with this convention is the **European Union General Data Protection Regulation (GDPR)** that entered into force in May 2018, and has a status of a directly applicable common law in the EU, but also the **United Kingdom Data Protection Act** (Data Protection Act, 2018), that is declared to be a complementary act to the GDPR.

At the time this book is written, the US does not have one unified act regulating the protection of personal data, but does have a number of acts and regulations regulating personal data protection in specific sectors both on the federal and state level and much is also left to contractual regulation between parties. For this reason, this section will focus on the provisions of the EU GDPR and provisions of the

Code of Ethics of the American Psychological Association that are relevant to the treatment of personal data in testing situations.

In line with the Convention, the GDPR defines personal data as any information relating to an identified or identifiable natural person. This natural person is called the data subject and needs to be identifiable from the data either directly or indirectly. This means that aside from name, identification number, an online reference and similar, if one or more factors "specific to the physical, physiological, genetic, mental, economic, cultural or social identity of that natural person" (GDPR, Art.4) alone or taken together allow the person to be identified, the data is considered to be personal data.

Processing, according to GDPR, is any operation or set of operations which performed on personal data or sets of personal data. Using automated processing of personal data to "evaluate certain personal aspects relating to a natural person, in particular to analyze or predict aspects concerning that natural person's performance at work, economic situation, health, personal preferences, interests, reliability, behavior, location or movements" (GDPR, Art 4.) is called **profiling**. A structured set of personal data accessible according to specific criteria is called a **filing system**. A natural or legal person processing personal data is called **processor**, while the natural or legal person (or other entity) that determines the purpose and means of the processing of personal data is called the **controller**.

From the standpoint of a psychologist, a key aspect of this definition of personal data is that not all data collected in the course of work of a psychologist or during psychological testing is personal data. Results of psychological testing represent personal data only if they contain information that could make the person who completed the test identifiable. However, it is not necessary that the test data contain the name, address or the ID number of the test-taker for it to be considered personal data. If it is possible to identify the test-taker based on his answers or configuration of answers, this is sufficient for that data to be considered personal. For example, if one school class is tested, but all children in it were born on the same year save for one child and the test data contain year of birth, but not names of children, data from these tests are still personal data at least for that one child whose identity can be determined from the year of birth. On the other hand, such definitions mean that psychological test data, when it is to be used solely for scientific or statistical purposes, can be anonymized by removing parts of data that could allow the identification of test-takers. Through **anonymization**, test data stop being personal data, allowing psychologists to use them with more freedom in future work (for example by presenting them in scientific publications). Legal protection mechanisms refer to personal data and test results that do not allow conclusions about the identity of test-takers are no longer personal data.

That said, the GDPR also defines the concept of **pseudonymization**, and this term refers to

> the processing of personal data in such a manner that the personal data can no longer be attributed to a specific data subject without the use of additional information, provided that such additional information is kept separately and

> is subject to technical and organizational measures to ensure that the personal data are not attributed to an identified or identifiable natural person.
>
> *(GDPR, Art.4)*

In pseudonymization, parts of data that could allow identification exist, but are kept separately, and the possibility still exists for them to be joined with the dataset thus allowing the identification of data subjects. Therefore, the main difference between anonymized and pseudonymized data is that with anonymized data, there is no longer any way to identify the natural persons (data subjects) the data referred to. On the other hand, with pseudonymized data, identifying information is kept separately from the main body of data, but the possibility still exists that these data be joined and natural persons the data belongs to be re-identified. Due to this, anonymized data is not personal data anymore and provisions of personal data protection regulations do not refer to it, while pseudonymized data is still personal data.

When considering the relationship between these legal provisions and psychological tests, it is clear that psychological tests are by their nature instruments for collecting personal data, while their administration and interpretation of results fits the definitions of processing of personal data and profiling, as long as the test-taker is identified or identifiable. A matrix containing test results or an archive of completed tests would in accordance with these regulations represent a filing system.

The GDPR states that **data processing is lawful if**:

- the data subject has **given consent** to the processing of his or her personal **data for one or more specific purposes**
- processing is **necessary for the performance of a contract** to which the data subject is party or in order to take steps at the request of the data subject prior to entering into a contract;
- processing is necessary for **compliance with a legal obligation** to which the controller is subject;
- processing is necessary in order to **protect the vital interests of the data subject** or of another natural person;
- processing is necessary for the performance of a task carried out in the public interest or in the exercise of official authority vested in the controller;
- processing is necessary for the purposes of the legitimate interests pursued by the controller or by a third party, except where such interests are overridden by the interests or fundamental rights and freedoms of the data subject which require protection of personal data, in particular where the data subject is a child.

(GDPR, Art 6.)

Purpose of data processing

An important concept of this regulation is the purpose of data processing. When personal data is collected and processed, on the basis on one of the legal conditions listed above, this has to be in order to achieve some purpose. This purpose must be clearly defined and should not change. Data that is collected needs **to be relevant for the purpose of data collection** (psychological testing in our case) both by their nature – by what data is collected and by their quantity. Personal data that does not serve the purpose of data collection should not be collected. In the same spirit, the quantity of collected personal data should not be larger than needed to fulfill the purpose of data collection. Aside from the requirement that personal data be needed for the fulfillment of the purpose of data collection, personal data must be complete and accurate. The data subject has the right to "obtain from the controller without undue delay the rectification of inaccurate personal data concerning him or her" (GDPR. Art. 16). The data subject also has the right to have incomplete personal data completed. If the accuracy of the personal data is contested, the data subject has the right to obtain from the controller a restriction of processing.

Processing the data for scientific, historical and archiving purposes

A separate article of the GDPR allows EU member states to provide for derogations from the rights of the data subjects in their national data protection laws for situations where personal data is processed for purposes of scientific or historical research or for archiving purposes in public interest. The same article also requires that special safeguards be implemented in such cases in order to protect the rights and freedoms of the data subject. Processing for these purposes should respect the **principle of data minimization**. When a purpose of processing in such cases may be served with pseudonymized or anonymized data, it should be fulfilled in that manner.

Informed consent in the GDPR

When considering different bases for collecting data, the most important for the practice of psychological testing is the concept of informed consent. **Informed consent** is defined in the GDPR as consent of the data subject to data collection and processing. Before asking for such a consent, or at the time that the data is obtained, the controller needs to provide the data subject with all of the following information:

- The identity and the contact details of the controller and, where applicable, of the controller's representative;
- The contact details of the data protection officer, where applicable;
- The purposes of the processing for which the personal data are intended as well as the legal basis for the processing;
- Where the processing is based on point (f) of Article 6(1), the legitimate interests pursued by the controller or by a third party;
- The recipients or categories of recipients of the personal data, if any; and
- Where applicable, the fact that the controller intends to transfer personal data to a third country or international organization and the existence or absence

of an adequacy decision by the Commission, or in the case of transfers referred to in Article 46 or 47, or the second subparagraph of Article 49(1), reference to the appropriate or suitable safeguards and the means by which to obtain a copy of them or where they have been made available. (GDPR, Art. 13).

The same article also requires the controller to inform the data subject about the period for which the personal data will be stored, or if that is not possible, the criteria used to determine that period and about important rights the data subject has according to this regulation, including the right of rectification and erasure, the right to withdraw consent, to lodge a complaint with a supervisory authority, the legal basis for data collection and about the basic properties of automated decision making that will be carried out, with significance and envisaged consequences for the data subject. Should the controller intend to process the data for a purpose other than the one for which it was collected, information about this needs to be given to the data subject prior to the processing, along with any other relevant further information, thus effectively providing the data subject with an opportunity to withdraw his/her consent before processing for a different purpose has begun (GDPR, Art. 13).

The controller has the responsibility to be able to demonstrate that the data subject has given his/her consent for the processing of his/her personal data. If the consent is given in the context of a written declaration that also concerns other matters, GDPR obliges the controller to make the request for consent clearly distinguishable and "in an intelligible and easily accessible form, using clear and plain language" (GDPR, Art. 7).

The data subject has the right to withdraw a given consent at any time and withdrawing consent must be as easy as it was to give it. When applied to a situation of psychological assessment this means that a test-taker is free to withdraw his/her consent for participating in the testing procedure at any moment during the testing procedure and at any moment after the testing is finished. The psychologist has an obligation to accommodate such a request without undue delay and erase all data collected up to that point (if not agreed otherwise with the test-taker). The test-taker is obliged to cover the costs of testing if such costs exist and he/she was informed about them when giving consent. For example, in a commercial testing situation, the test-taker who withdrew consent would be obliged to cover the costs of testing and also any other costs the psychologist or his/her organization had in regard to the testing, such as travel expenses, etc. However, if the test-taker refused to pay or objected to paying the expenses that would create the basis for the psychologist or the organization he/she was working for to request that payment through legal means, but would not free the psychologist from the obligation to delete the collected personal data immediately after the consent was withdrawn. Personal data should be erased immediately after the test-taker has withdrawn his/her consent.

After the data have been collected, the data subject, i.e., test-taker in the case of psychological assessment, has the right to access the data and obtain a copy of it (GDPR, Art. 15) and the GDPR precisely lists additional information that the controller needs to provide about what has and is being done with the data and his/her rights about it. Considering the right of access and to obtain a copy in the context of psychological practice, a question arises of what exactly constitutes the personal data of the test-taker and what should be included in the "copy", having in mind the general need to protect the secrecy of testing materials, the need that is upheld in psychological ethics codes of many countries. A good practice in such situations is that the psychologist provides his/her own report containing results of the test taker or another document containing conclusions he/she created and used in the further procedure, if such documents exist. The psychologist may also provide a copy of answers the test-taker gave, but not of the testing materials themselves, and certainly not of the supplementary test materials, such as test manuals, norms, etc. A problem might arise when responses of the test-taker are recorded on a sheet containing test items, or other test materials and therefore, if there is a need to provide a copy or access to test results to the test taker, it is a generally good practice to record the answers separately. The test-taker also has the right to transfer the copy of the data to another controller. To this end, the copy of results given to the test-taker should be provided "in a structured, commonly used and machine-readable format" (GDPR, Art. 20). This right also includes the right to have the data directly transferred from one controller to another where technically possible.

When a psychologist is working in a cross-cultural context and conducts testing in different languages or different cultural versions of a test on members of different cultures, and especially when there is a need to compare test results of test-takers who completed different versions of a test, a psychologists should take very good care that there is a sufficient level of equivalence between test versions that are to be compared for the comparisons to be valid.

The regulation also provides for the right of data subjects, test-takers in the case of psychological testing, to have incorrect or incomplete data rectified (GDPR, Art 16.). In such cases, a psychologist should, when it is possible, allow for repeated testing of test-takers who believe that their test data are invalid or outdated. Psychologists should also, in accordance with this regulation, allow the test-taker to provide additional personal non-test data, when such data is important for the purpose the data is used for but was not available initially. This provision, however, does not mean and should not be interpreted as a right to violate the testing procedures by correcting incorrect answers to individual test items after the testing is finished or in any way that would compromise the validity of the testing.

When collecting data from children, this regulation states that for children below 16 years of age, consent needs to be obtained from the holder of parental responsibility over the child. EU member states are allowed to decrease the age of consent for children by national laws, but not below the age of 13 (GDPR, Art. 8). It should be emphasized that the holders of parental responsibility over a child are not always parents, and it is possible that only one of the parents hold parental responsibility or that parental responsibility has been taken away from biological parents in the legal process. Care should be taken that the person consent is obtained from indeed holds parental responsibility.

The regulation declares certain types of data to represent special categories of personal data. This category includes data revealing:

- Racial or ethnic origin;
- Political opinions;
- Religious or philosophical beliefs;
- Trade union membership;
- Genetic data or biometric data for the purpose of uniquely identifying a natural person;
- Data concerning health; or
- Data concerning a natural person's sex life or sexual orientation.

Processing of such data is prohibited, but this prohibition may be lifted by the explicit consent of the data subject for one or more specified purposes and a limited list of other situations when processing such data is necessary, such as scientific, historical or statistical purposes, medical and public health reasons, etc. It should be noted that other laws may prohibit processing of certain of these special categories of data for certain purposes (such as employment, for example) and, in such cases, prohibition for processing remains even if the data subject has given explicit consent.

Transfer of personal data to third countries. GDPR states that, in general, personal data may be taken to a third country, territory or an international organization if it is ensured that an equal level of protection will be provided for the transferred data both in the location of immediate transfer and in any other locations data may be transferred to. If the EU Commission has decided that a certain third country, territory or an international organization ensures an adequate level of protection, this transfer may be done without any specific authorization. If the destination of the data transfer is not subject to such a decision of the EU Commission, then the controller or processor may transfer data only if they have provided appropriate and enforceable safeguards to protect data subject rights and legal remedies for data subjects through adequate legal means (GDPR, Art 46).

Data protection in the US

Although consideration for personal data protection issues, including personal data protection in relation to psychological testing has a tradition in the US that is as long as the tradition of psychological testing, unlike the situation in European countries, in the United States of America there is so far no single law regulating data protection in general. Instead, data protection is regulated by a number of laws that regulate issues including data protection in specific sectors that exist both on the federal and state levels. These laws are principally based around the protection of the right to privacy and they generally refer to the rights of US citizens. The main principle is that an individual has an expectation and a right to privacy unless otherwise agreed or regulated by law. Protection of personal data and various issues regarding psychological testing have been subject of multiple court rulings. A good example of this is the famous case of Detroit Edison Co. v. National Labor Relations Board (NLRB), 440 U.S. 301 for 1979 (https://supreme.justia.com/cases/federal/us/440/301/) in which the court refused the request of the petitioner – the NLRB – to have test materials (the test itself, manuals, etc.) disclosed to them and also to have the individual results of test-takers disclosed without the consent of the test-takers. A comprehensive list of norms regarding psychological testing in the US that will be discussed in more detail in another part of this book is provided by the American Psychological Association in their Code of Ethics, and there are cases in which certain provisions from this document have been included in regulations of various US states. In the US legal system, a significant emphasis is placed on the protection of personal data through contracts and self-regulation by organizations. To this end, an important development is the EU-US and Swiss privacy shield www.privacyshield.gov/welcome issued by the US. The EU-US and Swiss privacy shield provides a framework helping US companies adapt their privacy policies to include the protection of personal data of EU and Swiss citizens in line with the requirements of EU (GDPR) and Swiss regulations, thus enabling easier transfer of personal data of European data subjects to the US. It enables companies to self-certify that their privacy policies and procedures provide equal protection of the personal data to that in the EU and Switzerland. The necessary components and procedures of such privacy policies are listed in detail and there is a step-by step guide through which a company can demonstrate that it has adopted such a procedure.

Ethical rules of the psychological profession related to psychological testing, rights of test-takers

Ethical rules of the psychological profession refer to ideas and understandings of what constitutes good practice and valid conduct in performing the profession of a psychologist. Ethical rules are based on general moral principles that should guide psychologists in their work. The principles are formally codified in codes of ethics that are created by national associations of psychologists in each country. The American Psychological Association (APA), the national association of psychologists in the United States of America, lists the following general ethical principles that should be followed by psychologists (American Psychological Association, 2016):

- **Beneficence and Nonmaleficence** – psychologists should strive to be benefit those they work with and should take care not to cause harm or damage
- **Fidelity and Responsibility** – psychologists form relationships of trust with people they work with and are aware of their responsibilities to those people and the society.
- **Integrity** – psychologists seek to promote accuracy, honesty and truthfulness in what they do.

- **Justice** – psychologists recognize that all who use their services have the right to an equal quality of psychological procedures, processes and services, and that psychologists have to take precautions that would prevent their own potential biases, boundaries of competence and limitations of expertise to lead to the acceptance of unjust practices.
- **Respect for People's Rights and Dignity** – psychologists respect the dignity and value of all people and their rights, privacy, confidentiality and self-determination, especially with persons or communities with vulnerabilities that impair autonomous decision-making.

In the United Kingdom, the **Code of Ethics and Conduct of the British Psychological Society** (Code of Ethics and Conduct, 2018) lists the following **four ethical principles** that constitute main domains of responsibility within which ethical issues are considered. These principles are:

- **Respect for the dignity of persons and peoples** – psychologists value the dignity and worth of all persons with sensitivity to the dynamics of perceived authority and particular regard to people's rights. In applying this principle, psychologists should consider privacy and confidentiality, respect, communities and shared values within them, impacts on the broader environment, issues of power, consent, self-determination and the importance of compassionate care.
- **Competence** – psychologists value the continuing development and maintenance of high standards of competence in their work and work within the recognized limits of their knowledge, training, education and experience. In applying this principle, psychologists consider possession or otherwise of appropriate skills and care needed to serve persons and peoples, limits of their competence and the potential need to refer on to another professional, advances in the evidence base, the need to maintain technical and practical skills, matters of professional ethics and decision-making, any limitations to their competence to practice taking mitigating actions as necessary and caution in making knowledge claims.
- **Responsibility** – psychologists accept appropriate responsibility for what is within their power, control or management in order to ensure that the trust of others, power of influence and duty toward others are not abused. In this regard, psychologists consider issues of professional accountability, responsible use of their knowledge and skills, respect for the welfare of human, non-human and the living world and potentially competing duties.
- **Integrity** – requires psychologists to be honest, truthful, accurate and consistent in their actions, words, decision, methods and outcomes, to set aside self-interest and be objective and open to challenge of their behavior in a professional context. To this end, psychologists consider issues of honesty, openness and candor, accurate unbiased representation, fairness, avoidance of exploitation and conflicts of interests including self-interest, maintaining personal and professional boundaries and addressing misconduct.

Although all these basic principles of both codes of ethics have their application and should form the general context in which psychological testing is performed, there are additional provisions that directly refer to the testing practice. **APA Ethical Principles of Psychologists and Code of Conduct (2016)** in their article 3.10 explicitly require psychologists to obtain informed consent of "the individual or individuals using language that is reasonably understandable to that person or persons except when conducting such activities without consent is mandated by law or government regulation or as otherwise provided in this ethics code". Article 9.03 of the same code states that informed consent "includes an explanation of the nature and the purpose of the assessment, fees, involvement of third parties and limits of confidentiality and sufficient opportunity for the client/patient to ask questions and receive answers". The duty to provide an explanation remains also with persons who are legally incapable of giving informed consent, such as children for example, and this explanation needs to be provided in a language that is reasonably understandable to the person being assessed.

Psychologists using services of an interpreter need to obtain informed consent from the client/patient for the use of that interpreter and "ensure that confidentiality of test results and test security are maintained, and include in their recommendations, reports and diagnostic or evaluative statements, including forensic testimony, discussion of any limitations on the data obtained" (Art. 9.03).

The Practice Guidelines of the British Psychological Society (*Practice Guidelines (Third edition)*, 2017) also require psychologists to seek and receive consent of those they work with before starting assessment or any other procedure or activity, and they describe procedures and consider specificities of obtaining informed consent from different types of people. Aside for general rules for obtaining informed consent, these guidelines also discuss specifics of obtaining consent from children and young people, people who may lack capacity, employees and detained persons.

These guidelines require the psychologist to consider providing the information about:

- **What the psychological activity for which the consent is asked involves**, as far as this is consistent with the model of interaction;
- **The benefits of the activity**, either directly to the client or indirectly through service improvements, theoretical advances and the like;
- **Alternative assessment options** and their availability;
- **Foreseeable risks, potential benefits and costs** from engaging or not in the activity; and
- **The client's right to withdraw their consent**.

Psychologists also need to make sure that prospective clients are informed of the extent and limitations of confidentiality, the purposes of any assessment, the nature of procedures to be employed, and intended uses of notes or recording be before the assessment starts. The psychologist should also ask whom they would like to be informed of their assessment, if anyone, and what information they would be willing to share with others.

Considering the obtaining of **consent of children and young people**, these guidelines require the psychologist to provide additional information and explanations to the child in an accessible way on various topics regarding their work as a psychologist, reasons for their involvement, properties of the procedure, rights of the child and how they will be protected, etc. The idea is that the child is supported to exercise his/her rights in accordance with the child's evolving capabilities. The children should be supported to express their views and contribute to decision-making. In case there is disagreement between the child and the parent/caregiver, the psychologist should try to resolve it and if that is not successful, the psychologist should draw on his/her experience to "act in the best interest of the child".

When obtaining informed consent from people who may lack capacity to consent (due to difficulties in mental functioning such as brain injury, dementia, neurological conditions and the like), the psychologist needs to make a judgement about a client's ability to give informed consent by evaluating if the person is able to understand the information relevant to the decision, retain it, use it in making the decision and communicate this decision. Conduct in these cases should be in line with the principles of the **UK Mental Capacity Act** which requires that the client be supported and assisted in making their own decision, respecting the right to make an "unwise" decisions and that anything done on behalf of a person with mental capacity issue be in their best interest, while any intervention should be on the bases of the "less restrictive option".

With regard to the informed consent of people assessed as employees, where the psychologist has been commissioned and payed by the employer to make an assessment of the employee, the psychologist should protect the employee and collect only what is needed and can reasonably be used for the purposes of employment and nothing else. To this regard, prior to the assessment, agreements should be made that explicitly state what information can be shared with the commissioning organization and this information should be sent to the client prior to being shared with the organization.

These guidelines also discuss the need to obtain informed consent from detained person, such as prisoners and people in mental health detentions. In such situations, psychologists should be aware of the power imbalance and the need to observe provisions of the UK law and a number of conventions the UK is signatory to, such as the UN Convention on Torture that bans the application of "psychological pressure" to elicit a confession or compliance with a regime. Psychologists working with prisoners should particularly be aware of the power imbalance, which is much greater than in other non-forensic settings.

Aside from the provisions about obtaining informed consent, APA Ethical Principles of Psychologists and Code of Conduct (2016), 11 articles of Section 9 dealing with assessment contain provisions for the use of assessments in general, release of test data, test construction, test scoring, interpretation and providing explanations for assessment results and also about maintaining test security.

This code requires psychologists to base their reported opinions only on information and techniques that are sufficient to substantiate their findings. These opinions should be provided only after an examination that is adequate to support it and when this is practical, in spite of reasonable effort, they should limit the nature and extent of their conclusions as well as clarify the probable impact of the limited information they have on validity and reliability of their assessment.

Psychologists should use tests and other assessment techniques in manner and for purposes that are appropriate in light of the available evidence and research data. The validity and reliability of these instruments should be established for use with members of the population tested and they should also be appropriate to individual's language preference and competence unless otherwise required. When this is not so, psychologists should describe strengths and limitations of such test results and interpretation.

APA code defines **test data** as referring to "raw and scaled scores, client/patient responses to test questions or stimuli and psychologists' notes and recording concerning client/patient statements and behavior during an examination." (Ethical Principles of Psychologists and Code of Conduct, 2016, Art 9.04). The same article specifies that portions of test materials containing answers of the test-taker also constitutes test data. On the other hand, manuals, instruments, protocols, and test questions or stimuli constitute test materials (Ethical Principles of Psychologists and Code of Conduct, 2016, Art 9.11) and psychologists should make a reasonable effort to maintain their integrity and security consistent with law and contractual obligations. Psychologist may provide test data to the test-taker at his/her request (client/patient release) either to the test-taker or to other parties that he/she designates. Psychologists may refuse to release data to protect the test-taker or others from substantial harm, misuse and misrepresentation, but must, in deciding this, recognize existing legal regulations. Aside from this, psychologists may only provide test data as required by law or court order.

In test construction, psychologists are obliged to use appropriate psychometric procedures and current scientific or professional knowledge in this area in all phases or aspects of test construction.

When interpreting test results psychologists take into account the purpose of the testing and various factors other than test scores that might influence the psychologists' judgements and accuracy of interpretations and indicate any significant limitations of their interpretations. These other factors include test-taking abilities, situational, linguistic, cultural differences, etc. Psychologists do not base their data on obsolete results or obsolete tests and measures. When offering assessment or scoring services to others, psychologists are required to accurately describe "the purpose, norms, validity, reliability and applications of the procedures and any special qualification applicable to their use" (Ethical Principles of Psychologists and Code of Conduct, 2016, Art. 9.09). When psychologists use scoring and interpretation services, they should select them based on the evidence on their validity. Whether they score and interpret tests themselves or use automated or other services, psychologists retain responsibility for the appropriate application and interpretation of tests. Psychologists also take reasonable steps that testing results be explained to the test-taker or his/her representative whenever this is not precluded by the nature of their relationship. If the latter is the case, this needs to be explained to the person in advance (American Psychological Association, 2016).

APA code also obliges psychologists to not promote use of psychological assessment techniques by unqualified persons, except for training purposes under supervision.

To summarize, provisions described above can be summarized as five categories of rights of test-takers:

- Right to be asked for informed consent to testing
- Right to be informed about the results of testing
- Right to privacy
- Rights to respect and dignity, to be categorized in the least stigmatizing way (Fajgelj, 2003)
- Right to confidentiality

Right to be asked for informed consent to testing

The right to be asked for **informed consent** to the testing refers to the duty of the psychologist to obtain the consent of the test-taker before the start of the testing and after the psychologist has provided required information to the test-taker in a clear way using language that the test-taker can understand. Regulations of different countries and organizations specify somewhat different pieces of information that need to be provided to the test-taker for his/her consent to be valid, but all of these include the following information:

- **Information about the identity of the psychologist** – full name, the organization he/she conducts the testing for and all the other information necessary for the identity of the person performing the testing to be clear to the test-taker.
- **Information about the purpose of the testing** – what exactly the data will be used for. The purpose of the testing needs to be clear, accurate, meaningful and true, and the testing procedure needs to collect only data necessary for the stated purpose. The declared purpose of testing needs to justify the use of all the tests that will be administered to the test taker.
- **Information about how the data will be used** – will the results be interpreted individually in order to create an individual report or assessment of the test-taker, or will the results be interpreted only on the group level, for example, by calculating aggregate measures that describe the whole sample or groups of test-takers, such as frequencies, means, standard deviations, etc.? Also, if the data will be used in some special way that is not clear from the purpose of the testing, the test-taker should be informed about that.

- **Information about the identities or the categories of people that will have access to the data** – if the data will be used by a limited number of concrete people, their names should be listed. If the persons who will have access to the data are not defined by name, but by their organizational affiliation or function or position within an organization, the psychologist needs to inform the test-taker about all the categories of people that will have access or about the criteria determining who will have access to the data. Special care should be taken with information about this if someone other than the psychologist doing the testing will have access to the data and especially if the data are to be shared with persons or legal entities outside of the organization the psychologist works for.

Aside from these, informed consent should also include various other pieces of information required by applicable legal regulations such as the basis for testing – is it voluntary or required by law or a contractual obligation; the rights the test-taker has, such as the right to withdraw consent at any time, with the consequences of withdrawal; the right to access the data; benefits or costs of participating or not participating; rights and procedures in case of unlawful processing of data; and other pieces of information that would be relevant for the decision of the test-taker. Additional information or information should be provided in a special way in case the test-takers are children or persons lacking capacity to consent. Special care in formulating and asking for informed consent should be taken with people from vulnerable groups, detained persons and employees.

Although regulations typically do not exclusively require the informed consent information to be presented in a written form, if the testing procedure is involved in any kind of legal process, it will typically be up to the psychologist to prove that he/she did obtain informed consent prior to testing. For this reason, it is very advisable that informed consent information be presented in a written form and have the test-taker indicate his/her consent by signing the form containing the informed consent information.

Right to be informed about the results of testing

The psychologist is obliged to inform the test-taker about results of testing and to provide him/her access to reports or other assessments the psychologist has created about him/her. These results should be explained to the test-taker as much as possible in a way he/she can understand. The test-taker is also entitled to obtain a copy of the test data and other materials reporting on his results the psychologist has created. It should be noted that this right does not exist when testing is anonymous (for example, when it is done for research purposes) or after data has been anonymized, as it is then impossible to identify personal results of the test-taker. Psychologists should make a clear distinction between test results (portion of the test containing test-taker's responses) and test materials (parts of the test that do not contain test-taker's responses, such as test items, manual, stimuli etc.). The right to be informed about the test results does not imply access to test material. In fact, good practice demands that psychologists preserve the integrity and secrecy of test materials as much as possible, because many tests would be invalidated if their test materials were available to test-takers.

Right to privacy

The test-taker has the right to withdraw his/her consent at any time before, during or after testing and psychologists have a duty to respect such a decision. In case the test-taker decides to quit the testing procedure, the psychologist should treat that as a withdrawal of consent. In such a case, the psychologist is obliged to erase all data collected in the course of the testing procedure for which the consent has been withdrawn. When consent is withdrawn, legal consequences of the withdrawal, if any, come into effect. If there are legal consequences of consent withdrawal (or of not giving consent in the first place), these should be listed in the text of the informed consent. It is possible that during testing, the test-taker refuses to answer an individual item or several items or a question included in the test or the assessment procedure. The psychologist should decide in advance and provide information to the test-taker in the scope of obtaining informed consent, whether such refusal (to answer a certain item or question) constitutes consent withdrawal or not.

Psychologists recognize that in their relationship with test-takers there is a power imbalance and the decisions and assessment made by the psychologists can have profound consequences for the life of the test-taker. Given this, it is very important that psychologists in their work respect the dignity and worth of all people and their rights and cultural, individual and role differences between people. Psychologists also employ special safeguards to protect rights and welfare of vulnerable communities and groups.

Rights to respect and dignity, to be categorized in the least stigmatizing way

When interpreting test results, psychologists will typically be in a situation when they have to put the test-taker in one theoretical category or another, or make inferences about characteristics of the test-taker or his/her test performance. When, in such cases, the test-taker is described with words or categories that carry a negative meaning, and these descriptions become accepted and used in by people in the social environment of the test-taker, the test-taker will become negatively marker or "stigmatized". Maybe the most important manifestation of stigmatization is the use of derogatory, insulting nicknames to address a person or to talk about a person by other people in his/her social environment. For example, if we noted that a man named Martin is referred to as "Crazy Martin" by people from his social environment or that a woman named Anna is referred to as "Juicehead Anna", this would be an example of stigmatization, although stigmatization also has much subtler manifestations.

The word "stigmatization" itself originates for the Ancient Greek term for markings or tattoos that were, in the times of Ancient Greece, burned or carved into the skin of criminals, slaves and traitors to identify them as unworthy and morally compromised persons. Stigmatization leads to belittlement, rejection and ostracization of the stigmatized person, thereby causing harm to him/her and the consequences of this are especially hard when the stigmatized person is already vulnerable and in need of increased social support.

Performing their duty of supporting welfare and dignity of the test-taker, if there are multiple adequate ways in which test results can be named or presented, the psychologist should choose names and ways of presentation that carry the least amount of additional negative content, i.e., which can be least expected to contribute to the stigmatization of the person. This, however does not mean that a psychologist may present the results untruthfully. For example, if the test-taker failed a qualification test, this may not be presented as if he/she passed it, nor may there be any misinterpretation of the results. The requirement that psychologists be truthful and accurate in their reports is something that is included in psychological codes of ethics worldwide. However, this does mean that, when there are alternative ways to describe results, primarily the negative ones, the psychologist should choose the way that is the least likely to contribute to the stigmatization of the person. In doing the, the psychologist should also be aware of the **Barnum effect**. The Barnum effect might happen if the psychologist, trying to present the results in a least stigmatizing way, presents only general statements that apply to all people and thus do not contain any specificities of the test-taker in comparison to other people (the Barnum effect is described in the chapter about interpretation of individual results).

Right to confidentiality

Both codes of ethics and laws require the psychologist to maintain the confidentiality of the information they receive from people they work with, test-takers in the case of psychological testing. That means that psychologists should take all available reasonable measures to ensure that nobody, save the persons permitted access to test-taker's data by his/her informed consent, have access to that data. These measures include technical, personal and organizational measures to protect confidentiality of the data. In practice, this means that psychologists need to keep their test results locked away in places where unauthorized persons cannot reach them without performing an illegal act, such as braking in, hacking, lock picking and the like. Both when working with test data and when archiving, psychologists must treat test data with due care and pay attention not to leave them in places in which unauthorized persons could access them by chance or while performing their regular work. Old test results also contain personal data, the confidentiality of which is to be protected, so these should either be destroyed when they are no longer needed, or anonymized if they are to be used for research purposes only, or protected with the same care as the new data, if there is a need to keep old data for archiving or some other reasons.

If people other than the psychologist come into contact with the data per the nature of their work, these people should be contractually obliged to respect the confidentiality of the data. If the data are kept in an electronic form, such as in the form of an electronic database, these data should also be protected using available means such as password protection, encryption or using other protection forms. Care should be taken about where databases with personal data of the test-takers are physically stored. It is best that they be stored in a local computer owned or exclusively controlled by the psychologist, but if there is need for such databases to be accessible over the internet, it is again best that they be physically stored on a computer owned by the psychologist or his/her organization. If the database with personal data is stored on an external computer or a computer system owned by a third party or organization, it is important that a contractual arrangement with this third party provides for the level and form of protection that is in line with legal regulations and the consent the psychologist obtained from the test-taker. If the data are to be taken out of the country, legal provisions about such transfers should not be forgotten.

References

American Psychological Association. (2016). *Ethical principles of psychologists and code of conduct*. American Psychological Association. Retrieved from www.apa.org/ethics/code/

Code of Ethics and Conduct. (2018). The British Psychological Society.

Convention for the Protection of Individuals with Regard to Automatic Processing of Personal Data. (1981). Retrieved from https://rm.coe.int/1680078b37

Data Protection Act. (2018). *UK parliament*.

Fajgelj, S. (2003). *Psihometrija*. Beograd: Centar za primenjenu psihologiju.

General Data Protection Regulation – GDPR. (2018). © *European union*, 1998–2019. Retrieved from https://eurlex.europa.eu/legal-content/EN/TXT/HTML/?uri=CELEX:32016R0679

Practice Guidelines (3rd ed.). (2017). The British Psychological Society.

INDEX